BIOEQUITY – PROPERTY AND THE HUMAN BODY

Medical Law and Ethics

Series Editor
Sheila McLean, Director of the Institute of Law and Ethics in Medicine,
School of Law, University of Glasgow

The 21st century seems likely to witness some of the most major developments in medicine and healthcare ever seen. At the same time, the debate about the extent to which science and/or medicine should lead the moral agenda continues, as do questions about the appropriate role for law.

This series brings together some of the best contemporary academic commentators to tackle these dilemmas in a challenging, informed and inquiring manner. The scope of the series is purposely wide, including contributions from a variety of disciplines such as law, philosophy and social sciences.

Other titles in the series

Altruism Reconsidered
Exploring New Approaches to Property in Human Tissue
Michael Steinmann, Peter Sýkora, and Urban Wiesing
ISBN 978-0-7546-7270-8

The Child As Vulnerable Patient
Protection and Empowerment
Lynn Hagger
ISBN 978-0-7546-7252-4

Disclosure Dilemmas
Ethics of Genetic Prognosis after the 'Right to Know/Not to Know' Debate
Edited by Christoph Rehmann-Sutter and Hansjakob Müller
ISBN 978-0-7546-7451-1

Critical Interventions in the Ethics of Healthcare
Challenging the Principle of Autonomy in Bioethics
Edited by Stuart J. Murray and Dave Holmes
ISBN 978-0-7546-7396-5

Law, Mind and Brain
Edited by Michael Freeman and Oliver R. Goodenough
ISBN 978-0-7546-7013-1

Bioequity – Property and the Human Body

NILS HOPPE
University of Hannover, Germany

ASHGATE

Published by
Ashgate Publishing Limited
Wey Court East
Union Road
Farnham
Surrey, GU9 7PT
England

Ashgate Publishing Company
Suite 420
101 Cherry Street
Burlington
VT 05401-4405
USA

www.ashgate.com

British Library Cataloguing in Publication Data
Hoppe, Nils.
Bioequity – property and the human body. -- (Medical law and ethics)
1. Human body--Law and legislation. 2. Preservation of organs, tissues, etc.--Law and legislation.
I. Title II. Series
344'.04194-dc22

Library of Congress Cataloging-in-Publication Data
Hoppe, Nils.
Bioequity – property and the human body / by Nils Hoppe.
p. cm. -- (Medical law and ethics)
Includes bibliographical references and index.
ISBN 978-0-7546-7280-7 (hardback) -- ISBN 978-0-7546-8932-4 (ebook)
1. Human body--Law and legislation. I. Title.

K564.H8.H67 2009
344.04'19--dc22

2009025222

ISBN 9780754672807 (hbk)
ISBN 9780754689324 (ebk)

Mixed Sources
Product group from well-managed forests and other controlled sources
www.fsc.org Cert no. SGS-COC-2482
© 1996 Forest Stewardship Council
FSC

Printed and bound in Great Britain by
TJ International Ltd, Padstow, Cornwall

Contents

List of Cases *vii*
List of Statutes *xi*
Acknowledgements *xiii*
Foreword *xv*

PART I BACKGROUND

1 Introduction 3

2 Concepts and Issues 13

3 Alder Hey and Public Opinion 33

4 Terminology 45

PART II LEGAL APPROACHES

5 Old Law for New Problems? 61

6 Protecting Entitlements 67

7 The Common Law Position 75

8 Legislation 91

9 A Look at Paradigmatic Case Law 107

10 The Law, Systematically 117

PART III BIOEQUITY

11 Equity 137

12 Developing New Property Classes 151

13 Concluding Thoughts 161

Bibliography *165*
Index *175*

List of Cases

Commonwealth and US Cases

AB v. Leeds Teaching Hospital NHS Trust [2004] EWHC 644, [2004] 2 Fam LR 365
Alcock v. Chief Constable of South Yorkshire Police (1992) 1 AC 310
Attia v. British Gas plc [1988] QB 304
Attorney General's Reference (No. 6 of 1980) [1981] QB 715
Bishopsgate Motor Finance Corp. v. Transport Brakes Ltd. [1949] 1 KB 332
Bolam v. Friern Hospital Management Committee [1957] 2 All ER 118
Borden (UK) Ltd. v. Scottish Timber Products Ltd. [1981] 12 Ch. 25
Bourhill v. Young [1943] AC 92
Bowman v. Secular Society Ltd. [1917] AC 406
Browning v. Norton Children's Hospital (1974) 504 SW 2d 713 (Ky)
Central London Property Trust Ltd. v. High Trees House Ltd. [1947] KB 130, [1956] 1 All ER 256
Chester v. Ashfar [2005] 1 AC 134, [2004] 4 All ER 587, [2004] 3 WLR 927
Church of England Building Society v. Piskor [1954] Ch 553, [1954] 2 All ER 85
Cobbs v. Grant (1972) 8 Cal.3d 229
Creswell v. Potter [1978] 1 WLR 255
Diamond v. Chakrabarty 447 U.S. 303 (1980)
Dobson v. North Tyneside Health Authority [1996] 4 All ER 474
Donaldson v. Beckett (1774) 4 Burr. 2408
Doodeward v. Spence (1908) CLR 406
Evans v. Amicus Healthcare Ltd. [2003] EWHC 2161, [2004] EWCA (Civ) 727
Exelby v. Handyside (1749) 2 East PC 652
F v. West Berkshire Health Authority [1989] 2 All ER 545
Gillick v. West Norfolk and Wisbech Area Health Authority [1986] 1 AC 112
Glass v. UK [2004] 1 FLR 1019
Greenberg v. Miami Children's Hospital Res. Inst. 264 F. Supp.2d 1064 (2003)
Hadley v. Midland Fertility Services Ltd. and Others [2003] EWHC 2161 (Fam)
Haynes's Case (1614) 12 Co. Rep. 113
Hecht v. Kane 16 Cal. App. 4Th 836 (1993)
Herring v. Walround (1682) 22 ER 870, [1681] 2 Chan Cas 110
Ingram and Another v. Commissioners of Inland Revenue [1999] 2 WLR 90, [2000] 1 AC 293, [1999] 1 All ER 297, [1998] UKHL 47
Macmillan Inc v. Bishopsgate Investment Trust plc (No. 3) [1995] 1 WLR 798
McLoughlin v. O'Brian [1983] AC 410

Millar v. Taylor (1769) 4 Burr. 2303
Ministry of Health v. Simpson [1951] AC 251
Moore v. The Regents of the University of California 793 P 2d 479 (Cal. 1990)
Page v. Smith [1994] 4 All ER 522
Perry v. British Railways Board [1980] ICR 743
Pilcher v. Rawlins (1872) LR 7 Ch. 259
Polly Peck International plc v. Nadir (No. 2) [1992] 4 All ER 769
Quick v. Coppleton (1803) 83 ER 349
R (on the application of Burke) v. GMC [2005] 3 FCR 169
R v. Bateman (1925) 94 LJKB 791
R v. Bristol Coroner, ex p. Kerr [1974] QB 652
R v. Brown [1993] 2 All ER 75, [1994] 1 AC 212, [1993] 2 WLR 556, [1992] UKHL 7
R v. Cheere (1825) 107 ER 1294
R v. Fox (1841) 114 ER 95
R v. Gibson [1991] 1 All ER 439
R v. Human Fertilisation and Embryology Authority, ex parte Blood [1997] 2 All ER 687, [1997] 2 WLR 806
R v. Kelly (1998) 3 All ER 741
R v. Lynn [1788] 2 Durn & E 733
R (on the application of Quintavalle) v. Human Fertilisation and Embryology Authority [2003] 3 All ER 257
R v. Rothery (1976) RTR 550
R v. Sharpe (1857) Dears & B 160
R v. Welsh (1974) RTR 478
R v. Wright (1603) Co. Lit. f. 127 a-b
Re Cole [1964] 1 Ch 175
Re Diplock's Estate [1948] Ch 465
Re F [1990] 2 AC 1
Re Goldcorp Exchange Ltd. [1995] 1 AC 74
Re GWW and CMW (1997) 21 Fam LR 612
Re W [1992] 4 All ER 627
Roche v. Douglas [2000] WAR 331
Rowland v. Divall [1923] 2 KB 500
Schloendorff v. NY Hospital (1914) 194 NE 92
Scott v. Brown [1892] 2 QB 724
Sidaway v. The Board of Governors of the Bethlem Royal Hospital [1984] QB 493
Somersett's Case (1771) 20 How. St. Tr. 1, 80-81 (KB)
Tingler v. Chamberlain (1899) 71 Conn. 566
United Scientific Holdings Ltd. v. Burnley BC [1978] AC 904
Wallis v. Smith 2001 NMCA 17
Walsh v. Lonsdale (1882) 21 Ch.D. 9
Washington University v. Catalona 437 F.Supp.2d 985 (2006)

Westdeutsche Landesbank Girozentrale v. Islington London Borough Council [1996] 2 All ER 961
Williams v. Williams (1882) Ch.D. 659
Winston v. Lee 470 US 753 (1985) (Sup. Ct.)
Yearworth and others v. North Bristol NHS Trust [2009] EWCA Civ 37

Other Jurisdictions

BGH, BGHZ 124, 52 of 9 November 1993
BGH, I ZR 135/87 of 8 June 1989
BVerfG, 1 BvR 2181/98 of 11 August 1999
OLG Frankfurt a.M., 2002, 183 of 26 April 2002

List of Statutes

United Kingdom Legislation

Adults with Incapacity (Scotland) Act 2000
Anatomy Act 1832
Anatomy Act 1984
Animal Welfare Act 2006
Civil Procedure Act 1997, *Civil Procedure Rules*
Corneal Tissue Act 1986
County Courts Act 1984
Human Organs Transplant Act 1989
Human Fertilisation and Embryology Act 1990
Human Tissue Act 1961
Human Tissue Act 2004, *Human Tissue Bill*
Law of Property Act 1925
Mental Capacity Act 2005
Offences Against the Person Act 1861
Road Traffic Act 1988
Supreme Court Act 1981
Supreme Court of Judicature Act 1873
Theft Act 1968

Statutory Instruments

Statutory Instrument 50 of 2005; The Blood Safety and Quality Regulations 2005

Hansard

Reading of the Human Tissue Bill; Standing Committee G, House of Commons, 3 February 2003

Foreign Legislation

Gesetz über die Spende, Entnahme und Übertragung von Organen und Geweben [Transplantationsgesetz] of 4 September 2007 (BGBl. I S. 2206) (Germany)

European Instruments

Charter of Fundamental Rights of the European Union
Commission Directive 2006/17/EC on technical requirements for the donation, procurement and testing of human tissues and cells.
Commission Directive 2006/86/EC on traceability requirements, notification of serious adverse reactions and events and certain technical requirements for the coding, processing, preservation, storage and distribution of human tissues and cells.
Common Position (EC) No 50/2003 on setting standards of quality and safety for the donation, procurement, testing, processing, preservation, storage and distribution of human tissues and cells.
Directive 2002/98/EC of the European Parliament and of the Council on Standards of quality and safety for the collection, testing, processing, storage and distribution of human blood and blood components.
Directive 2004/23/EC of the European Parliament and of the Council on setting standards of quality and safety for the donation, procurement, testing, processing, preservation, storage and distribution of human tissues and cells.
Directive 2005/61/EC of the European Parliament and of the Council on Traceability requirements and notification of serious adverse reactions and events.
Directive 2005/62/EC of the European Parliament and of the Council on Community standards and specifications relating to a quality system for blood establishments.
Treaty on European Union and of the Treaty Establishing the European Community

International Instruments

Declaration of Helsinki
European Convention for the Protection of Human Rights and Fundamental Freedoms
Universal Declaration of Human Rights

Patents

US Patent No. 4,438,032: *'Unique T-lymphocyte line and products derived therefrom."*
US Patent No. 5,679,635: *'Aspartoacylase gene, protein, and methods of screening for mutatons (sic.) associated with canavan disease.'*
US Patent No. 7,217,547: *'Aspartoacylase gene, protein, and methods of screening for mutations associated with Canavan disease.'*

Acknowledgements

The work leading up to this text has been fragmented across a number of different initiatives, some private and some public. Initially, my interest in the question of how the human body could be viewed from a property perspective was raised by a European Union funded research project which I was part of (PropEur, University of Birmingham). Some time later, I was successful – together with Christian Lenk – in obtaining funding for our very own EU research project on human tissue, which is ongoing (Tiss.EU, University of Göttingen). During the course of these projects it became evident that the legal and ethical aspects of working with human cells and tissue are far from resolved and that more thought and ideas in this area are needed. The book before you is an attempt to not merely repeat the ideas that are already being discussed but to add to the discussion with a novel idea – using the Law of Equity to address property questions in cases of unlawfully obtained cells. Very recent case law in England underscores the relevance of this theme, confirms some of the conclusions of this book and shows that progress is being made.

I am very grateful to a number individuals who have supported me in the production of this text and the underlying research – sometimes unwittingly by asking the right (or the wrong!) questions during conferences. I particularly want to express my gratitude to (in no specific order): Christian Lenk, Claudia Wiesemann, Asim Sheikh, Heather Widdows, Roger Brownsword, Graeme Laurie, Uwe Koreik, Paul Hoyningen-Huene and Marc Stauch. De ma part aussi un grand remerciement à mes collègues Florence Bellivier et Christine Noiville du Centre National de la Recherche Scientifique à Paris pour leur référence à mon projet 'bioequity' dans leur nouveau livre sous le même titre (Bellivier and Noiville (2009) 'La Bioéquité' Editions Autrement, Paris). I am particularly grateful to Stephan Meder, Nikolaus Forgó, Axel Metzger, Hermann Butzer and Volker Epping for facilitating a much earlier version of this text. I am very much indebted to Alison Kirk and David Shervington of Ashgate and an unknown reviewer for their comments, corrections and hard work. Finally, I am grateful beyond words for the support and love I am given every day by my family, particularly my wonderful wife Nina. As ever, all inaccuracies and errors remain my own.

For Gaby and Hans-Peter

Foreword

Not much has information survived about the Roman legal scholar Gaius.[1] Even his exact name is subject to considerable debate. He wrote much of his work between 130 and 180 AD and did not take part in the bureaucratic power games other lawyers played in those days – and therefore he did not have the privilege to give legal answers in the emperor's name (ius respondendi). He probably lived in a provincial town contemporary historians were not particularly interested in.

Gaius is the author of the *institutiones* – a legal textbook that became one of the most influential legal documents ever written. The *institutiones* were a kind of archetype for teaching the law. The text is organized in three parts – *personae*, *res*, *actions* – and four books. Even contemporary Civil Codes (like the Austrian or the Italian) are organized much in the same way once developed by Gaius.

In the second book Gaius introduces a distinction between tangible and non-tangible goods.

> *12. Quaedam praeterea res corporales sunt, quaedam incorporales.* Things are either corporal or incorporal.
> *13. Corporales hae sunt, quae tangi possunt, velut fundus, homo, vestis, aurum, argentum et denique aliae res innumerabiles.* Corporal things are tangible as land, a slave, clothing, gold, silver and innumerable others.
> *14. Incorporales sunt, quae tangi non possunt qualia sunt ea, quae in iure consistunt, sicut hereditas, ususfructus, obligationes quoquo modo contractae. [...].* Incorporal things are intangible like those existing simply in law as inheritance, usufruct, obligation however contracted.

A clear distinction is drawn between physical objects (*res corporales*) and entitlements (*res incorporales*). A slave is quite clearly a *res corporalis* – just like any other physical object. The rules of property (and torts) apply. The Roman law has no problem in measuring the price and value of physical objects (and therefore also of slaves). Gaius' distinction became one of the main sources for the fundamental split between property law on the one hand and law of obligations on the other in modern legal doctrine.

---

1 For a (short) introduction to biographical details see O. Brehrends, Gaius. In: Stolleis, M. 2001, (ed.). *Juristen. Ein biographisches Lexikon. Von der Antike zum 20. Jahrhundert, München*. München: Beck, 229; See also Honoré, A.M. 1962. *Gaius: A Biography*. Oxford: Oxford University Press.

In our times, the fundamental distinction between physical objects and their proper legal regime on the one hand and entitlements on the other hand tends to disappear. We speak about *intellectual property*, as if it were a physical good in the creator's possession. We use all kinds of financial products instead of hard cash. Research in many fields (medicine is only one of them) becomes less and less interested in physical objects and concentrates more and more on data and information about physical objects. The physical good becomes nothing more but a storage device for the (non physical) information. This *virtual reality* is our real reality – in research and in the regulation and organisation of research.

Nils Hoppe's book is a fundamental and groundbreaking study about the ethical and legal consequences the growing availability of body material *and* information about body material has on contemporary medical research and care. He develops a set of thoughts necessary to bring the different interests, rights and claims into a new legally and ethically convincing order when no clear distinction between *res corporales* and *incorporales* can be made. Equity, as a concept European legal thinkers with a continental background are not too familiar with, might indeed become a guiding principle in the debate. The future will show whether it will be as influential as Gaius' distinction.

Nikolaus Forgó
2009

PART I
Background

Chapter 1
Introduction

> [Basilio and Loretta] Jorges spent $30,000 for infertility treatment. Loretta took fertility drugs and produced multiple eggs, some of which were mixed with Basilio's sperm and implanted back in Loretta. Loretta did not get pregnant. But without her knowledge or consent, some of her eggs were successfully implanted in another woman. The recipient was apparently duped into thinking they were from a consenting donor. The recipient gave birth to twins, a fact that the Jorges learned a few years later. Now the Jorges are suing to gain visitation rights to the eight-year-old twins created with Loretta's stolen eggs. The Jorges were not alone in being victims of theft. Medical records indicated that other couples' genetic material had also been purloined.[1]

The criminal offence of theft, in the UK, requires the 'dishonest appropriation of property belonging to another with the intention to permanently deprive the other of it'.[2] Andrews and Nelkin, quoted above, use theft terminology flowing from an understanding of how the case of the Jorges should be assessed on a common sense basis. It comes easy to speak of *our* bodies, *your* arm, *my* foot. They are *my* cells, *your* eyes and *their* genes. So when someone takes them away from me without my consent, or talks me into letting go of them by pretending that they are wanted for analysis but then uses them for research, maybe even for personal gain, should that not be a theft offence? The law[3] says *no* in most cases, *maybe* in some cases and *yes* in very few cases.[4] It certainly does not amount to a satisfactory level of desirable legal certainty.

The discussion is by no means new. Much has been written on the complex legal and ethical issues raised by the way excised human tissue and expelled or extracted body products are dealt with in practice. As is often the case, a number of high profile scandals provided the debate with new impulses. The discussion

---

1 Andrews, L. and Nelkin, D. 2001. *Body Bazaar – The Market for Human Tissue in the Biotechnology Age*. New York: Crown, at p. 157.

2 Section 1, Theft Act 1968.

3 In the context of the subject matter of this book it is very difficult to restrict the discussion to only one jurisdiction. Much valuable work has been done in a number of countries. For the purposes of coherence, a reference to *law* denotes, in this text, primarily English and Welsh law. Where appropriate, I have indicated a deviation from this and other jurisdictions are cited.

4 Such as where body product and tissue samples taken as evidence (cf. section 7, Road Traffic Act 1988) are misappropriated by the delinquent (see, as an illustration, *R v. Rothery* (1976) RTR 550 (blood) and *R v. Welsh* (1974) RTR 478 (urine)).

was fuelled in the 1990s both by the outrageous case of John Moore[5] as well as seemingly routine organ retention practices in UK hospitals.[6] More recently, certain large-scale research undertakings have appeared on the scene. These undertakings are dependent on the procurement of tissue samples from a broad section of the population, along with the sustained provision of personal health data on these individuals and the linking of the data. They come at a time when the public's view of research dealings with, possibly unwitting participants' tissue is highly critical.[7] One thinks of such projects as the UK Biobank project,[8] as well as the Baltic states' and Iceland's population genetic databases.[9]

The dilemma can be segmented into a number of discrete elements of law and ethics. On the legal side there is an overall reluctance of the courts to address the issue of proprietary interests in human biological material. Many opportunities, particularly given developments in modern bio-technological research, have been missed in confronting or attempting to address particular issues. Instead, the law has generally reverted to principles set some one hundred years ago in a case concerning a two-headed foetus in an Australian countryside circus.[10] The critical question, whether this is appropriate in the context of modern day medical reality, is highly relevant. At the same time it is worth asking whether it ought to be up to judges to address these questions when the legislator is possibly better placed to intervene. Nonetheless, it is necessary to reflect why it is important to address the question in terms of 'property' at all, this question being, especially in connection with the human body, incredibly inconvenient to argue in an ethical sense. Dworkin and Kennedy (1993) can assist us with such questions and have ably described the rationale for this style of legal thinking:

> In some cases, the courts may have to determine whether or not something is property because it is only when that matter is settled that particular legal consequences flow: for example, the precise cause of action available, against

---

5 *Moore v. The Regents of the University of California 793 P 2d 479 (Cal. 1990).* Also see p. 107 below.

6 See Redfern, M. 2001. *The Report of the Royal Liverpool Children's Inquiry*. London: The Stationery Office.

7 Dickson, D. 2002. Human Tissue Samples More Difficult to Obtain for Academics. *Nature Medicine*, 8, 543.

8 See Brownsword, R. 2007. Biobank Governance: Property, Privacy and Consent. In: C. Lenk, N. Hoppe and R. Andorno 2007. *Ethics and Law of Intellectual Property: Current Problems in Politics, Science and Technology*. Aldershot: Ashgate. 11-25.

9 See Andorno, R. 2007. Population Genetic Databases: A New Challenge to Human Rights. In: C. Lenk, N. Hoppe and R. Andorno 2007. *Ethics and Law of Intellectual Property: Current Problems in Politics, Science and Technology.* Aldershot: Ashgate.

10 *Doodeward v. Spence [1908] CLR 406.* Also see Dworkin, G. and Kennedy, I. 1993. Human Tissue: Rights in the Body and Its Parts. *Medical Law Review*, 1(3), 291-319. 'The English common law has never got to grips properly with this issue: many of the relevant common law authorities are ancient and of little real value in modern situations'.

> whom, and the rights to trace the destination of the property when considering remedies.[11]

Establishing property rights is therefore a necessary condition for entertaining any sort of notion of proprietary remedies. But it may, conversely, be that certain suitable rights can attach to a subject matter only if that subject matter is first held to be property. They go on to describe the exasperating lack of pragmatism contained within this system:

> Thus, there is a circular analysis: property does not exist unless certain rights normally attach to it; but it may not be possible to determine whether those rights are attached to that subject-matter without first determining whether the subject matter is property![12]

The point Dworkin and Kennedy seek to make is quite clear: whichever way we turn the question, we will need to address the question of property in order to test the law's ability to deal with human tissue in a proprietary fashion. Here, it is important to bear in mind that everyday practices usually have already established a certain kind of treatment (such as a proprietary treatment) and the law merely needs to work out how to capture this reality. At the same time, it is necessary to acknowledge that some routine practices (such as riding motorbikes without a helmet or availing oneself of the services of sex workers) are nonetheless sometimes prohibited by law and their continuous occurrence in 'real' life does not favourably influence their illegal quality.

The second challenge, and, in essence, the necessary precursor to any valid legal regulatory attempt, concerns the design of an ethically acceptable manner of dealing with human biological material. In this context, it is necessary to carefully establish whether what we are struggling with is a question of ethics or one of language. It could be suggested that what we are really dealing with is a problem in a terminological dimension rather than one of actual meaning: we feel that the tools provided by everyday language do not adequately encompass the special status which the human body enjoys. Speaking, therefore, of *things*, *property* and *ownership* when referring to human bodies produces an uneasy feeling. This uneasiness is manifested in different ways, sometimes by reverting to terminology used by Marx in a derogatory sense.[13] This prejudices any sensible discussion of the issues by using negatively connotated notions such as *commodification*

---

11 Dworkin and Kennedy 1993 at p. 293.

12 Dworkin and Kennedy 1993 at p. 293.

13 '[...] labourers, who must sell themselves piecemeal, are a commodity, like every other article of commerce, and are consequently exposed to all the vicissitudes of competition, to all the fluctuations of the market'. Marx, K. and F. Engels 1848 Manifesto of the Communist Party, available at http://www.gutenberg.org/etext/61, accessed 3 June 2009.

or *propertization*. This terminology means to denote the ultimate alienability of something, the making of something into a thing rather than an entity enshrining deeper value than merely that of its raw material. Another example is that of the term *exploitation*: when used in connection to human beings it denotes a repulsive way of treating others. Where we use the term in an economical context, it merely indicates a certain amount of use gleaned from an available resource. Many commentators see the human body and many of the personal rights attaching to the person as being outside the realm of what can be made into such a resource:

> The idea is that there are limits to what can be bought or sold as commodities. Some things are so valuable, priceless or sacred that they should never be allowed into the marketplace. Selling human organs offends common notions of decency.[14]

Whilst there is sufficient empirical evidence that the human body is valuable (more on this later), its sacred status or even 'pricelessness' are products of subjective philosophical or religious views. These views will differ considerably from one individual to the next and as such do not lend themselves easily to academic comparison. Further, quite independent of whether individual authors are in favour of a regulated level of compensation for the source (such as in the case of de Castro, quoted above) or not, the negative association of terms such as *commodification*, *commercialization* and *propertization* mean that the debate often grinds to a halt before an adequate assessment of what we actually mean to say can be made.

Add to this the fact that, in many cases, commentators start their explorations of the theme with a preconceived notion that commercial dealings with human-derived materials must be wrong and only then go on to develop an argument to support this view. As Macklin states: 'A presumption appears throughout the literature that [...] it would be wrong to pay donors for their eggs. [...] However, nowhere is an explanation offered for why payment for eggs is ethically suspect'.[15] Macklin wrote these lines in 1996; since then, literature has endeavoured to provide clear and salient reasoning on the question why the sale of oocytes can be argued to be ethically inadmissible.[16] Nonetheless, in order to discuss these issues comprehensively, it would be more sensible to test one's own convictions

---

14 De Castro, L. 2003. Commodification and Exploitation: Arguments in Favour of Compensated Organ Donation. *Journal of Medical Ethics*, 29(3), 142-146.

15 Macklin, R. 1996. What Is Wrong with Commodification? In: Cohen, C. *New Ways of Making Babies: The Case of Egg Donation*. Bloomington and Indianapolis: Indiana University Press, cited in Cohen, C.B. 1999. Selling Bits and Pieces of Humans to Make Babies: The Gift of the Magi Revisited. *Journal of Medicine and Philosophy*, 24(3), 288-306.

16 See, for example, Fox, D. 2008. Paying for Particulars in People-to-be: Commercialisation, Commodification and Commensurability in Human Reproduction. *Journal of Medical Ethics*, 34(3), 162-166.

(which probably cannot be fully avoided) against the full range of contemporary possibilities and viewpoints before coming to a conclusion and expressing it in the literature. In order to be sufficiently systematic about reviewing one's assumptions in this fashion, a close look at the issues involved is essential. More often than not, different premises are intermingled and the debate therefore, regrettably, is unfocused.

A common theme running through much of the literature is that of an unquestioning adherence to the inalienability of the body under any circumstances, closely following a purportedly Kantian stance on dignity. Cohen states: 'according to Kant, [dignity] is not an attribute of isolated individuals, but of individuals who belong to a community, "the realm of ends". In that community, each member is suffused with dignity'.[17]

Any such attribute belonging not to the individual but, in some way, constituting a type of *res communis* opens it up to communal regulation. It is thus withdrawn from the realm of influence of the individual (and therefore also from his choice) and given to being decided on the basis of what is best for the community in question – if necessary overriding the interests of the individual. The criticism of seeking to revert to outdated legal principles may also be applied in the case of commentators rigidly adhering to philosophical viewpoints whose times have been and gone – and which, quite simply, may be interpreted somewhat out of context. Seeking the comfortable shelter of what some see as *Kantian* inalienability stipulations rather than testing our assumptions against current moral viewpoints and a contemporary biotechnological backdrop, appears to be naïve.[18] Can the view attributed to Kant seriously be considered to be any more than a mere guiding principle, a rudimentary starting point for one possible, very narrow, perspective of the issue, comfortably cushioned in the historical and scientific context of the late eighteenth century? 'In ethics and political philosophy, as in bioethics, Kant's principles of ethics are typically invoked in order to put forward strict restrictions on what should be allowed', Merle tells us.[19]

It rather seems to be the case that the Kantian stance is drawn on where a certain style of viewpoint seeks to find philosophical arguments to underpin its logic where it would be more persuasive to simply re-argue the issue on the basis of contemporary considerations. In particular, it is difficult to see why we would need to reinterpret Kant in a fashion which is commensurate with modern biotechnology – the question '*what would Kant have made of organ transplantation?*' simply promises no interesting answers over and above an entertaining analysis of the benefit of hindsight. In fairness to this text, the aim is not to provide an overview

17 Cohen 1999, at p. 292.

18 To my great relief, Cohen, whilst finding him instructive, does not feel either that we need to become fully fledged Kantians to benefit from his reflections. See Cohen (1999) at p. 292.

19 Merle, J. 2000. A Kantian Argument for a Duty to Donate One's Own Organs. A Reply to Nicole Gerrand. *Journal of Applied Philosophy*, 17(1), 93-101.

of the plentiful and intricate works of philosophy on this topic, nor can it achieve this. Rather, the criticism is levelled at the selective use of isolated passages of, sometimes ancient, philosophy, in order to underpin modern viewpoints. In many cases, these viewpoints could just as persuasively be argued without conscripting Kant, Locke or Aristotle to posthumously endorse them.

The result of arguing from different moral vantage points, whilst desirable in terms of diversity of debate, is that the discourse tends to focus on a number of questions which do not always give the appearance of homogenous semantics: some commentators ostensibly advocate the introduction of property rules for the purposes of encompassing entitlements to human tissue. Others suggest that the human body and its constitutents are inherently inalienable and the application of property rules goes against the grain of our moral fabric. Both groups use terminology, such as *property*, *entitlement*, *ownership*, *possession* and so forth in different, sometimes overlapping, often synonymous or seldom comparable ways – despite the fact that the argument is had in a fashion which suggests a dialogue of some kind. This may lead to a discourse situation where it appears prudent to always find a middle ground, regardless of how little persuasive quality or contextually appropriate relevance one or the other side's arguments may possess, which does not advance this important debate and is therefore counterproductive.

> This format usually encourages protagonists to collect into an unsorted heap whatever arguments look as though they might have any persuasive force on their side, and because people may be on the same political side for different moral reasons, or have the same moral principles but reach different political conclusions, the political arguments tend to obscure both the real issues and the logical structure of the controversy.[20]

Whilst proponents of the property approach often feel supported by an intransigent libertarian ethic of absolute individual autonomy (and, presumably, are as disappointed by the fact that they are required to wear a helmet when riding their motorbikes[21] as they are about their inability to sell their spare kidney), those who side with the notion of an absolute inalienability of the body tend to call the, already mentioned, classic reasoning of Christian ethics to their aid and argue that whatever renders the body a means, rather than an end in itself, ought to be proscribed. An obvious marriage of the two views, a certain degree of respect for both the special status of the human body on the one hand and a deferential bow

20 Radcliffe Richards, J. 2003. Commentary: An Ethical Market in Human Organs. *Journal of Medical Ethics*, 29(3), 139-140.

21 See, e.g. Moser-Jones, M. and Bayer, R. 2007. Paternalism and its Discontents: Motorcycle Helmet Laws, Libertarian Values, and Public Health. *American Journal of Public Health*, 97(2), 208-217.

to the necessities of everyday medical practice on the other, appears eminently persuasive and is thankfully also regularly discussed.[22]

Nonetheless, it is rather simplistic to attempt to compartmentalize views in this complex area into any small number of distinct groups. Each nuance of differing opinion in terms of the utilization of the human body for research or therapy creates, in turn, a new stance on the issue, generally deserving of serious consideration and debate.

In this brief introduction, a first outline of a criticism of the obfuscation of terminology and belief in these debates is taking shape and will be further developed in subsequent chapters. The emotional charge on these debates and the helplessness with which we strive to make old law work for new challenges will be highlighted. Emotional encumbrance, high profile scandals and subsequent fast-track legislative reactions have led to a debate which is no longer in a position to provide the answers needed. It is acknowledged that what we are dealing with is an area of human life which is eminently difficult to pin down normatively. Many of the questions we are facing are a direct result of these questions' coordinates moving from what is ethically acceptable to what is ethically unacceptable[23] and from what is technically impossible to what is at some point routine.[24] Parts and products of the human body, severed from their original setting, increasingly represent valuable raw material for research and therapy.[25] Biomedical feasibility has in the past had a notable tendency to overtake legal admissibility at great speed and the law is thus predictably slow to develop novel strategies of dealing with these new challenges. Human beings, on the other hand, interact in this new arena in much the same way they have always interacted: where the ownership of something valuable is vaguely unclear, it is best to lay claim to it and wait to see what happens. Possession is a powerful state of affairs: force, only rarely acceptable, is required to overcome another's possessory right. It will become clear in Chapter 5 that past attempts to use established proprietary norms in this context have either failed or yielded unsatisfactory results. The reflex reaction,

---

22 Herring, J. and Chau, P. 2007. My Body, Your Body, Our Bodies. *Medical Law Review*, 15(1), 34-61.

23 Such as using executed prisoners' bodies for anthropophagic medical use and, later, for anatomical dissection.

24 The first successful heart transplantation by Christiaan Barnard in 1967 is a very good example of this. At the time, the survival time of the recipient – Louis Washkansky – was considered a success at 18 days. He died of bilateral pneumonia. Mean survival time nowadays is ≈ 12 years and some 80,000 people have received donor hearts worldwide. See Hoffenberg, R. 2001. Christiaan Barnard: His First Transplants and Their Impact on Concepts of Death. *British Medical Journal*, 323(7327), 1478-1480; German Heart Institute Berlin (DHZB) (2008) 'Long Term Results after Heart Transplantation', available at http://www.dhzb.de/aktuell/veranstaltungen/long_term_results_after_heart_transplantation/, accessed 19 May 2008.

25 At a recent experts' meeting I attended, the phrase 'Gold of the 21st Century' was used to describe its status.

applauded by those who feel the body must remain inalienable, is to assume that these proprietary strategies have failed because the body and its parts reside outside the sphere of what can be owned or possessed and thus we must trouble ourselves with questions of personal rights, human rights or dignity rather than questions of theft, conversion or trespass. Chapter 12 contains the proposition that this is an unusual way to attempt to address these questions. In the past, the law has, at regular intervals, encountered novel ideas and has had to work with them: when intellectual property rights became an issue, the law had to develop strategies to establish proprietary remedies in relation to something quite ethereal. Traditional concepts of property had to be reframed to encompass the notion of ownership in ideas and concepts, lines of poetry, pieces of music. The law thus knows two kinds of property: tangible property and intangible property. It is argued that it is time to introduce a third kind of property to capture the rights and entitlements attached to the human body and its parts. By doing so, we avoid the terminological flaws of using ordinary proprietary terminology to refer to the body and we create an elegant and efficient legal framework within which we address questions of ownership and possession in human body parts and products. The transition from traditional concepts of property to revolutionary proprietary concepts (such as intellectual property and *choses in action*) was in many aspects based on the flexible concepts of the Law of Equity. These concepts of Equity can do more than merely assist us in creating a plausible and convincing legal structure for our dilemma.

This text is structured into thirteen chapters, divided into three parts. The first part, 'Background', explains the complex conceptual questions involved. It starts with a criticism of undifferentiated uses of terminology, such as *commodification,* as well as the inhomogenous structure of the debate. It further introduces a matrix which seeks to facilitate the categorization of retention cases and the identification of legal and ethical issues involved. This part sets the scene for the two parts which follow, providing a useful reference for the subsequent discussions.

The second part, 'Legal Approaches' represents an overview of the current state of play in relation to legally capturing proprietary entitlements to human tissue. Starting from basic questions of how the law seeks to protect entitlements, a discussion of the distinction between using rules of liability or rules of property to protect entitlements and the question of the inalienability of certain entitlements is given. This is followed by a discussion of the Common Law legal situation and some very recent developments are shown: the introduction of the Human Tissue Act, The EU's *Tissue Directive* and recent case law, such as the *Moore*, *Catalona* and *Greenberg* cases, as well as the very recent *Yearworth* case. The part culminates in a criticism of the current regime and the identification of a pressing need for reform in Chapter 10.

In the third part, 'Bioequity', an introduction to the nature and history of Equity and a suggestion how a reformed normative framework for treating human tissue in a proprietary fashion might look are given. Equitable property concepts, often used to make a distinction between moral entitlements and legal entitlements in the context of subject matter the Common Law fails to see as property, are applied to a modern biomedical setting. As an introduction to the concept, a short history of the development of Equity is set as a backdrop to a more detailed analysis of equitable property concepts. By way of example, the presented logic is applied to the paradigmatic case of *Moore* in order to demonstrate its workings and thereby suggest a novel normative property framework for dealing with human tissue.

There is a respectable amount of very good literature on questions of property in human tissue and the human body.[26] The idea of this text is not to reinvent the wheel but to add something new to this library: to show some, but, by necessity, not all of the problems in relation to how the matter is generally discussed. This work seeks to show the inequitable way the law deals with the issues at stake and propose a workable design to resolve some of the issues by applying the Law of Equity. In order to accomplish all this, a sensible, structured discussion is a necessary precursor. If the aim is to find a workable design for legally and ethically encompassing questions of property and human tissue, a lowest common denominator must initially be identified as a skeleton and then, actions and concepts which are legally practicable and ethically admissible should form the flesh upon those bones. What we have at the end of such an exercise is a body of law and ethics which may be put to work.

26 See, for example, Dickenson, D. 2007. *Property in the Body: Feminist Perspectives*. Cambridge, UK; New York: Cambridge University Press; Nwabueze, R.N. 2007. *Biotechnology and the Challenge of Property: Property Rights in Dead Bodies, Body Parts, and Genetic Information*. Aldershot: Ashgate; Wilkinson, S. 2003. *Bodies for Sale: Ethics and Exploitation in the Human Body Trade*. London: Routledge; and some excellent chapters in Mason, J.K. and Laurie, G.T. 2006. *Law and Medical Ethics*. Oxford: Oxford University Press; Herring, J. 2006. *Medical Law and Ethics*. Oxford: Oxford University Press; Lenk, C., Hoppe, N. and Andorno, R. 2007. *Ethics and Law of Intellectual Property: Current Problems in Politics, Science, and Technology*. Aldershot: Ashgate.

Chapter 2
Concepts and Issues

'Property and the human body' is an academic theme populated by more than one discipline. Lawyers, philosophers, medical professionals, economists and representatives of many other subjects crowd the scene. The introduction to this book contained a description of how the debate is sometimes slowed down by an inconsistent use of terminology and a confusing mixture of beliefs about how certain concepts work in reality. The question of *exploitation* is one where this confusion is thrown into stark relief. There appears to be an overriding fear that an increase in the 'propertization' of the human body automatically leads to dark and sinister organ trading cartels taking over the world of medicine. It remains a fact that the post-mortem removal of organs for transplantation purposes can only take place where the source of the organs has died in an intensive care setting. This very often fails to find adequate attention but rules out a number of practices suggested by some to be the natural consequence of a higher level of propertization of the body: exploitation practices ranging from back alley kidney sales all the way to stealing corpses from the morgues to sell on their organs for transplantation.[1]

This chapter will introduce a number of concepts which are vital to the subsequent discussion as they will establish a systematic framework. This framework determines the setting in which the discussion is taking place. A look will be taken at the kinds of tissue and body products that have already been made the subject of property (in which case it could be suggested that the law is trying to catch up with reality) before looking at some of the reasons for the recent increase in debating propertization issues – the organ retention scandal at Alder Hey[2] featuring prominently. Finally, a number of pivotal concepts will be illustrated, the distinction of each of which might come easier to the lawyer than to the non-lawyer. In particular, the accurate and careful differentiation between notions of *entitlements*, *property*, *ownership* and *possession* is paramount to the remainder of this book.

---

1 See, e.g. Remigius Nwabueze's comments on the genesis of the Human Tissue Act 1961. Nwabueze, R. 2007 at p. 47; Savulescu, J. 2003. Is the Sale of Body Parts Wrong? *Journal of Medical Ethics*, 29(3), 138-139 at p. 138; Keller, M. 2008. *Ausgeschlachtet – Die menschliche Leiche als Rohstoff* [Butchered – The Human Body as Raw Material]. Berlin: Econ.

2 In the 1980s and 1990s, some 2,000 organs were retained without appropriate consent at a Liverpool hospital. See Chapter 3 below for a detailed account and discussion.

Systematically Discussing Propertization

A central criticism made here, is that there is no homogeneous structured discussion of the problem of capturing proprietary entitlements in human tissue. One author might speak of issues in relation to live organ donation whilst another addresses the retention of children's organs after post-mortem examinations. An argument develops and the two commentators ostensibly cannot agree. In reality, the subject matter of the discourse is inappropriate for a comparison to be made. A slight but significant difference in their premise (such as between the taking of tissue from live and from post-mortem sources) is sufficient to totally unhinge the comparability of their logic and their analysis. A further issue might be the, sometimes hidden, methodological and educational differences between members of the different sciences engaged in this interdisciplinary field. Nonetheless, there are a number of important core features of the debate which all protagonists can agree on.[3] For the purpose of guiding one through the debate and to facilitate the identification of the different issues which present themselves in this complex thematic environment, a matrix will be introduced here. It is supposed to serve two purposes: on the one hand, it is intended to provide us with a more systematic and schematic method for displaying absolute differences in concepts. On the other hand, it will give the next part of this text a structure which makes sense, hopefully providing a trail of breadcrumbs running through the exploration of the problems.

The matrix (Figure 2.1) is an attempt at visualizing conceptual differences. No claims can be made as to its absolute accuracy or validity. Its primary purpose here is to raise awareness of the different issues which are all too often intermingled in the discussion. To start off with, questions on the treatment of human tissue have been segmented into a number of discrete individual problems, the characteristics of which will, in individual cases, mean different legal and ethical consequences. These have been put in horizontally declining order of contextual relevance, starting with the nature of the source from which the material derives. Next is the overarching notion of consent, and the quality of such consent, which needs to be discussed. The validity of consent is interdependent with the solution of the third column, which looks at the level of impact which the excision has on the source. It will be shown later that one cannot consent to all types of harm and thus the value returned by the third column is paramount to deciding whether, under current law, the excision was lawful at all. The second part of the matrix consists of the motive for the excision, the type of tissue excised, an element of *mens rea*[4] and one of pecuniarity. The final two columns – potential appropriation *mens rea* and pecuniarity – are necessary to underpin the proposals contained in the last part

3 The relevance of consent in the larger context and discussions of conscription of organs, for example, tend to be rejected by the majority in each discipline on the basis of its incompatibility with shared notions of individual autonomy and choice.

4 'Guilty mind' – the state of mind that the prosecution must prove a defendant to have had at the time of committing a crime in order to secure a conviction.

	Source A	*Consent* B	*Impact* C	*Motive* D	*Type of tissue* E	*Appropriation* F	*Pecuniarity* G
1	Live, compos mentis	Informed	No contact	Individually therapeutic	Body products	Honest	No
2	Post mortem, ex-ante provisions	Other consent	Non-invasive	3rd party therapeutic	Regenerative tissue	Dishonest	Yes
3	Post mortem, no ex-ante provisions	None	Invasive	Individually beneficial, non-therapeutic	Reproductive material		
4	Unknown			Non-therapeutic	Non-regenerative tissue		
5	Live, non-compos mentis, child			Non-therapeutic + genetic analysis			

Figure 2.1 Matrix – different aspects of tissue retention

of this text – the principle behind developing fresh proprietary approaches using the Law of Equity.

Where a matrix such as this one is introduced, it may raise the expectation that it is a tool to produce simple answers. It would, of course, be a very elegant solution if it were possible to create a checksum x to determine the ethical or legal admissibility of a certain tissue retention act. Moore, as an illustration would score a *16*:

- live, *compos-mentis* (1)
- no consent (3)
- invasive excision (3)
- non-therapeutic motive (4)
- body products[5] (1)
- dishonest appropriation (2)
- pecuniary interest (2)

What if it could simply be said that:

$$\textit{if}\ \mathrm{x} > 12 = \text{inadmissible}$$

This is neither the idea behind the matrix, nor does it work.[6] The law rarely lends itself to arithmetic solutions. The matrix is to be used to illustrate the mixed character of the discussion and to provide a structure for discussing different elements of the problem. On the following pages, the categories will be introduced and their relevance in the discussion on property and the human

5 I have given Golde and Quan the benefit of the doubt in terms of the type of tissue.

6 The concept already falters on the basis that each cell in each column would have to be accorded different values, the source and thus authority of which is quite unclear.

body will be underlined. Subsequently, the same structure will be applied to illustrate how the law currently views the issues at stake here. In the following, an illustration of the matrix's categories will be provided whilst more detailed sources and references in relation to the individual underlying concepts can be found in Chapters 7 and 10. I will refer to where in the matrix the current discussion takes place by including the 'coordinates' in brackets.

Source

Speaking of the source of the tissue as a 'donor', such as in the term 'organ donor', prejudices the debate based on a wrong premise: donation implies some sort of voluntary giving of a gift to another. It also presumes property rights which must be present to validate the act of gifting.[7] Even though the notion of a gift relationship is often used to demonstrate an ethical best practice model in relation to parting with tissue, stripping elements of voluntary giving out of the equation decisively weakens the arguments in favour of calling the process a donation.[8] The term *source* seems to be more appropriate. This is particularly relevant where the source of the material is unaware of the '*gift*' or, quite simply, deceased.

One of the lessons from public scandals such as Alder Hey[9] is that any public discourse on tissue retention incidents will be influenced by what could be called the 'emotional' status of the source. Had the tissue retained at Alder Hey not been that of children, whose grieving parents were deprived of an opportunity to bury them intact, the situation may have been different. For example, organs retained from post mortem examinations of octogenarians in the interests of a longevity study may well have generated less (or at least a different kind of) uproar and possibly a more sensible debate.[10] Add to that the fact that, on condition of the source's competence to express his or her own wishes, it is the source's desire which steers the procurement and retention of tissues. This means that the nature of the source is of paramount importance. Live patients, capable of understanding the proposed intervention and capable of giving consent, are very much medical

7 The conceptual flaw of using property notions for the purposes of constructing a gift will be addressed as part of the discussion of the *Greenberg* and *Catalona* cases in Chapter 9.

8 See Plant, R. 1977. Gifts, Exchanges and Political Economy of Health Care. *Journal of Medical Ethics*, 3(4), 166-173; Boyes, M and Ward, P. 2003. Brain donation for schizophrenia research: gift, consent, and meaning. *Journal of Medical Ethics*, 29, 165-168.

9 The Alder Hey scandal is discussed in detail below. See Chapter 3.

10 A public survey on attitudes towards organ donation found that there were particular sensitivities in relation to children's organs being taken. Presentation given by K. Shearn of Opinion Leader Ltd. at the IQPC conference on Biobanking and Sample Management, Frankfurt, 26 May 2009.

law's darling[11] (and, in our matrix, A1). They are in a position to consent to the extraction of tissue and, in barring aspects of an inability to consent to certain kinds of harm,[12] this will provide sufficient justification for a subsequent use of the tissue.

Where the source has died but has made *ex ante* provisions (A2), e.g. an effective provision as to what is to be done with his or her body after death, including provisions in relation to the excision of tissue and its subsequent use, this situation is, in terms of expressiveness, almost equivalent to a living patient's express consent. The adherence to these kinds of *ex ante* provisions is, however, rather an expression of respect for the deceased's wishes than a legally binding instruction.[13] Harris argues that this is because whilst a sense of interest prevails, the 'I' to whom the interest attaches does not.[14] Two practical problems do, however, play a central part in this situation: on the one hand, regardless of how much foresight the source may have had, *ex ante* provisions are often simply not clear enough to provide sufficient guidance for clinicians (or – even worse – they may just not be found in time to influence proceedings). On the other hand, clinicians will very often revert to the deceased's relatives and ask for their permission, in some cases despite being in possession of valid *ex ante* provisions. Pattison asserts that this was very much the normal state of affairs under the old regime for tissue acquisition in the UK.[15] If the relatives decide, against the express wishes of the deceased, that they do not wish tissue or organs to be extracted and used, the clinicians rarely go against this. It is quite simply an issue of pragmatism: the deceased will not start legal action against the hospital to enforce a donation,[16] whilst the relatives may well. Conversely, it appears to be quite safe for physicians to override the relatives' desires to donate where the source's opposing wishes are known – after all, the physicians cannot be forced to take tissue.

---

11 A deliberate analogy to 'Equity's darling': the *bona fide* purchaser for value without notice. 'Equity's darling' fulfils all the requirements for an innocent purchaser who is favoured by the Law of Equity. See *Polly Peck International plc v. Nadir (No 2)* [1992] 4 All ER 769 and *Macmillan Inc v. Bishopsgate Investment Trust plc (No 3)* [1995] 1 WLR 798, cited in Worthington, S. 2006. *Equity*. Oxford: Oxford University Press, at p. 96.

12 *Attorney General's Reference (No. 6 of 1980) [1981] QB 715* as per Lord Lane: '[...] even the most complete consent, by the most competent person, will not suffice to legalise an assault which there are public grounds for prohibiting', cited in Dworkin and Kennedy 1993, at pp. 291-292.

13 Though the Human Tissue Act 2004 contains provisions of an appropriate consent given *ex ante*, numerous questions remain in relation to the proprietary disposability of the body of a deceased person. See Sperling, D. 2008. *Posthumous Interests: Legal and Ethical Perspectives*. Cambridge: Cambridge University Press. p. 88ff.

14 Harris, J. 2002. Law and Regulation of Retained Organs: The Ethical Issues. *Legal Studies*, 22(4), 527-549, at p. 537.

15 Pattinson, S.D. 2006. *Medical Law and Ethics*. London: Sweet & Maxwell Ltd, at p. 434.

16 And how would you compel a physician to take tissue?

This leads to the third source scenario – that of the post mortem extraction with no *ex ante* provision (A3). Here, the relatives will in most cases be asked and the resulting permission to use the source's body for tissue harvesting is correspondingly weaker than any permission manifested, in some form or the other, by the source him or herself.

Continuing our look at the different categories of the matrix, we encounter an even more problematic situation: where there is no knowledge of the source's identity (A4). Many of the specimens retained at Alder Hey will fall into this category. Given that there was a complete lack of a system for cataloguing the tissue preparations, it will in almost all cases be unrealistically difficult to find relatives of sufficient standing to provide *ex ante* consent to the continued use of the tissue.[17] Most researchers, at this stage, tend to revert to continuing their research using these tissues as, conversely there is no way the relatives can know of the use of the tissue, no-one is likely to come and complain about it. Not knowing *whom we harm* or the harmed not knowing that *he is being harmed* does not, however, justify harming.

Finally, a look at the most protection-worthy class of sources is in order: those unable to give consent and children (A5). Those unable to consent to the use of their tissue through incompetence or age are used as sources in a surprising number of cases.[18] Such use is, both legally and ethically, highly questionable. Consent given on behalf of others in the shape of *by proxy* consent, in particular where the intervention is non-therapeutic is, in the absence of positive law, also a matter of concern.

Consent

Having established the nature of the source, and thus his or her ability to consent to what is yet to come (or at least who can consent on their behalf, if anyone), a look at the type of consent that has been obtained is necessary. As will be shown below (Chapter 3), the notion of informed consent (B1) has yet to fully percolate into English medico-legal reality.[19] The admissibility of weaker forms of consent (B2), or lack of consent altogether (B3), will be discussed in detail, as well as questions of providing blanket consent for the use of material in biobanks, the future potential research outlook being unknown at the time of donation with

17 Again, the Human Tissue Act 2004, discussed in detail later on, makes provisions in relation to existing collections. For the purposes of systematizing the discussion, existing collections are nevertheless discussed here.

18 As an example, see the Australian case of *Re GWW and CMW [1997] 21 Fam LR 612* where the court used its *parens patriae* jurisdiction to authorize a bone marrow donation from an *incapax*.

19 There is a convincing argument, discussed below in Chapter 7, that there is in fact no need for full informed consent in order to lawfully carry out medical treatment.

legislators and researchers seeking to introduce a generic blanket consent model (also B2).

Impact

The ability to consent to medical intervention is dependent on the level of impact that this particular intervention involves. As will be illustrated below, the law has been fickle when the question of permissible harm is to be addressed: having adornments permanently etched into oneself, piercing holes in body parts and having potentially fatal fistfights with others in the name of sport have been deemed to be largely unproblematic,[20] whilst consensual sado-masochistic activity for sexual gratification amongst adults is seen as inadmissible.[21] The notion hinges on the 'lawfulness' of the activity representing the impact. Therapeutic surgery, as an illustration, is of course a lawful activity. When investigating the level of impact and its interconnecting characteristics with the other categories which have been established (such as consent and source), it will be possible to narrow down the bases upon which society decides whether certain rights are inalienable or not.

The least problematic kind of impact is evidently one where no physical contact is made (C1). An example of this may be the donation of sperm or the retention of urine and faeces in cases where the source him or herself provides the material. There is sufficient evidence that even in these situations, however, harm may be the result of the taking. In circumstances where the taking is non-invasive or of very low invasive quality (C2) but the taking is done by someone else (such as a doctor or a nurse), the potential for harm increases. An example of this situation might be a swab of saliva and a borderline case may be the cutting of hair samples or the scraping of skin cell samples. There is a fluid threshold between a C2 impact and a C3 impact, with the invasiveness of the taking of skin cells being ever so close to the invasiveness in terms of taking larger combinations of cells, such as the removal of a growth on the patient's skin (C3). It will be

---

20 'In some circumstances violence is not punishable under the criminal law. When no actual bodily harm is caused, the consent of the person affected precludes him from complaining. There can be no conviction for the summary offence of common assault if the victim has consented to the assault. Even when violence is intentionally inflicted and results in actual bodily harm, wounding or serious bodily harm the accused is entitled to be acquitted if the injury was a foreseeable incident of a lawful activity in which the person injured was participating. Surgery involves intentional violence resulting in actual or sometimes serious bodily harm but surgery is a lawful activity. Other activities carried on with consent by or on behalf of the injured person have been accepted as lawful notwithstanding that they involve actual bodily harm or may cause serious bodily harm. Ritual circumcision, tattooing, ear-piercing and violent sports including boxing are lawful activities.' *R v. Brown* [1993] 2 All ER 75, [1994] 1 AC 212, [1993] 2 WLR 556, [1992] UKHL 7, as per Templeman LJ at 9.

21 See the ratio in *R v. Brown* cited above and discussed in more detail below, in Chapter 7.

described below how harm is singularly individual, so the exact quality of the impact very much depends on the individual patient's personal attributes. This is particularly relevant where the possibility of secondary harm (such as post-traumatic stress disorder) is discussed.[22]

Motive

Some thoughts on whether the motive for the removal of tissue plays any part at all in whether the excision itself is admissible will be expounded at a later stage. It is sometimes argued that it makes no difference,[23] but in terms of the Common Law assessment of the excision (prior to being able to apply proprietary concepts to the tissue) it is vital to check the motivation for the removal in order to ascertain whether it is possible to lawfully consent to a certain procedure.

> The destination and use of human tissue removed from the body varies. Some body or clinical waste ordinarily will be destroyed, discarded or otherwise disposed of immediately; some material may be used for medical purposes, for the therapeutic benefit of the patient who was the source of the material or, for example in transplantation situations, for the medical benefit of another; some may be used for medical research or teaching; some may be stored in tissue banks (or archived for record or other purposes); and in some cases, the body material may be used for non-medical purposes: for example, in research and development of non-therapeutic cosmetic product.[24]

It is also worth noting at this stage that the lawfulness or unlawfulness of the excision plays an important part when determining the possibility to follow or trace an entitlement in removed human tissue.[25]

In terms of the motivation for a certain activity, there is another category which overlaps in part with the preceding and following categories (in fact, the overlap is such that it is clear that any distinct lines drawn by the matrix schematically must falter when put to a test of categorical exactitude. For the purposes of schematically displaying the debate, its utility remains undiminished). Where the motive is to save or substantially improve the patient's life (D1), it is acceptable to remove non-regenerative tissue (such as amputations, for example) and to introduce one's own conception of what is required in the space left by a lack of consent or *ex ante* provisions on behalf of the unconscious patient (see 'Necessity', in Chapter 7). Where the motive is to provide a life saving treatment for another (such as a kidney transplantation) (D2) the latest state of play in the UK is that we can now

22 See Chapter 9.

23 Van Diest, P.J., Lopes Cardoso, N.W.J. et al. 2003. Cadaveric Tissue Donation: A Pathologist's Perspective. *Journal of Medical Ethics*, 29(3), 135-136.

24 Dworkin and Kennedy 1993, at pp. 291-292.

25 See Chapter 12.

consent to the non-therapeutic harm of the explantation, even where we do not know the recipient.[26] In the very same way, future possible methods and therapies must be kept within the realm of the possible, otherwise innovation and research will be stifled. That is why the law must remain flexible in this regard:

> This flexibility is necessary, if, in the absence of appropriate legislation, the courts are to keep up with medical reality. The legality of live organ transplantation demonstrates this. The very first transplants, insofar as they could not be categorized as therapeutic from the point of view of the donor, were questionable – there was no judicial authority to establish whether there was sufficient 'just cause' to provide a defence.[27]

One very prominent example of this is the first successful heart transplantation: Christiaan Barnard waited until the brain dead donor had stopped breathing spontaneously rather than relying on the irreversibility of the cessation of her brain functions for fear of criminal prosecution. In most other jurisdictions, a close personal relationship to the recipient is required to fulfil the conditions for the lawfulness of the donation. The law has neglected, so far, to introduce concrete criteria for evaluating the quality or proximity of relationships. The same kind of deficiency can be seen in the lack of a satisfactory explanation of how the voluntariness of the giving is improved by a high degree of personal proximity between the giver and the receiver.[28] Other scenarios might include the participation in research projects which have a direct impact on the source's own condition (D3) or the giving of tissue and body products for the purposes of pure research, independent of one's own medical condition or even for industrial purposes (D4). The motive for the extraction projects a designation on the material and not only provides important medico-legal criteria for establishing the admissibility of the excision, it also underpins the principles outlined by Harris in that it may or may not represent the *good moral reasons* used to justify the later use of such tissue.[29]

---

26 Section 33, Human Tissue Act 2004; Human Tissue Authority (2006). 'Code 2 – Code of Practice – Donation of Organs, Tissue and Cells for Transplantation', available at http://www.hta.gov.uk/guidance/codes_of_practice.cfm, accessed 3 June 2009.

27 Dworkin and Kennedy 1993, at pp. 299-300.

28 Examples from other jurisdictions include the relevant provisions of the German *Transplantationsgesetz* (Transplantation Act). Criminalizing all participants involved in the giving of an organ in a situation where no proximity between giver and receiver can be established was the subject of much criticism and a decision by the *Bundesverfassungsgericht* (Constitutional Court): in particular, it was criticized that, whilst the surgeon could be found to have neglected to ensure all requirements for a lawful transplantation were given, the criminal act of the giver and the receiver would be limited to failing to have a proximate relationship. *BVerfG, 1 BvR 2181/98 of 11.8.1999.*

29 Harris, J. 2002. Law and Regulation of Retained Organs: The Ethical Issues. *Legal Studies*, 22(4), 527-549 at p. 528.

The ethical status of a D4 excision for the purposes of research and an excision for the purposes of creating cosmetics in an industrial setting is difficult to assess. Would a different status be accorded to these two activities? In particular, would the taking of tissue for the purposes of research, which has no connection with the individual from whom the tissue is taken, be deemed to be qualitatively different to the excision of the tissue for the purposes of creating cosmetics? There seems to be an overriding feeling that as soon as some sort of pecuniary incentive or ulterior monetary motive is attached to dealings with the human body, the practice is deemed to be out of bounds. Giving blood for the sake of giving blood is commendable, receiving (sometimes disproportionate) disbursements for the trouble the donor goes to is acceptable, obtaining money's worth for the vendor's blood carries a stale taste and would by most be described as inappropriate.

It therefore appears that donation is fine, sale is not: self-deception by means of providing large sums labelled as compensation for expenses for the 'donation' of certain body products[30] are commonplace where, in reality, it is probably more accurate to speak of at least a monetary incentive for the donation and quite possibly a sale. The question of the relevance of the motivation for the excision is clear in terms of consenting to grievous bodily harm for the purposes of therapy or where the law permits it.[31] Contrast to that a situation where one consents to grievous bodily harm in the context of extracting one's own cells for one's own cosmetic treatment.[32] We can go one step further and consider the situation where material is taken to produce a commercial product which is not for the source but for others. The lines in this setting are very difficult to draw and it is prudent to bear this in mind when discussing these issues.

Type of Tissue

An interdependency exists between the categories of *impact* and *type of tissue*. Depending on what kind of tissue is taken, the level of harm inflicted on the source of the tissue can be gauged (taking blood requires more harm to be done than taking hair, for example). The relative degree of transience or permanence of an injury has a decisive impact on the kind of proscription, if any, the law deems necessary in relation to the activity which causes the injury. The law distinguishes between qualitative categories of harm (take, for example, the distinction made between *common assault* and *assault occasioning grievous bodily harm*) and provides for a proportionate degree of punishment. Where, therefore, the harm or injury is thought

30 Blood plasma, for example, is taken for between $9 and $20. There appears to be no problem labelling the transaction as a sale in this context. See Anderson, L., Newell, K. and Kilcoyne, J. 1999. 'Selling Blood': Characteristics and Motivations of Student Plasma Donors. *Sociological Spectrum*, 19, 137-162.

31 Such as the giving of a kidney or part of a liver for transplantation.

32 Cf. the relocation of fat from one's own body for the purposes of cosmetic surgery.

to be deserving of a special kind of interference to prevent it from happening, the law interferes. Where the harm does not exceed this basic trigger threshold, the law does not interfere. After all, the law does not concern itself with trifles – *de minimis non curat lex*. The injurious consequence is therefore one consideration when determining whether, in interplay with the other established categories, we are entitled to engage in the activity. Injury or harm, in this context, should also include notions of consequential ramifications of an activity. The creation of an embryo, part of whose genetic make-up will have been taken from the gametes of a source (E3), can (if the resulting foetus is brought to term) technically be described as economical harm. This is possibly terminologically suspect[33] but certainly a construct deserving of clarification and discussion. It is suggested below that the law must accord a higher level of protection to reproductive fluids than to other tissue samples containing genetic material. This holds true as long as the somewhat futuristic notion of producing human life from raw DNA data is just that – a futuristic notion – and not reality.

The taking of body products, such as waste products (E1), poses interesting additional questions of abandonment and waste analogies[34] but involves very little in the way of problematic intervention between the researcher (physician) and the research participant (patient). Indeed, it could be argued that the material would have been produced and ejected regardless of what, in terms of subsequent research activity, was planned for the material. The category E2 describes regenerative tissue, which in itself probably ought to be categorized in a finer grid: this may refer to top layers of skin, hair, fingernails (though there is an argument that, at some stage, hair and fingernails turn into a waste body product (E1) rather than remaining in the category of regenerative tissue (E2)). E2 refers to any type of tissue which, if taken, can be replaced by the body. The next category, E3, refers to reproductive material, i.e. gametes. Again, the category does not adequately do justice to the sizeable differences between the different kinds of gametes deserving discussion. The taking of sperm from a donor involves a considerably lower impact (C1) than that of taking oocytes (C3). The preparation of the donor for the harvesting of oocytes also involves a considerable health risk.[35] The category E4, finally, captures tissue which is non-regenerative. This includes all tissue

33 Though if reasonably argued to its conclusion is possibly inescapable. Dickenson is quite right when she timidly refers to babies as 'products' in this technical context. Where there is a product, there may be fault and liability in much the same way as a consequence may be described as 'harm'. See Dickenson, D. 2007. *Property in the Body: Feminist Perspectives*. Cambridge, UK; New York: Cambridge University Press at p. 12.

34 See McHale, J. 2000. Waste, Ownership and Bodily Products. *Health Care Analysis*, 8(2), 123-135.

35 See, e.g. Berg, J. 2001. Risky Business: Evaluating Oocyte Donation. *American Journal of Bioethics*, 1(4), 18-19; Giudice, L., Santa, E. and Pool, R. (2007). *Assessing the Medical Risks of Human Oocyte Donation for Stem Cell Research: Workshop Report*. Washington D.C.: National Academies Press, at pp. 13-50.

and tissue constructs which cannot be replaced by the body. No distinction is made within this category between redundant tissue structures (such as a kidney) and non-redundant structures (such as a limb). Again, some tissue types fall in-between categories (in this case, notably, the liver). The removal of such tissue by third parties for non-therapeutic or non-life-saving treatment is seen as *prima facie* illegal.[36] Where the tissue is severed by the source him or herself, it is still necessary to address the question of whether proprietary entitlements come to exist by virtue of the removal.

Appropriation and Pecuniarity

Finally, the last two categories in the matrix provide an important entry point to the third part of this text, as it underscores the current system's failure to attach negative consequences to a dishonest appropriation of tissue. It is argued that, despite the generally outrageous nature of source disenfranchisement such as in the case of Moore,[37] the real problem with the decision was that the court let itself be seen to let the gross illegality of the scientists' conduct remain without consequences.[38] An action for the assault would have been sure to succeed if Moore had successfully shown that the vast proportion of sample taking after his splenectomy was for ulterior research purposes rather than for his treatment, and therefore lacking appropriate consent. But Golde and Quan, the two scientists, were licensed by the court to profit directly from their unlawful act:[39] they had, it is submitted, sufficient *mens rea* for a theft offence (F2) and obtained a pecuniary profit from the illegal appropriation of Moore's cells (G2). This is inappropriate and demonstrates that the law is woefully wanting in this regard. The suggestion for a normative model, contained in the final chapters of this text, is based on the premise that downstream profit, generated from an illegal act, should under no circumstances remain with the wrongdoer.

The matrix therefore is intended to show category differences in discourse and is to serve as a structure for the debate for the purposes of this text. Rather than fall into the trap inherent in this theme and mix up different notions with countless

36 This follows from the decision in *R v. Brown* and the relevant stipulations in the Offences Against the Person Act 1861 (such as section 18) resulting in an inability to consent to certain harm and the qualitative unlawfulness of the harm inflicted.

37 The case is discussed in detail in Chapter 9.

38 Though the disenfranchisement issue can really be argued to serve as a fairly unsophisticated protection mechanism in favour of the source: were constituents of the human body to be classified as medical products from the outset, the source would possibly be liable for defects in the product. In the case of infections or other contamination of the constituent, this could have unforeseen ramifications and it could be suggested to be rather in the source's interest not to have proprietary interests.

39 'The greatest incitement to crime is the hope of escaping punishment'. Cicero, Pro Milone c. 50 B.C., cited in Van den Haag, E. 1975. *Punishing Criminals: Concerning a Very Old and Painful Question*. New York: Basic Books, at p.153.

numbers of different tissue retention scenarios, the matrix will be used to recall where in the debate we are and it is hoped that it will serve the reader as a point of reference when it becomes necessary to locate where we stand in discussing the notion of uses for human tissue, to disentangle notions and provide clarity of concept.

Distinguishing Tissue Types

What has been discussed so far leads to the overriding question in this section: can, in the light of what has been said already, the notion of uses for human tissue be discussed universally? What about problems in relation to using gametes for in vitro fertilization treatment – what about the fertilized ovum or an embryo, or even a foetus? As Cohen notes, most people shirk away from questions of selling reproductive material,[40] whilst in reality we already do: 'Money is the chief inducement for stranger oocyte "donation"'.[41] It could be argued that money is the chief inducement for the 'donation' of gametes in general. What must be kept in mind, though, is the fact that oocyte giving is considerably more invasive and dangerous than giving sperm.[42] This is an illustration of the matrix working in a practical setting: the item *reproductive material* in category *E*, *type of tissue*, makes no distinction between sperm and oocytes; category *C*, *impact*, sets the two kinds of activity well apart from each other. It is time to ask how these kinds of differences are reflected in legal terms.

> Blood and sperm banks must surely be protected by the law of theft. Nor need the status of 'property' be denied to parts of living donors removed for transplantation or even removed for in vitro fertilization. The case of an ovum fertilized in vitro is, to say the least, more doubtful.[43]

Cohen continues to set side by side the sale of hair (which she deems to be ethically unproblematic) and the sale of gametes (which she feels is ethically problematic). A distinct differentiation of why hair is less worthy of protection than other types of tissue does not take place.[44] This, it could be argued, is merely a snapshot of

---

40 Cohen, C. 1999. Selling Bits and Pieces of Humans to Make Babies: The Gift of the Magi Revisited. *Journal of Medicine and Philosophy*, 24(3), 288-306.

41 Cohen 1999, at p. 290, referring to the message carried by newspaper advertisements for oocyte donors.

42 Berg, J. 2001. Risky Business: Evaluating Oocyte Donation. *American Journal of Bioethics*, 1(4), 18-19.

43 Griew, E. 1978. *The Theft Act 1968 and 1978*. London: Sweet & Maxwell. At para 2-18, cited in Dworkin and Kennedy 1993, at p. 301.

44 Though it has been conclusively established that hair cannot play a role in certain crimes against the sovereign: 'Stay friend, until I put aside my beard, for that never

Cohen's contemporary moral evaluation of circumstances. Part of why the debate on ethically acceptable practices in a biomedical setting will just not go away is that the requisite reference point of *what is possible* constantly changes. If it were possible to routinely produce a human embryo using DNA from the root of hair samples, the sale of hair would no longer be as straightforward as Cohen suggests. This brings the discussion back to the original question: whether all types of tissue can be treated in more or less the same way. It has been shown that the legal and ethical evaluation must, by necessity, change with what is scientifically possible (something which has not happened in relation to the use of human tissue). Treating hair differently (legally and ethically) to gametes is something which most people would probably agree to. Moving on to other types of tissue, can the same sets of rules and values be applied to, say, the transplantable heart as those sets of rules and values we attach to corneal tissue? The one saves a life, the other restores eyesight. There is clearly an overlap with the *motive* for the extraction: 'the preservation of life is a greater value than that of exterior beautification'.[45] Presumably, the restoration of eyesight is to be found somewhere on the spectrum between the preservation of life and exterior beautification – to illustrate the two extremes. From these few examples, it appears to be clear that, for the purposes of this text, it may well be necessary to restrict the scope of what can be achieved. A plethora of different problems and aspects are raised by different kinds of tissue – it would hardly be feasible to address notions of entitlements in a blood sample in the same breath and breadth as notions of entitlements in gametes. Going further, the idea of discussing entitlements in embryos or foetuses has little in common with the original question of entitlements in basic human tissue as some argue that it is too close for comfort to the notion of slavery.[46] It is imperative to be clear about which kind of tissue we are referring to when discussing certain aspects of dealing with this tissue in a property-like fashion, just as it is important to be clear about other categories, such as *use* or the *type of consent* obtained. Not only is it important, therefore, to distinguish between broad categories such as regenerative and non-regenerative tissue, but also to distinguish within these categories. As shown at the outset, each nuance of perception of the circumstances changes the problem profoundly. For the purposes of this text it is generally intended to try to address rudimentary issues of types of human tissue which have no direct reproductive function and are not organs for transplantation.[47] Specific problems in relation to other types of tissue and body products are addressed individually.

---

committed treason', Sir Thomas Moore getting his view of the Cartesian dualism across some 100 years before Descartes, in a remark to his executioner, before placing his head on the block (1535), quoted in Frost-Knappman, E., Shrager, D.S. et al. 1998. *The Quotable Lawyer*. New York: Checkmark Books, at § 124.8, p. 292.

45 Cohen 1999, at p. 291.

46 Mason and Laurie 2006, at p. 516.

47 Though the threshold is sometimes difficult to fix: a perfectly transplantable heart, for example, may be rendered subject to our contemplation where the explanting entity

Uses for Tissue

The retention of certain kinds of tissue or body parts has a long tradition to look back on. Andrews and Nelkin provide an interesting account of the disappearance of Albert Einstein's brain, the pathologist in charge assuming that some sort of novelty value factor gave him sufficient justification to remove and keep the brain in a (clearly sizeable) jam jar in his office.[48] Other prominent body parts which were subject to being taken without sufficient consultation include the brain of the convicted German Red Army Faction (RAF) terrorist Ulrike Meinhof,[49] who committed suicide whilst serving her sentence, and British journalist Alistair Cooke who had died in the United States and whose (technically unsuitable) bones were reported to have been harvested illegally for transplantation purposes.[50] A surprising number of more or less useful practices are dependent on the steady supply of tissue, body parts or complete bodies of deceased individuals.[51] The factual usefulness of the human body in biomedical research and therapy is undisputed.

> For modern biomedical businesses and research, human tissue samples are an irreplaceable source, collected in large numbers for transplantation, training, research, drug testing, clinical audit, cell line development and trade.[52]

Liddell and Hall illustrate the usefulness of human tissue by providing some interesting numbers: there are approximately 345 public sector tissue collections for transplantation purposes and five tissue banks for research in the UK. More than 150,000,000 tissue samples are taken every year for diagnostic purposes.[53] Therapy, diagnosis and research are all very different types of motivation for taking tissue samples from individual patients or research participants. The question therefore arises whether, when we speak of the use of human tissue, we need to distinguish between the actual use of the tissue and the motivation for the use of the tissue, or whether we just contemplate use as such, without addressing these questions.

---

feels it prudent to make it into a medical product by harvesting the heart valves rather than using the organ for transplantation.

48 Andrews and Nelkin 2001, at pp. 9-10.

49 Frankfurter Allgemeine Zeitung, 8 November 2002, Wirbel um den Verbleib von Ulrike Meinhofs Gehirn, available at http://www.faz.net/s/Rub02DBAA63F9EB43CEB421272A670A685C/Doc~E817795BD38B545C49C8E6156BDB20E13~ATpl~Ecommon~Scontent.html [Quick URL: http://alturl.com/6ssb], accessed 3 June 2009.

50 See http://news.bbc.co.uk/2/hi/americas/6667875.stm, accessed 3 June 2009.

51 For a number of examples, see Roach, M. 2004. *Stiff: The Curious Lives of Human Cadavers*. New York: Norton & Co.

52 Liddell and Hall 2005, at p. 175.

53 Liddell and Hall 2005, at p. 175.

> Strictly speaking, it should be possible to separate questions as to the existence of property and title from any indecent or otherwise unacceptable use made of such property.[54]

In other words, do we make a difference – legally and ethically – between the use of a human head for practising the art of surgery,[55] storage for possible future research[56] or display in an art exhibition?[57] We will look at the genesis of the Human Tissue Act in detail at a later stage.[58] This may, however, be a good opportunity to look at the difference Parliament made between different types of use when debating the Human Tissue Bill:

> In the [Human Tissue] Bill presented to Parliament the government's policy was that under no circumstance should tissue-based medical research take place without the consent of the person from whom the tissue was obtained. This policy was to apply regardless of whether the person was living or deceased, the tissue was a microscopic cell sample or organ, the research was a part of of the education of medical students, the tissue was going to be discarded as waste (e.g. with other refuse from surgery), or the tissue was anonymised.[59]

Liddell and Hall paint a somewhat bleak picture of the genesis of one of the principles underlying what is arguably Europe's premier attempt at legislating for the storage and use of human tissue: the Human Tissue Act. Its ambivalent provisions on consent will be discussed in detail further below (see Chapter 8). What becomes clear from this initial assessment of the Act's provisions on the permitted use of tissue shows that, though the legislator felt the need to draw clear lines in order to facilitate clinical reality, the reality perceived by those drafting and passing the legislation seemed to differ considerably from reality as perceived by clinicians and researchers. According to Liddell and Hall: '"Research is different from care", the government opined'.[60] Whilst few would disagree with this assessment, it is also clear that the two are inseparable. Without continuing research, patients would not be able to insist on the best

---

54 Dworkin and Kennedy 1993, at p. 295.

55 Roach 2004, at pp. 19-33.

56 Redfern 2001, summary at para. 20 (available at http://www.rlcinquiry.org.uk/contents.htm, accessed 14 November, 2007).

57 See, e.g. Miah, A. 2004. The Public Autopsy: Somewhere between Art, Education and Entertainment. *Journal of Medical Ethics*, 30, 576-579 and Dewar, S. and Boddington, P. 2004. Returning to the Alder Hey Report and Its Reporting: Addressing Confusions and Improving Inquiries. *Journal of Medical Ethics*, 30, 463-469 at p. 468.

58 See Chapter 8.

59 Liddell and Hall 2005, at p. 195.

60 Rosie Winterton, Minister for State, Department of Health, Hansard [HC Rep.] 28 June 2004, col. 105, cited in Liddell and Hall 2005, at p. 196.

possible treatment being available.[61] Research and care are co-dependent; but whilst good research is a *conditio sine qua non* for good care, good research is often dependent on access to patients, the quality of care for whom is not decisive in obtaining access. Liddell and Hall agree with this in saying 'Thus the idea that research is categorically and intrinsically distinct from audit, monitoring and quality assurance is less than convincing',[62] though it would have been preferable to have seen them stress this point more. Much in the same way, university lecturers cannot seriously be expected to teach (their subject matter being up to date, current and thus useful) without permitting them to engage in their own research, and clinicians cannot be expected to give patients the best possible treatment without them or their colleagues indulging in extensive research. But not only is there an interdependency, the line between the two concepts is traditionally difficult to draw. Distinguishing clearly between standard therapy, experimental therapy, experimenting without therapeutic benefit and pure research is nigh on impossible. The research community, health systems and governments strive to provide treatment for some of today's most devastating diseases, placing their hopes almost completely on therapies being developed in an experimental setting. Often, the kind of research undertaken is difficult to connect with a clinical application until the application is found – sometimes by accident. Put simply, there will always be times in research where you need to find the question to an answer you already have. Examples of this are the discovery of penicillin or the off-label use of drugs for purposes never thought of and discovered purely by experimentation. One prominent illustration of this is that of thalidomide: after being sidelined following unforeseen teratogenic side-effects, thalidomide (itself a serendipitous discovery) has now found a new marketability altogether as treatment against leprosy,[63] thrombosis[64] and obesity.[65] It is not difficult to envisage a similar potential contained in using human derived substances for research; indeed this potential is regularly suggested to be boundless. 'Tissue and organs which have been archived are an invaluable asset for medical research',[66] comments Redfern.

61 'Progress in medicine often depends upon physicians, such as those practicing at the university hospital where Moore received treatment, who conduct research while caring for their patients'. *Moore v. The Regents of the University of California* (1990) 271 Cal. Rptr.146, (1990) 793 P2d 479, per Panelli J at p. 151, 484.

62 Liddell and Hall 2005, at p. 197.

63 See Rocha, J. 1994. Thalidomide Given to Women in Brazil. *British Medical Journal*, 308, 1061.

64 See, e.g. Silingardi, M., M. Iotti et al. 2004. Thalidomide, Deep Venous Thrombosis and Vasculitis. *Journal of Thrombosis and Haemostasis*, 2(11), 2062-2063.

65 Also see Laffitte, E. and Revuz, J. 2004. Thalidomide: An Old Drug with New Clinical Applications. *Expert Opinion on Drug Safety*, 3(1), 47-56.

66 Redfern 2001, at p. 445.

Commercialization

Further, it is quite clear that any market for human tissue would be a seller's market. The demand outstrips supply many times over. The American Association of Tissue Banks comprises 98 accredited institutions, which it reports to be performing more than 1,500,000 million allografts from approximately 30,000 donors.[67] Transplant UK reports that between 1 April 2006 and 31 March 2007, some 4,021 corneas were explanted in the UK alone, about 2,512 of which were suitable for transplantation purposes.[68] Not only therapeutic tissue types are difficult to obtain: a growing concern in terms of acquiring sufficient tissue for research leads to a pragmatic approach to costs and the economics of tissue used for research.

> It should by now be clear that although freely given, donor eye tissues for research are not harvested, processed, and delivered for free.[69]

Curcio writes on the shortage of available eye tissue for research. She goes on to outline that until the mid-1990s, eye banks received between $26 and $100 for research tissue, if any reimbursement at all. Actual costs of between $400 and $900 per donor eye were established recently and Curcio advises researchers to include these increased costs in their research grant applications. In the context of the evident economic viability of human tissue, Bellivier and Noiville pose the valid question whether the law does not have an inherent duty to respond to this change in social circumstances:

> [...] blood is transformed then sold, perhaps in the form of medication, cells are isolated, transformed into lines, from which therapeutic substances can be derived; organs are removed, donated then transplanted; in some countries, a woman's uterus is rented for the gestation of a child, which is then handed over to a sterile couple, etc. Human biomaterial circulates and is traded. In this sense, it has become the subject for legislation, under the general consensus that the legal expert cannot ignore the appearance of new entities that are the object of commercial exchange.[70]

---

67 American Association of Tissue Banks website: http://www.aatb.org/content.asp?content_id=453, accessed 3 June 2009.

68 Transplant UK 2007. *Transplant Activity in the UK*. London: The Stationery Office at p. 32.

69 Curcio, C. 2006. Declining Availability of Human Eye Tissues for Research. *Investigative Ophthalmology & Visual Science*, 47(7), 2747-2749 at p. 2748.

70 Bellivier, F. and Noiville, C. 2004. The Commercialisation of Human Biomaterials: What Are the Rights of Donors of Biological Material? *Journal of International Biotechnology Law*, 1(3), 89-97 at p. 89.

What is interesting and seems quite appropriate is the reference to new entities that are already the 'object of commercial exchange'. In reality, we already treat material derived or taken from the human body as property. Bellivier and Noiville however, go a step further and use property terminology in that they speak of 'rented' uteri. It is probably the case that they use the term as an analogy to renting out one's labour rather than renting out one's spare room.

Savulescu makes a strong proclamation of a right to make the decision to sell a body part. 'People have a right to make a decision to sell a body part. If we should be allowed to sell our labour, why not sell the means to that labour?',[71] he says. Whilst people probably have a right to make that kind of decision, society may well take the position that there ought to be no purchaser or that the realization of the decision is deemed illegal. Further, selling a body part is quite different from selling one's labour. Nonetheless Savulescu uses both concepts in a single argument. Indeed, the distinction between making available one's labour and making one's body available for profit in order to bear someone else's child tends to be portrayed as fuzzy. It is clear that in most jobs nowadays, we are free to refuse to carry out a task or to plainly not go to work and we need not fear the application of force to compel us (with the notable exception of army service and forced labour). We may lose the job, but will not face the application of physical force in terms of making ourselves limitlessly available. Once a life matures within the body of the surrogate, which the law deems worthy of protection, the compelling factor becomes harder to ignore.[72]

71 Savulescu, J. 2003. Is the Sale of Body Parts Wrong? *Journal of Medical Ethics,* 29, 138-139 at p. 138.

72 And the law has seen fit to interfere in this particular constellation. See section 2 of the Surrogacy Arrangements Act 1985, which makes it an offence to make commercial arrangements for surrogacy.

Chapter 3
Alder Hey and Public Opinion

Properly mandated tissue harvesting from post mortem donors poses few legal or ethical problems – notwithstanding a possible fundamental disagreement with using material derived from the human body. The routine harvesting of tissue from deceased patients, assuming that the material is put to better use on a lab bench rather than in a casket,[1] does raise a number of issues which have so far eluded systematic solution. Attention should, in particular, be drawn to the schism between a lay person's, sometimes highly emotionalized, view of separating parts from a human body and the clinicians', sometimes rather clinical, view of the same problem: 'In the end, the choice is between using leftover materials further for valuable scientific/educational purposes and throwing it away!'[2] This view of the matter, namely that once the material has been taken it does not infringe the patient's rights if it is subsequently used for research is questionable for a number of reasons but can certainly only be deemed possible at all where the physician and the researcher are unconnected. The matter was discussed in the Californian Supreme Court's judgment in the case of *Moore*:[3]

> Golde [the physician treating Moore] argues that the scientific use of cells that have already been removed cannot possibly affect the patient's medical interests. The argument is correct in one instance but not in another. If a physician has no plans to conduct research on a patient's cells at the time he recommends the medical procedure by which they are taken, then the patient's medical interests have not been impaired. In that instance the argument is correct. On the other hand, a physician who does have a preexisting research interest might, consciously or unconsciously, take that into consideration in recommending the procedure. In that instance the argument is incorrect: the physician's extraneous motivation may affect his judgment and is, thus, material to the patient's consent.[4]

---

1 This is the position of van Diest et al. 2003. Cadaveric Tissue Donation: A Pathologist's Perspective. *Journal of Medical Ethics*, 29(3), 135-136. See also the level of paternalism criticized in Morrison, D. 2005. A Holistic Approach to Clinical and Research Decision-making: Lessons from the UK Organ-retention Scandals. *Medical Law Review*, 13, 45-79 at pp. 54-56.

2 Van Diest, P., Lopes Cardoso, N. et al. 2003, p. 136.

3 See the discussion of the Moore case in Chapter 9 below.

4 *Moore v. The Regents of the University of California* 793 P 2d 479 (Cal. 1990) at p. 484.

Even in the context of the remarkably cavalier approach to the physician-patient relationship in *Moore*, the confusion over what may or may not be done with tissue appears to be pervasive and adequate solutions difficult to find. Brought to the fore by scandals, such as at Alder Hey Royal Liverpool Children's Hospital and at Bristol Royal Infirmary, the public outrage has prompted a hectic and busy attitude amongst academics and legislators. Many of the solutions which were discussed did not appear satisfactory to everyone and considerable confusion remains on the issue of legality or illegality of what happened at Alder Hey. The general consensus seems to be, however, that to just keep tissue without asking for it was not a good thing to do. The awkward feeling remains that the greatest regret of all those involved in routinely retaining tissue for decades without consent is having been caught, rather than honest repentance for the injustices done (if any). What is indeed regrettable is the fact that the whole problem was caught up in a tidal wave of negative publicity which prevented a sensible discussion of the practice. As Dworkin and Kennedy have said: 'attitudes to property issues may well be affected by the particular circumstances of a case, especially by any sense of outrage that may be felt about the case'.[5]

Whatever the public response was in detail, the result is unambiguous: the name Alder Hey is now synonymous with the wantonly paternalistic practice of retaining organs from deceased children without their relatives' consent. It is often reported that such practices were widespread throughout the UK and that the Royal Liverpool Children's NHS Trust Alder Hey has fallen victim to being labelled the only perpetrator in the public's view. The Redfern Report does indicate that there seemed to have been a general policy of retaining organs and tissue after the originally designated use was no longer an issue. The scale of retention at Alder Hey has so far not been matched however, and the reputation therefore appears to be fully deserved:

> The practice we have described seems to have been of general application. The medical justification is a manifestation of the paternalistic approach, namely the policy of restricting the freedom and responsibility of parents in their supposed best interests. In mitigation, it is stated that the heart collection has served to reduce the mortality rate following cardiac surgery for some serious conditions and malformations from 33% to 3%. This benefit cannot be ignored, but it is no justification for ignoring the parents' rights.[6]

Alder Hey

Some details of the affair at Alder Hey are needed to put the frequent references in context. Whilst organs had been taken and retained at Alder Hey during post mortem examinations of children continuously between the years 1948 and 1988

5 Dworkin and Kennedy 1993, at p. 295.

6 Redfern 2001, summary, para. 13.

(this is the heart collection referred to in the Report), it can probably be said that the years 1988 and 1995 were to blame for the public's perception of the scandal. Before 1988 only those samples were retained which had been fixed for analysis (a process that took between six and eight weeks) as the burial of the remaining body tended to be before the samples were ready. During the latter years (referred to as 'the van Velzen Years' in the Inquiry Report), the retention practice was intensified under the reign of the now disgraced pathologist Professor Dick van Velzen who issued orders to his staff to retain every organ of every child.[7] Overall, the tissue collection at Alder Hey included 2,128 hearts, up to 4,020 foetuses (only 442 of which were at van Velzen's Myrtle Street unit), 13 post-natal heads or parts thereof, 22 late premature/term foetus heads, 188 eyes, one whole body of a child and a receptacle containing the head of an 11-year-old.[8] The specimens retained by van Velzen tended to be badly catalogued or not catalogued at all and in general were useless for research.[9]

The nature of the collection makes for gruesome reading and it is hardly surprising that the public response was explosive.[10] The Alder Hey affair illustrates an important rift between the public's perception of bodies and body parts and the perception of medical practitioners, in this case pathologists. If we revert briefly to the generalized two primary classes of views outlined at the beginning – namely those who follow a libertarian stance and those who adhere to the view of the body's inalienability – it becomes clear that both would have condemned the behaviour of those responsible at Alder Hey. The libertarians could argue that the children's respective estates should have been consulted and that some sort of trespass to property occurred. Those opposed to this view may be outraged by the objectification of the children's bodies and their treatment as mere material – it may be fair to say therefore that the practice could be condemned as universally wrong.[11] Nonetheless, a certain – but not limitless – amount of empathy for the unenviable and hazy legal position of clinicians is in order:

> After completing the usual diagnostic procedures within the framework of the autopsy, there is usually a rather large volume of leftover material comprising sections, paraffin blocks, and wet material (organs and tissue samples kept

---

7 See, e.g. Price, D. 2003. From Cosmos and Damian to van Velzen: The Human Tissue Saga Continues. *Medical Law Review*, 11(1), 1-47.

8 Redfern 2001, paras. 14-20.

9 Redfern 2001, para. 38.

10 *The Sun* used the headline 'Tot Body Snatcher Banned' to report the result of the GMC's inquiry into the Alder Hey pathologist in June 2005. The acrimonious tone of the article reflects popular opinion (Available at http://www.thesun.co.uk/sol/homepage/news/article108908.ece, accessed 3 June 2009). *The Guardian*, on balance, reported the same story with the headline 'Former Alder Hey Pathologist Struck Off' (Available at http://www.guardian.co.uk/uk_news/story/0,,1511058,00.html, accessed 3 June 2009).

11 Neglecting minority viewpoints such as conscription and absolute *res communis* for the moment.

> in formalin). It is common practice to keep paraffin blocks and sections for reasons of quality control, and for future diagnostic procedures requested by family members – for example, in case of hereditary diseases. This is very much justified, and can be considered to be covered by the permission given for the autopsy itself, but the Alder Hey affair has taught us that it is wise to properly inform those giving permission about this.[12]

Van Diest et al. clearly label their views as being representative of the pathologists' perspective of the issues raised by the Alder Hey affair. It does appear to be clear that whilst those involved feel that they were morally and legally within their rights to retain the tissue,[13] they also seem to suggest that a certain amount of lip service to the desire for autonomy and dignity of the patients and their families may be required to procure something akin to the much-quoted flak jacket[14] against liability.

Consent as a Flak Jacket

The Inquiry Report was geared towards notions of consent and criticized the lack of such consent for the storage of the tissue. This red thread can be followed all the way into the drafting of the Human Tissue Act,[15] which also very much centres on the requirement of a proper mandate by consent. This is hardly surprising, as consent issues are at the very heart of good medicine: it is virtually impossible to explore any aspect of medico-legal thinking without reference to elements of consent and this certainly does not stop when looking at the subsequent use of tissue after excision (the excision itself not being subject to the provisions of the Human Tissue Act).[16]

> ... where relatives of equal standing disagree, it is lawful to proceed provided one of them consents. In doing so, [the policy] departs from the government's

12 Van Diest et al. 2003, at page 135.

13 And possibly not wrong in that assessment: cf. the US case *Browning v. Norton Children's Hospital* 1974 504 SW 2d 713 (Ky) where it was held that when subjected to hospital treatment, the patients were also subjected to common hospital practices, arguably therefore also including the subsequent reuse of tissue taken for pathology purposes for other research.

14 See below, Liddell and Hall 2005. at p. 193.

15 See Chapter 8.

16 I have written on the importance of consent in medico-legal decision-making elsewhere (and in German). See Hoppe, N. 2008. Normative Modelle zur Regelung der Kommodifikation menschlichen Gewebes in Forschung und Therapie: Fragen der Zustimmung aus der Common Law Perspektive. In: *Kultur und Bioethik: Eigentum am eigenen Körper*. Edited by C. Steineck and O. Döring. Nomos: Baden-Baden at pp. 51-63.

> rhetorical claims about consent. *It implies a jurisprudence wherein consent is a flak jacket against liability rather than a meter of respect.*[17]

Describing consent as a flak jacket against the threat of liability flowing from the subjective feeling of the patient's legitimate wishes being overridden is a very accurate metaphor which can be traced back into case law.[18] It also fits in with the reality of medicine. It will be described later on how it must be first and foremost in the 'medical man's'[19] mind to restrict not only one's own liability but also one's own culpability. Taking the individual patient's autonomy as a basis for accepting that anything which flows from the voluntary consent of that individual as being *right*, the medical professional is then, by and large, exculpated. Proper consent is, therefore, very much and rightly so a flak jacket against the vicissitudes of medical reality, not only in terms of being liable for one's actions (which medical professionals already are to a much higher degree than others)[20] but also to a moral culpability which attaches to acts which could otherwise be interpreted as *wrong*.

> Although the new regulatory framework emphasises the importance of consent and is intended to improve the clarity of the law, the Act does not define the meaning of consent. This is surprising since confusion and disagreement surrounding the requirements of valid consent were the very issues that caused the problems at Bristol and Alder Hey, and the requirements for valid consent remain particularly contentious as a matter of law and bioethics.[21]

It would, in this context, clearly be too much to ask of an individual item of legislation, such as the Human Tissue Act, to provide exhaustive guidance on an area as complex as it is well-defined as consent. The Common Law already contains rules and provisions in relation to almost every conceivable individual case of consent. It has also chosen to reject an absolute provision of informed consent, and rightly so. As Liddell and Hall comment, 'Strictly speaking, there is no doctrine of "informed consent" in UK law'.[22]

---

17 Liddell and Hall 2005, at p. 193 (emphasis added).

18 *Re W [1992]* 4 All ER 627 at 633.

19 Cf. McNair J's use of the term in *Bolam v. Friern Hospital Management Committee* [1957] 2 All ER 118.

20 'The test is the standard of the ordinary skilled man exercising and professing to have that special skill.' *Bolam v. Friern Hospital Management Committee* [1957] 1 WLR 582, per McNair J at p. 586. But also see *R v. Bateman* (1925) 94 LJKB 791, per Hewart LCJ at p. 794: 'The jury should not exact the highest, or very high standard, nor should they be content with a very low standard'. Both sources courtesy of Mason and Laurie (2006), at p. 310.

21 Liddell and Hall 2005, at p. 190.

22 Liddell and Hall 2005, at p. 190.

Since *Sidaway*,[23] it is quite clear that the courts do not expect medical professionals to reveal all available information to a patient normally necessary in order to come up to the standard generally accepted to be informed consent. The law bows to the supremacy of what is accepted as best practice in this particular area of life, as it often does in medical matters.[24] This is appropriate as the law simply has to take a back seat when it comes to the question of life and death decisions being taken in hospitals. It is plausible to side strongly with an argument against fully informed consent in the therapeutic context. At the same time one does not need to be convinced as to the validity of the same argument when it comes to research. Are the strong arguments for a weaker standard of consent in the therapeutic setting easily translated to the research setting?

In terms of questions of therapy, it is proposed as a generally acceptable argument that the doctor cannot provide the patient with the exact information necessary to procure real informed consent. He can only ever achieve an approximation: if he provides all of the information he has, he will bamboozle the patient with the sheer weight of detail. If he provides purely that which he considers to be relevant for reaching a treatment decision, he is in serious risk of paternalistically curtailing the patient's autonomy and thus failing to meet the standard required of him. He therefore needs to tread a delicate balance. What he is primarily dealing with, just as in the case of *Sidaway*, are questions of risk attached to a certain treatment, such as permanent spinal cord damage where surgery takes place on the patient's back. Where tissue is removed, there is a similar category of risk involved in an excision. The cutting of the patient may already entail a number of risks which cannot be realistically distinguished from the kind of risks arising during the course of an excision of tissue for therapeutic or diagnostic purposes. It is at this stage that we need to ask whether we need to distinguish between the different motives for the excision (see column D in Figure 2.1).

What happens with tissue in terms of consent after the tissue is excised? Provided the patient has been properly informed about the risks involved in such an excision and the therapeutic or diagnostic primary purpose is satisfied – should the rules change if the tissue is then used for something else? Going one step further: what happens in situations where the doctors excise tissue purely to further establish the exact pathogenesis of this particular patient, possibly for the benefit of a class of sufferers? And another step: what if the doctors realize, in a *Mooreian* way, that the individual patient's physical characteristics give rise to important and socially valuable research? There is no question about the fact that the law provides more than enough mechanisms to deal with the invasive intervention involved in the context of taking this tissue. The question which spins into the focus of attention at this stage is that of consent for the subsequent use

23 *Sidaway v. The Board of Governors of the Bethlem Royal Hospital* [1984] QB 493.

24 As in, for example, the discussion on which criteria are appropriate for establishing the death of a person. See Goff, R. 1995. A Matter of Life and Death. *Medical Law Review*, 3, 1-21.

of the tissue. This is a completely different issue which is all too often mixed up. Consent for surgery is one thing; consent for the use of the tissue is something quite different. And whilst one need not, as outlined above, argue strongly for informed consent in the therapeutic or diagnostic setting, it would be convincing to do so in the research setting. We are not speaking of life and death decisions for the individual patient whose material is in question.[25] Nor are we speaking of an intervention, the omission of which may lead to individual harm to the patient. The intervention is more burdensome to the patient than it is beneficial as long as he does not substantially and directly profit from the research. In these circumstances it is quite acceptable to ask of the researchers (not the treating physicians) that they disclose fully what they intend to do with the tissue. An additional dimension of difficulty is added to this question where the researchers simply do not know what kind of research is going to be undertaken using the tissue. They may know that they want the tissue for a certain purpose but they realize that, at some subsequent stage, there might be an ulterior use for the tissue in research. The consent that was obtained for the use of the tissue for the initial purpose would then, of course, not cover the use of the tissue for the ulterior motive and the use thus be inadmissible. The solution, some suggest, is to just ask for consent to use the tissue in research, without being overly specific in relation to exactly what kind of research is done with the tissue. This so-called blanket consent is by many deemed to be exactly the kind of lip-serving flak jacket construction which appears to be so undesirable.[26]

> However, a growing band of commentators dispute such arguments, claiming that broad, relatively unspecific disclosure would in many circumstances suffice for meaningful consent (particularly where the risks of physical and psychiatric injury is low).[27]

The argument sets out that if it is not necessary in therapy to have fully informed consent, then it is clearly not necessary to obtain fully informed consent for the removal and storage of tissue for research.[28] The unadjusted transposition of these consent concepts from the therapeutic to the research setting is unconvincing. It does, of course, make it substantially easier for tissue banks not to have to be in a position to ask tissue donors for fresh consent in cases where a new research focus

25 I acknowledge that an argument might be spun for the life and death character certain research may have for others.

26 See in particular Liddell and Hall 2005, at p. 192; Jamrozik, K. 2000. The Case for a New System for Oversight of Research on Human Subjects. *Journal of Medical Ethics*, 26, 334-339, at p. 338. Also see Jones, M.A. 1999. Informed Consent and Other Fairy Stories. *Medical Law Review*, 7(2), 103-134.

27 Liddell and Hall 2005, at p. 190.

28 See for example, Loff, B. 2000. Informed Consent for Tissue Retention Discussed in Australia. *The Lancet*, 356, 1663. Also see Brazier, M. 2003. Organ Retention and Return: Problems of Consent. *Journal of Medical Ethics*, 29, 30-33.

arises in relation to the material. What we really have is a problem in at least two different dimensions: (a) the necessity of conducting the research even where no consent for the new research can be sought and (b) the infrastructural difficulties in obtaining subsequent fresh consent. Relying on a regime of blanket consent, in the shape of a general, unspecific consent to research *per se*, fundamentally deprives the individual tissue donor of being able to reject certain research. He may not, for example, wish for his material to be used for furthering ethically controversial research topics, such as pre-implantation diagnostics or stem cell research (however remote such a research possibility might be). One should insist on a higher quality of consent in the research setting than in the therapeutic setting, but it is useful to underscore the previous criticism of informed consent in relation to its pragmatism: it is simply not feasible. '... The critical issue' comment Liddell and Hall, 'is not specificity, but that the informational content is reliably truthful and that patients have an opportunity to decline activities according to personal convictions'.[29]

All in all, it is clear that consent procedures in relation to therapeutic/diagnostic purposes and research need not be identical. In fact, if they were identical they would probably be inappropriate and unsuitable. Whilst all arguments seem to be in favour of having a higher density of information in terms of research than in terms of therapy and diagnostics, those drafting the Human Tissue Act did not feel that this was the case.

> Let me state clearly that the Bill does not require consent to be specific to each research project for which tissue might be used. Consent can be broad. Consent to research can be generic and enduring.[30]

This is rather too close for comfort to a complete blanket consent. Neither the Bill nor the Act did, in fact, define the level of consent required at all.[31] The overriding idea seems to be the same which was criticized when discussing the level of harm involved in excising tissue – namely that the problem is regularly suggested to be moot where the source of the material cannot be identified, e.g. not knowing whom is harmed. This does not, in fact, solve the problem but represents the equivalent of closing one's eyes to the potential of harm. Just because it cannot be seen does not mean it is not there.

Returning briefly to a point made above – that of the infrastructural insufficiency which leads to the present dilemma – if there is the opportunity to store tissue in a fashion which enables identification of and contact with the original source in

29 Liddell and Hall 2005, at p. 190.

30 Lord Warner, Parliamentary Under-Secretary of State for Health, quoted in Liddell and Hall 2005, at pp. 190-191.

31 The Act suggests that appropriate consent should be sought (Sections 2 and 3), that it sometimes ought to be in writing (Section 3(3)) and that sometimes witnesses are necessary (Section 3(5)b).

order to ask for fresh consent, should use not be made of this technology and the individual's autonomy be respected as much as possible?

The question raises a completely new thematic area, which is necessarily well outside the remit of this text: that of anonymization or pseudonymization of material, removing or blocking the tracing of the original source of the material. It may, in some contexts, be rather in the source's interest not to be in a position to be found.[32] Even in situations where the original source can be found, some tissue and biobanks have a policy of not getting in contact with the original source.[33]

> Some argued that the government's shift from the maxim 'Always Ask' to 'Ask or Anonymise' or 'Ask us for Regulations to Ask the High Court' did not yield sufficiently to form an overlapping moral consensus. Anonymisation is difficult for epidemiologists who clean and update large amounts data in longitudinal studies, and also for clinician-researchers who routinely come into possession of identifying information.[34]

Individual Choice or Public Good?

It is precisely this point which procures the most sizeable problems in the debate on how material can or should be anonymous or use pseudonyms: the fact that as long as the material contains analysable DNA information, it can be matched to a source.[35] The higher the density of interconnected data from different sources, the more likely it is that such data can be matched to an individual. The question whether anonymity or pseudonyms in this context works at all is therefore justified.

> [Human Bodies, Human Choices][36] included the idea that *anonymised* cell lines might be used or stored without consent and that donors might be asked to give up property and other economic rights in cell lines.[37]

---

32 Such as in the context of criminal prosecutions or insurance companies' assessment of risk.

33 The UK Biobank project, for example, will not get in touch with participants, even where there is evidence of a disease susceptibility which the participant may wish to be informed of. See http://www.ukbiobank.ac.uk/faqs/results.php, accessed 3 June 2009, in particular the answers to questions 2 and 3.

34 Liddell and Hall 2005, at p. 201.

35 A striking illustration of the powerful character of this fact is the increasing number of crimes which are now solved, many years later, following forensic DNA analyses of evidence gathered at a time when such an analysis was not yet possible.

36 Department of Health 2002, *Human Bodies, Human Choices – The Law on Human Organs and Tissue in England and Wales.* London: Stationary Office.

37 Liddell and Hall 2005, at p. 203.

We have seen that not only the perspective of those drafting the Human Tissue Act but also that of the pathologists appears to very much remain that there need not be a proper consent procedure in cases where the privacy of the original 'donor' can be safeguarded. The 'umbrella problem' of individuals' proprietary interests in genetic data remain the same: the question whether one individual can ever have an exclusive entitlement to such data, given that the entire family shares part of the same genetic make-up and, potentially, the same disease susceptibility.

> On this issue, the struggle for moral balance was foreshortened by the government's fixation on personal autonomy and consent. The government largely ignored the argument that some genetic information is more accurately regarded as familial rather than personal information.[38]

Alarmingly, it is sometimes suggested that principles of 'solidarity' – meaning in this context, presumably, conscription-style participation in medical research in terms of an inability to refuse consent once tissue has been excised – should, argue some pathologists, be the overriding interest.

> To ensure that enough material continues to be available for the training of future medical generations, it will remain necessary to reuse left over tissue and organs on a small scale from today's patients. *We believe that the principle of solidarity should take priority over the right of self determination here.*[39]

This appears to be an unjustified utilitarian approach. Van Diest et al. are, it appears, not concerned with issues of solidarity but with the unshackled flourishing of current practices in pathology. This approach is regrettably very much mirrored in pertinent case law, as in the much-cited *Moore* case where the judges painted the gloomy picture of the autonomous and fully informed homo oeconomicus: 'he [Moore] could conceivably go from institution to institution seeking the highest bid and, if dissatisfied, claim the right simply to prohibit the research'.[40]

And why not? The impertinence of Moore, potentially putting a price on his physical integrity, not willing to surrender it for too little profit, seemed to have been a guiding principle in the judgment. Whether this suggests that the judges ogled a principle of conscription[41] for acquiring tissue for research or whether they

38 Liddell and Hall 2005, at p. 188.

39 Van Diest et al. 2003, at p. 135 (emphasis added).

40 Dworkin and Kennedy 1993, at p. 308, quoting from the majority opinion on the first appeal in *Moore v. Regents of the University of California*. Also cited in Dworkin, G. 1997. Should There Be Property Rights in Genes? *Philosophical Transactions of the Royal Society, Biological Sciences*, 352(1357), 1077-1986, at p. 1078; Winter, H. 2005. *Trade-offs: An Introduction to Economic Reasoning*. Chicago: University of Chicago Press, at p. 25.

41 Aaron Spital clearly wanted to talk about the notion of conscription for therapy. See Spital, A. and Erin, C. 2002. Conscription of Cadaveric Organs for Transplantation:

felt that sources may only agree or refuse to be a research participant but not name a price for their participation is unclear. What can be said with certainty is that, regardless of the sometimes overly forceful feelings of subjective entitlement felt by some clinicians in the times before and immediately after Alder Hey, medical practitioners who were dealing with obtaining or storing tissue samples from patients and research participants were largely left to their own devices by the law. Womack and Gray write that:

> In the year or so leading to the tissue bank launch in June 1996, we could find no relevant law in the UK and our approach to the legal and ethical issues of supplying human tissue for research predominantly in the commercial sector was led by the Nuffield Council Report published in April 2005 [sic.].[42]

Being guided by the Nuffield Council Report of 1995 was probably as good as following the law, but it shows that whilst lawyers argue over points which have the air of a philosophical quandary rather than an application in reality, reality has moved on and the new needs of physicians are ignored. One possible answer to this may be the introduction of a combination of primary legislation and clearly defined codes of conduct. This model, followed in the Human Tissue Act and the relevant codes of conduct issued by the Human Tissue Authority, is discussed in detail later on.

Let's at Least Talk about It. *Am Journal of Kidney Disease*, 39, 611-615; Spital, A. 2003. Conscription of Cadaveric Organs for Transplantation: Neglected Again. *Kennedy Institute of Ethics Journal*, 13, 169-174; Spital, A. 2005. Conscription of Cadaveric Organs: We Need to Start Talking about It. *American Journal of Transplantation*, 5, 1170-1171; Spital, A. 2005. Conscription of Cadaveric Organs for Transplantation: A Stimulating Idea Whose Time Has Not Yet Come. *Cambridge Quarterly of Healthcare Ethics*, 14, 107-112; Spital, A. 2006. Conscription of Cadaveric Organs for Transplantation: Time to Start Talking about It. *Kidney International*, 70, 607. But also see: McGovern, T. 2002. Flawed Proposal for Universal Conscription of Cadaveric Organs Neglects Moral, Long-term, and Societal Implications, *American Journal of Kidney Disease*, 36, 609-610.

42 Womack and Gray 2007, at p. 212.

Chapter 4
Terminology

It does not appear easy to achieve an appropriate degree of precision when trying to discuss whether property might be an issue in relation to biological material. Not only is there some difficulty in the context of the many different concepts which were discussed at the outset, there is also considerable confusion as to the question of what kind of biological material we feel is to be part of our considerations. Cohen chose to refer to the different constituents of the human body under the umbrella term 'bits and pieces'.[1] The underlying rationale for this, at first glance, surprising terminology was probably to avoid inadvertently narrowing down the application of her ideas only to some types of tissue. This does, in many ways, mirror the linguistic inconsistency which leads to so much confusion in the literature. The notion of the human body within the realm of the *ownable* is fraught with terminological and conceptual difficulties, some of which are to be illustrated in this chapter. Whilst it would be technically correct to refer to the excised tissue as a *thing* in terms of it being movable, tangible and subject to possession, the label clearly conjures up undesirable connotations. This leaves us with a conundrum: how are we to refer to the excised tissue, which kinds of tissue do we mean and how shall we refer to the different concepts surrounding such tissue?

Tissue and Body Products

Biologically speaking, the term tissue encompasses protective tissue layers, muscle and nerve tissue as well as connective tissues, such as blood and bone. Some products of the human body contain tissue detritus, such as urine and seminal plasma. It is virtually impossible to draft a finite list of constituents of the body that are meant when speaking of tissue and body products. To use an umbrella term for all types of constituents would also go against the notion of the myriad of different legal and ethical concerns as shown in the matrix in Chapter 2. The idea is that we do not exclude parts of the body which are made subject to propertization and which should sensibly be included in our assessment.

> The terms 'human tissue' or 'biological material' are used to describe every aspect of a person's being, ranging from body waste (such as urine, faeces, hair, nail clippings), to a list representing an atlas of the human body; for example,

1 See Cohen 1999.

> blood, skin, bone, bone marrow, organs such as the cornea, liver, heart and kidneys, amputated limbs, fetal tissue, the placenta and other accompanying fluid and membranes (i.e. the contents of the uterus, other than the fetus resulting from pregnancy), fetal tissue, semen, ova.[2]

It is a good idea to refer to the matrix again when assessing our use of terminology here. We aim to be as inclusive as possible, whilst at the same time making sure that we pay appropriate attention to the different problems attached to different kinds of tissue.[3] This is undoubtedly a complex task.

Entitlements

Before creating a normative framework of protective rules, it is necessary to identify an initial entitlement which the law determines as being worthy of protection. Only then can we decide which kind of mechanism (such as property or liability) we want to employ in order to obtain a sufficient level of protection for this entitlement. Let us take a quick look at what the concept of entitlement means to assist in the determination of its use in this context.

Literature provides many different approaches and notions of entitlements. It would not serve the purpose of this text to consider all of them. To develop a first understanding of the notion of entitlements, we will look at the very attractive way proposed by Calabresi and Melamed (1972) to structure an assessment of *entitlements*.[4] Their model commences with an *initial entitlement* which society has granted to someone. It then seeks to ascertain whether the character of the entitlement makes it economically more sensible to protect this entitlement using rules of property or rules of liability. In cases where it is in society's interest not to permit transfer of the entitlement in question, Calabresi and Melamed use the concept of *inalienability*, which gives an individual the initial entitlement but not necessarily the right to part with the entitlement in all circumstances.

If we add to these considerations (of an economic nature) those of ethical admissibility, the categorization of things which can be protected by rules of liability, property or absolute inalienability turns into a very sensible blueprint for exploring our problem.

---

2 Dworkin and Kennedy 1993, at p. 291.

3 The example given in the context of the matrix was that of the difference between reproductive and non-reproductive tissue.

4 Calabresi, G. and Melamed, A.D. 1972. Property Rules, Liability Rules and Inalienability: One View of the Cathedral. *Harvard Law Review*, 85(6), 1089-1128.

Property Rules to Protect Entitlements

Protecting an entitlement using rules of property is appropriate in cases where letting the protagonists negotiate the value of a certain entitlement autonomously leads to a cost-efficient and practicable system. Calabresi and Melamed use the context of pollution and nuisance as an example:

> First, Taney may not pollute unless his neighbor (his only neighbor let us assume), Marshall, allows it (Marshall may enjoin Taney's nuisance). Second, Taney may pollute but must compensate Marshall for the damages caused. Third, Taney may pollute at will and can only be stopped by Marshall if Marshall pays him off (Taney's pollution is not held to be a nuisance to Marshall).[5]

In this example, the first and second rules are rules of liability (injunction, damages). The third rule is one of property (Marshall can buy out Taney's entitlement to pollute). Their system seeks to maximize economic efficiency and the authors write at length about costs of negotiating, freeloading agents and holding out for better deals. This kind of model could, in part, be used to systematize our conceptualization of entitlements in relation to human tissue.

There is also a valuable terminological point to be made here. It is helpful to note that we are speaking of entitlements, rather than ownership, property, and so forth (a point made in detail further below). An entitlement, as the description of some kind of right to something,[6] provides much more flexibility when attempting to encompass the complex medical reality of dealings with human tissue. It avoids the negative connotations of the use of the term ownership whilst also being legally more accurate. The opportunity to outline notions of different kinds of ownership (e.g. legal ownership and the idea of equitable ownership) will arise in Chapter 12 when looking at how the law has dealt with splitting up entitlements to satisfy several individuals' interests. There remains one question to be discussed in light of Calabresi and Melamed's idea of structuring entitlements. This is whether, when we speak of entitlements in human tissue, we can easily let individuals negotiate the value of the entitlement autonomously – this aspect ties in strongly with the basic question of inalienability which we will move on to discuss in detail.

Ownership

We will quickly take a look at the term ownership and how helpful it is in our context. Ownership, in the legal context, appears to be of little practical use. Its theoretical value lies in the assumption that, as an owner, you have the right to full enjoyment of something and can exclude everyone from that *something*. In

5 Calabresi and Melamed 1972, at p. 1116.

6 The terminological limits of the term *something* are acknowledged.

reality that is just not the case. Enjoyment of something is always restricted by all sorts of rules (it is well established that rights also include duties). Ownership of a fast car does not entitle you to drive it as fast as you want (and thus to fully enjoy it); ownership of shares in a company does not entitle you to sell these shares as you please.[7] One may own land but one's right to exclude those who have walked across it to get to the shops for the last 20 years may be severely limited.

The common understanding of ownership not as a full set of entitlements but simply a better set of entitlements than others appears to hold more promise. Ownership is therefore only really an expression of just that: the best possible entitlement under the circumstances, relative to the nature of the *something* in question and the entitlements of others.

Property

The term '*property*' is part of the terminology discussed at the outset at being a principal thorn in the side of the debate on normatively handling human tissue. It is very much a social and legal concept, namely that of describing a powerful relationship of control over a certain thing. As such, it is a creature of the law rather than one of circumstance: 'property and law are born and must die together. Before the laws, there was no property: take away the laws, all property ceases'.[8]

It follows that property is a quite legalistic, but socially necessary, principle which governs the interaction between people in relation to objects (which, in turn, are capable of being property). Where there is no respect for the property of individuals and the law fails to protect proprietary interests, there is a strong argument that society fails: 'A state that does not sufficiently respect property rights' say Smith and Zaibert, 'is likely to be a totalitarian state, and will also be likely to fail to respect rights of other sorts'.[9]

The numerous views of the nature of property include those who feel that the notion of property is an antecedent to any societal structure[10] or those who feel that property arises out of networks of social rules.[11] It is certainly not an easy concept, partly due to the ambiguous use of the term in everyday language. Here, the word *property* tends to denote one (or, sometimes confusingly, both) of two things. First, it may describe the physical presence of a concrete object ('this book is property'). Secondly, the legal and social concept of certain entitlements to concrete or

---

7 Examples courtesy of Worthington, S. 2006. *Equity*. Oxford: Oxford University Press, at p. 56.

8 Bentham, J., Dumont, E. et al. 1843. *Principles of the Civil Code. The Works of Jeremy Bentham*. London: J. Bowring.

9 Smith, B. and Zaibert, L. 2001. The Metaphysics of Real Estate. *Topoi*, 20, 161-172 at p. 161. Smith and Zaibert quote the Locke-Nozick position but disagree with it.

10 See, e.g. Nozick, R. 1974. *Anarchy, State, and Utopia*. Oxford: Blackwell.

11 Bentham, J., Dumont, E. et al. 1843. Chapter 8.

abstract objects ('this book is my property').[12] These notions of property have been extended to include intellectual property in terms of the ephemeral character of ideas rather than the tangible manifestation of objects, as well as a remarkable number of other objects and things.[13] It is, admittedly, also clear that the use of expressions such as 'this is property' is not as easily equated with saying 'this is a thing' as might be convenient for the assertion that there is a twofold way of using the term *property* in this chapter. The important point, however, can be made: the meaning applied to and use of the term *property* is semantically inconsistent and qualitatively non-homogenous.

The extent of this ambiguity becomes very clear when we consider a second illustration such as *tangible property* and *intangible property* which are in common usage, even in scholarly legal discourse. If *property* denotes the entitlement or the relationship we have to an inanimate[14] object, it cannot be categorized as tangible and intangible. It should rather be *property in the intangible* and not *intangible property*. The terminological helplessness is evident. Concentration on the second notion of the term *property* (that of it describing a relationship of control and entitlement to an object) can be suggested to be more useful in terms of analysing property systematically.

Bundles of Sticks

Additionally, there are a number of different notions of how to describe the idea of 'property'. As mentioned at the outset, the concept is certainly not as straightforward as we would probably like: resting with the principle that 'property' denotes a certain entitlement we have in relation to an object, and that such an entitlement carries with it the right to defend the entitlement against others, we can make good use of the bundle theory of property rights in order to explain what 'property' may mean.[15] Here, the quality of the entitlement is reflected in the number and designation of *sticks*, which make up the property *bundle*. Sticks in such a bundle could, for example, be the right to enjoy the object, deplete it, destroy it and so on. The idea of property being represented by sticks in a bundle

---

12 Also see Herring, J. and Chau P.-L. 2007. My Body, Your Body, Our Bodies. *Medical Law Review*, 15(1), 34-61 at p. 40.

13 See, e.g. Becker, L.C. and Kipnis, K. 1984. *Property: Cases, Concepts, Critiques*. Englewood Cliffs: Prentice-Hall, at pp. 3-5.

14 Animals tend to be treated like objects more often than not but there is agreement that they inhabit a class outside property classifications. For a view against a proprietary approach to animals, see Hilden, J. 2008. A Contractarian View of Animal Rights: Insuring against the Possibility of Being a Non-Human Animal. *Animal Law Review*, 14(1), available from http://www.juliehilden.com/animal_rights.html, accessed 6 September 2009.

15 For an overview, see, e.g. B. Björkman and Hansson, S.O. 2006. Bodily Rights and Property Rights. *Journal of Medical Ethics*, 32, 209.

has been around for quite some time and has been very ably described in the literature.[16] The convincing aspect is its plasticity. The law, whilst failing on the question of plasticity, has nonetheless described the concept of ownership in a very similar fashion. According to Pollock, ownership means 'the entirety of the powers of use and disposal allowed by law'.[17]

This description is as fitting as it is purposively restrictive: the law defines a certain number of lawful options in relation to an asset. This indicates an important point to remember in the context of either the propertization or the making inalienable of the human body. Something may, according to both the philosophical idea of bundles of sticks and the legal ideas of a range of permissible powers of use and disposal, be property which can be owned without losing its special status. Ownership merely describes a strong right – it is the exact number and kind of sticks in this bundle or the powers prescribed by law which define the character, not the label.

Looking at the different sticks and their denomination makes another issue very clear. An increase of sticks with different denominations, and different powers in relation to an asset, mounts up to a level of control over tissue which will result in the same uneasiness (even without using the label ownership). It is, in the end, all about the powers the law grants us.

> In each of these cases the central issue is one of control. Property is a powerful control device for the bundle of rights that it confers. It also carries a particular message – one of the potential for commerce and trade; of market advantage and disadvantage. To recognise a 'quasi-property' claim to [human] material is to support a normatively strong connection to that material and, accordingly, to establish a strong, justiciable legal interest; by the same token, these examples indicate that 'full' property rights will only be recognised where there is little or no prospect of exploitation or other harm, which can include the 'harm' or disrespect for the dignity of the human organism.[18]

There really are two important points contained in this quotation: first, we need to be careful to not be drawn into making assumptions about ulterior motives of commercialization and propertization purely because economic terminology is deployed when describing dealings with human tissue.[19] Secondly, the application

---

16 See Björkman and Hansson 2006, at p. 211 for a good summary of different bundle theories.

17 Pollock, F. 1896. *A First Book of Jurisprudence for Students of the Common Law*. London and New York: Macmillan, at p. 166.

18 Mason and Laurie 2006, at pp. 514-515.

19 This may just be for lack of other terminology; we cannot invent new terms every time we wish to describe the handling of human tissue. Where I have tissue and I give it to someone else and I get money in return, why call it something other than 'sale' only because tissue is involved?

of normative property concepts to human tissue leads to a manifest increase in defensible rights and entitlements for the rights-holder, not a decrease in rights. This strong justiciable legal interest is in favour of the source (as long as we agree that the source ought not to be disenfranchised).[20] We will take a quick look at this suggested augmentation of source entitlements versus the argument of exploitation.

Exploitation or Exploitability

Mason and Laurie are very convincing in asserting that recognizing a property claim to human material creates a strong justiciable legal interest. This is one of the aspects of propertization which can serve as a counterweight to the problem of exploitability[21] which may be the result of such a propertization: what we have, in effect, is an increase in the rights a person has (as long as we recognize an individual's initial entitlement in his own body). The argument of exploitability is strong and has to be taken seriously, though there is a convincing line of reasoning which suggests that uncompensated organ donation is more likely to foster exploitability than a regulated (property-based) system of compensated organ giving:[22] 'discussion of the sale of organs is overshadowed by cases of exploitation, murder and corruption'.[23]

It is probably true that those entering a market for organs or tissues as vendors are likely not to be well-off. A person who is reasonably wealthy will in all likelihood not feel the need to sell an organ or tissue for gain (or, at least, the level of financial incentive necessary would be disproportionate). It would be quite an impressive *non sequitur* to conclude on this basis that therefore poor people should be barred from taking the decision to sell their tissue or organs.

> Poverty which is acceptable to a society should not be a circumstance which prevents a person taking on a risk or harm to escape that poverty. It is double injustice to say to a poor person: 'You can't have what most other people have and we are not going to let you do what you want to have those things'.[24]

Nonetheless, the threat of exploitability of a certain section of society (a section which, it is suggested, is unable to look after its own interests) appears to be a

---

20 See the discussion of *Moore* in Chapter 9 below.

21 I use the term *exploitability* rather than *exploitation* deliberately here. The possibility, even the probability, of exploitation does not necessarily lead to exploitation. Speaking of exploitation *per se* in this context therefore arguably prejudices the discussion.

22 De Castro, L. 2003. Commodification and Exploitation: Arguments in Favour of Compensated Organ Donation. *Journal of Medical Ethics*, 29, 142-146 at p. 145.

23 Savulescu 2003, at p. 138.

24 Savulescu 2003, at p. 139.

principal reason for rejection of any suggestion of propertizing human tissue or of opening it up to a limited market solution.

> Most of the individual arguments are of a kind that implies the second view [of the rejection of organ selling], because they are about anticipated harms of allowing the practice: coercion, exploitation, shoddy standards, profiteering, misinformation, undermining altruism, deterring donation, and the like.[25]

Raising the spectre of exploitation serves, in most cases, the purpose of pre-emptively terminating the debate of propertization. Where we can show that there is a reasonable expectation of exploitation being the consequence of a certain state of affairs, the tendency very often is to then reject this state of affairs as untenable. It is, after more thoughtful consideration, evident that there are more constructive ways to approach the issue. We should rather address the need to prevent the metamorphosis of exploitability to exploitation. The sensible way forward in this context would then be to permit the state of affairs and regulate the consequences of exploitability, rather than proscribing the state of affairs in order to prevent the exploitation. In many cases the debate does, however, stop when we have identified an undesirable level of exploitation as a possible consequence. It is regularly argued that this mechanism is usually deployed by those who have the rejection of propertization as a primary aim rather than the assessment of all possible points of view: 'This format usually encourages protagonists to collect into an unsorted heap whatever arguments look as though they might have any persuasive force on their side [...]'.[26]

As academic scholars it is our duty to consider these issues all the way to their conclusion rather than start with pre-formed opinions which we then seek to underpin using a questionable rationale. The ownership of human bodies and their parts and products is no exception to this duty.

As pointed out above, even if we accept that there will inevitably be a certain level of exploitation as a result of the propertization of human tissue, it should not automatically lead to a prohibition.

> [...] when you find real dangers and difficulties, you will try to devise techniques for avoiding the harm while keeping the good. This is, after all, what we automatically do in other contexts. The existence of rogue builders and medical quacks does not lead us to try to stop building or medicine altogether: obviously, we aim for controls that will minimise the bad and keep the good.[27]

Rogue builders and medical quacks have been shown to be a threat to all manners of individuals, rich and poor. Where, in our context, we tend to concentrate on

25 Radcliffe-Richards 2003, at p. 139.

26 Radcliffe-Richards 2003, at p. 139.

27 Radcliffe-Richards 2003, at p. 140.

the weak and the sick, they are only one category of vulnerable individuals who we assume will end up being exploited. The exploitation of animals, though commonplace and in many ways necessary in modern life (think of agricultural livestock), is still limited by appropriate animal protection legislation.[28] These rules are intended to curb exploitative and abusive practices in relation to human interaction with animals, rather than proscribe the use of animals *per se*. Animals therefore inhabit a space between property and non-property. Nonetheless, such animals are generally thought to be assets which can be owned and traded. We simply do not have the full set of sticks in the bundle: in many cases we are not free to destroy or alter the animal. The law therefore limits the number of sticks in our bundle of rights in relation to the animals we own. This limitation of rights in the bundle does not mean that the bundle does not represent property, however.

> Each of the sticks that make up the property right can, in principle at least, be the object of negotiations independently of the remaining sticks in the cluster, and whatever the outcome of such negotiations, the property right – the absolute relation of belonging – remains ontologically speaking intact. Someone can give away some of the sticks without giving away his property over the thing in question. Thus it is not uncommon to see cases in which someone has given away (or has had taken away) virtually all the sticks in the bundle (in the case, for example, of the possession of his land by squatters); but even then, however, his residual property right over the thing itself remains.[29]

The question does not seem to hinge on having more sticks in the bundle than others but on the kind of sticks: as the owner of land, one can lease the land to someone else and give up the vast majority of sticks for a limited time.[30] One still has the stronger ultimate entitlement. We part with some of the sticks for a finite time (for life, for 99 years, etc.) but they are to revert at some stage.

For the duration of this transfer of sticks, we give up the rights attached to them. If someone has a mortgage over someone else's land, she cannot invoke the strength of her sticks unless the mortgagor fails to adhere to the conditions of the mortgage – again there is a limitation how or when she can make use of the sticks, but not an ultimate diminishing of ownership. Society's, and thus the law's, duty is to ensure that it is not the strength of the individual which dictates the use of property but the strength of the individual's entitlement which does. To follow Bentham then, property without law, is very much non-existent.

> Suppose we begin with the initially attractive idea that social circumstances and people's relationships to one another should develop over time in accordance

---

28 See, for example, the provisions of sections 4-8 the Animal Welfare Act 2006.

29 Smith and Zaibert 2001, at p. 167.

30 Given that we only have a limited number of sticks in the first place: in England, the outright owner of land is the Crown.

> with free agreements fairly arrived at and fully honored. Straightaway we need an account of when agreements are free and the social circumstances under which they are reached are fair. In addition, while these conditions may be fair at an earlier time, the accumulated results of many separate and ostensibly fair agreements [...] are likely in the course of time to alter citizens' relationships and opportunities so that the conditions for free and fair agreements no longer hold. The role of the institutions that belong to the basic structure is to secure just background conditions against which the actions of individuals and associations take place. Unless this structure is appropriately regulated and adjusted, an initially just social process will eventually cease to be just, however free and fair particular transactions may look when viewed by themselves.[31]

If we focus for the time being on the second concept of property advanced above (the abstract concept of a bundle of entitlements in relation to a concrete object, neglecting intellectual property), we should ask a number of questions in relation to how property comes into existence. If I create something with my own hands, there is a strong social presumption in favour of my ownership of that something. Where I assume physical control of something, there may well be someone else who has ownership of the thing and I am merely the possessor – still a strong entitlement but likely to be quashed by the owner's entitlement if push came to shove (legally). In the next section, we will consider the differences raised by a person's status as a *possessor* and as an *owner*.

Ownership and Possession

> [...] possession is nine-tenths of the law. Your possession of a shirt constitutes a strong presumption in favor of your ownership of the shirt.[32]

Roman law has traditionally known a strong dividing line between the concepts of ownership and possession in relation to one and the same asset. In terms of evidence it is, of course, sometimes considerably easier to prove possession and dispossession than it is to prove ownership.[33] One of the reasons why it is evidentially simpler to prove possession is because it involves a strong element of tangibility. We can traditionally only really possess that which is tangible. The asset we possess can be held up and shown to the world. Whilst possession is therefore a sturdier concept, ownership is one which appears to be more appropriate in the

---

31 Rawls, J. 1971. *A Theory of Justice*. Cambridge, MA: Harvard University Press at pp. 265-266.

32 Smith and Zaibert 2001, at p. 161.

33 Which, again, underlines the categoric difference between the two concepts. One (possession) is simply a question of actual fact whereas the other (ownership) is one of social fiction.

context we are dealing with. A more elaborate reflection on this follows further below.

Possession and ownership are not interchangeable concepts. They are qualitative degrees of the same thing as well as spatial statuses in terms of the entitlement to a certain asset. If we continue to envisage the collection of activities we are entitled to in relation to an asset as a bundle of sticks (each stick making up an individual right) we can see that ownership at the same time of possession represents in most cases the largest number of sticks in the bundle. As discussed above, ownership at the same time of possession in relation to a dog (or any other animal) represents fewer sticks than ownership as well as possession of a book – but we can still speak of property, ownership and possession. Ownership by itself is also a sizeable bundle of sticks, whilst possession is a smaller but still a very useful selection of sticks. To accomplish possession (and therefore a strong entitlement) all that is usually required is physical control of the asset, even though this notion also attracts considerable criticism from many fundamentally opposed thinkers:

> The first person who, having fenced off a plot of ground, took it into his head to say 'this is mine' and found people simple enough to believe him, was the true founder of civil society. What crimes, wars, murders, what miseries and horrors would the human race have been spared by someone who, uprooting the stakes or filling in the ditch, had shouted to his fellow men; Beware of listening to this imposter! You are lost if you forget that the fruits of the earth belong to all and the earth itself to no one![34]

There is a very persuasive notion contained towards the end of Rousseau's exclamation. Things which we have not created but which are given in the surroundings which we inhabit should not simply by virtue of laying claim to their possession become our property.[35] Occasionally there are good reasons for going against this notion. As well as ensuring that entitlements are justly enforced and protected, the law fulfils another important task: that of maximizing social benefit. The law is therefore not simply a blunt instrument used to give shape to feelings of justice and fairness. It will also accept unfairness and injustice in individual circumstances where such unfairness and injustice maximizes an overriding societal benefit.[36] The fruits of the earth, for example, may very well be

34 Rousseau, J.-J. 1992. *Discourse on the Origin of Inequality*. Indianapolis: Hackett at p. 44.

35 As an aside, this is also a stance mirrored in the discussion of the patentability of life. See *Diamond v. Chakrabarty* 447 U.S. 303 (1980).

36 This may well be argued to go against my hypothesis of using Equity in individual cases. If the law assumes a utilitarian stance of maximizing society's benefits, the individual fairness of a decision (such as that to disenfranchise a person) is no longer a relevant consideration.

finders keeps where this leads to desirable socio-economic activity.[37] It follows, that possession is an excellent starting point for claiming a strong entitlement to a thing, including tissues and cells.

On previous occasions, I have argued strongly in favour of a focus on the concept of possession when it comes to human tissue and body products rather than one of ownership.[38] The reasons for this have been elucidated above. The term *ownership* describes a certain quality of entitlement (ostensibly a good quality of entitlement, or rather: a better entitlement than most others). In contrast, the term *possession* describes the idea of physical control over a certain object. Whilst *de iure* stronger protection tends to be afforded to the owner than to the possessor, possession is *realiter* the more sturdy concept, much easier to assess and terminologically less controversial. The question may be distilled to this: would a financial incentive to purchase possession of human biological material attract the same moral disquiet as a financial incentive to purchase ownership in the material?

Using Force

Any person vested with possession of a certain object has a powerful control right over the object. Regardless of his title to the object in question, any attempts at removing the object from his control without his voluntary cooperation would entail some degree of force. Such an interference will, in most cases, be illegal – unless the use of force is properly mandated for that particular purpose and is deemed to be proportionate. Even in cases where there is an elevated interest in the recovery of an object from someone else's possession, such a recovery is not always proportionate. An excellent, as well as quite memorable, example in this context is the case of *Winston v. Lee*, the facts of which are outlined below:

> A shopkeeper was wounded by gunshot during an attempted robbery but, also being armed with a gun, apparently wounded his assailant in his left side, and the assailant then ran from the scene. Shortly after the victim was taken to hospital, police officers found respondent, who was suffering from a gunshot wound to his left chest area, eight blocks away from the shooting. [...] The Commonwealth of Virginia moved in state court for *an order directing respondent to undergo*

37 Quite aside from the usual examples of oil-drilling, gold-digging and diamond-mining, we can also apply this notion to assets which are not fruits of the earth but fruits of someone else's labour: abandoned ships at sea and treasure troves. Maybe even other people's abandoned genes?

38 Hoppe, N. 2009. Reflections on Entitlements in the Human Body from an Equity Perspective. In: *Altruism Reconsidered: Exploring New Approaches to Property in Human Tissue*. Edited by M. Steinmann, U. Wiesing, and P. Sýkora, Aldershot: Ashgate.

> *surgery to remove a bullet lodged under his left collarbone, asserting that the bullet would provide evidence of respondent's guilt or innocence.*[39]

The respondent in this case was the suspected robber. The forced surgery was intended to provide clarity on whether the bullet in the wounded man was from the shopkeeper's gun or not. The application failed, but only because it was deemed necessary to extract the evidence under general anaesthetic and the respondent was able to show that such an anaesthetic carried with it an inherent and real risk of injury or death. Had the procedure required no such anaesthetic and would have merely induced discomfort, the court may well have ordered it to be carried out against his will. This decision would have been proportionate on the basis that there was an overriding public interest in solving a gun-related crime, outweighing the respondent's entitlement to physical integrity.

This may suggest that it is in fact the concept of possession (in real terms, rather than in legal terms) which is pivotal in defining our relationships with regard to objects. The respondent had legally inseparable possession of the item and thereby frustrated the applicant's course of action. This case is clearly quite singular on the facts; it is unlikely that the legislator will regulate for these circumstances. The law therefore tries to apply abstract rules to work out whether it can solve the problem using existing norms. The question of property only comes to the court's attention in terms of ascertaining possession and underpinning its dominant character. Were the court to consider the property effects of such a status, the discussion may yield highly interesting results for our problem. The question of bailment, as an example, has not been satisfactorily discussed in this context.[40] The shop owner (if it was in fact his round in the first place) may have abandoned the round by firing it into the respondent or the respondent may merely be the bailee of the round, which was transferred to him (admittedly at great speed) for safe keeping for a limited time. It is prudent to resist the temptation to dissect the problem in *Winston v. Lee* in terms of ownership versus possessive interest in the round that is lodged in the respondent's body, though it is clearly an interesting question. The overriding point made here is an illustration of the dominance of possession in cases where the integrity of an individual's body is at stake.

In summary, we can conclude that the legal concept of ownership really only describes a theoretical construct of absolute entitlement, whereas possession is a *de facto* manifestation of control. As long as no one contests the status of possession and seeks the mandate to forcefully remove the object, control continues. When applying these notions to our problem of the possession of human tissue, we

39 *Winston v. Lee* 470 US 753 (1985) (Sup. Ct.) (emphasis added).

40 An interesting discussion of the law of bailment in this context would exceed the remit of this text, but I am grateful to my friend Asim Sheikh (UCD) for stimulating discussions and impetus for future work. The issue of bailment was also discussed in the Court of Appeal's recent judgment in *Yearworth v. North Bristol NHS Trust*, discussed in Chapter 9.

need to add another dimension. In our initial consideration, all that is required to remove something from the possessor's control is either his voluntary consent or a proper mandate to use force. In terms of removing tissue from the initial possessor (the source), the source cannot voluntarily consent to the tissue's removal outside a range of very narrowly defined circumstances.[41] These circumstances include lawful consent to a therapeutic or diagnostic procedure, at which point complex questions of entitlements arise principally after the material is to be recycled for purposes other than its original designation.

Having identified and discussed the issues involved in our systematic approach to the problem, we will now turn to a description of how the law has approached these issues and how we can argue that this approach has failed in many aspects.

41 See Chapter 7 for issues of consent.

PART II
Legal Approaches

Chapter 5
Old Law for New Problems?

> Parts are taken from the body without either the deceased's or their family's approval. Put to the use of medicine, these body parts become, as if by magic, property, but property owned by persons unknown, for purposes unforeseen by the deceased. If that represents the law, the law is an ass. [...] Even within the 'complexity and obscurity of the current law', some line must be drawn.[1]

In this chapter we will introduce a criticism of the different possible approaches for finding a normative system for handling human tissue used in the past. Subsequently, the mechanisms which the law provides for defining entitlements in the first place will be discussed. Then, some light will be shed on those mechanisms which serve to protect these initial entitlements. Having established the basic requirements for determining the legal status of tissue, a brief outline of the different approaches taken in the past will be given. A discussion of some of the developments in the Common Law precedes a look at recent developments in terms of the Human Tissue Act 2004. Following on from that is a glance at supranational legislative activity, focused on the European Union's Human Tissue Directive, before the next chapters culminate in a look at the United States and three paradigmatic cases there and a very recent English case.

The kernel of this part's reasoning follows on from this introduction: a systematic analysis of the law using the matrix introduced in Chapter 2 as a guiding tool. Issues of propertization and law will be addressed using the same structure provided there. Matching different approaches to human tissue to the matrix's thematic context prevents losing track of different elements of the debate. The idea here is to provide a natural follow up to the matrix structure. Having identified the different issues at stake, we can now test how the law is applied to these issues before embarking on an attempt, in the final part of this book, of creating a new normative approach to them.

Before developing a systematic approach to the normative treatment of human tissue, we need to address one of the many myths surrounding the issues at stake here. It sometimes looks deceptively as if the law has been slow to deal normatively with a recent development in biomedical progress – in this case the treatment of human tissue as material eligible for proprietary classification. The law is certainly slow to come to terms with new developments, but there is a very plausible argument that the development in this particular area is certainly not new. It has been suggested that recent progress has introduced the human body to the realm of

1 Brazier, M. 2002. Retained Organs: Ethics and Humanity. *Legal Studies*, 22(4), 550-569 at 563.

propertization (more commonly: *commodification*)[2] and this is usually not intended to denote a positive development. In fact, it is quite obvious that the routine use, commercial or non-commercial, of the human body has been widespread before the case of Moore made the headlines.[3] Merely the industrialization of the process has increased and with it the fear of an uncontrolled commercialization of the human body. Ranging from the use of parts of dead adversaries' bodies as decoration[4] to ritual cultural anthropophagic consumption of executed prisoners' blood,[5] there have always been uses and applications:

> In the nineteenth century there was a flourishing trade in New Zealand and elsewhere in preserved and tattooed Maori heads. Although this practice was declared illegal by the Governor of New South Wales in 1831, its legality was not challenged elsewhere. Indeed, proceedings were instituted in 1989 by the Maori Council in New Zealand, supported by the New Zealand Government, to halt the proposed sale of such a preserved head at a London auction. However, the head was withdrawn from the auction and the matter settled prior to trial.[6]

It would certainly be outside the remit of this text to provide an exhaustive history of the propertization of the human body and so we will linger on just a few examples. The most well-known, and with the benefit of hindsight possibly least problematic, use for the human body which has been in practice since earliest times is that of science; early anatomical knowledge is thought to have come either from dissection and vivisection or, at the very least, from keen observation of ritual sacrifices.[7] What follows from this realization is the question whether we

2 The difference between the two terms hinging on the question of disposability: making something into property (*propertization*) does not necessarily expose it to disposability and transferability. When something is made into a commodity (*commodification*) it is transferable. Here, we have different sticks in either bundle.

3 Also see Harris 2002, at p. 527: 'Organ retention has been with us for millennia. Walk into virtually any cathedral and many a church in Europe and you will find an array of retained organs and tissue, allegedly originally the property of assorted saints, or even of God, and almost certainly collected without proper informed consent and retained in less than secure conditions'.

4 See, e.g. Chacon, R. and Dye, D. 2007. *The Taking and Displaying of Human Body Parts as Trophies by Amerindians*. New York: Springer.

5 Bergmann, A. 2004. *Der entseelte Patient - die Moderne Medizin und der Tod.* Berlin: Aufbau-Verlag at p. 172. For an opposing view, see Arens, W. 1980. *The Man-Eating Myth: Anthropology and Anthropophagy*. Oxford: Oxford University Press.

6 Dworkin and Kennedy 1993, at p. 296. Withdrawing heads has also, of course, been a commonplace response of the judiciary when asked to adjudicate on proprietary notions in relation to human tissue.

7 Edelstein, L. 1987. The History of Anatomy in Antiquity. In: *Ancient Medicine.* Edited by O. Temkin and C.L. Temkin, Baltimore and London: The Johns Hopkins University Press, 247-301 at p. 248.

really think that, with the benefit of hindsight, we will disapprove of paternalistic retention practices in Liverpool hospitals in one hundred years' time – when the large-scale retention of such tissues has led to a reduction in morbidity or mortality of the magnitude similar to the one resulting from the heart collection at Alder Hey.[8] Not only will time heal these wounds, the benefit ultimately gleaned from inflicting these wounds will also play a significant part in its doubtless romanticized view in due course. This should not, however, distract from the fact that an injustice was done to the parents which the law did nothing to prevent or penalize.

The fact that Alder Hey caused such a landslide change in the public's level of response to, regrettably fairly routine, medical practices can be explained easily: the rift that is developing between patient and doctor is widening steadily the more the patient on the one side turns into an autonomous, self-determined customer and, on the other side, the doctor turns into a researcher. The degree of metamorphosis from the one state to the other for the two parties respectively determines the level of outrage expressed by the public. The more the member of the public feels 'enabled' and independent in his decision-making (i.e. moving away from the traditional 'the doctor knows best' doctrine), the more he feels defrauded when the newly won autonomy is disrespected (and feels rightly justified in expressing this in the available media). The researcher, on the other hand, often feels morally legitimated to use the material in this way in order to attempt to find the cause or cure to diseases – the end justifying the means. The practical implications of outrage expressed in public are, and this can be best illustrated using the example of the Human Tissue Act, political responses which tend to all too quickly try and solve all problems and hush all fears. It is a fact that they often represent mere lip service to the public and create new problems and hinder the work of researchers more than a retention of the status quo would have done.

The status as researcher does not, however, completely explain the protagonists' astonishing detachment from the kind of values commonly felt by members of the public. The problem narrows down to one of guidance. Doctors, more so than any other profession, are uniquely dependent on accurate guidance in relation to what is legally admissible and what is not. The consequence of acting in a 'wrong' way is, in this setting, much more volatile than in another setting. By adhering to the letter of the law, the medical professional feels that he or she is much more likely to be 'doing the right thing' than by assessing issues in an abstract moral sense. Whilst the law, more often than not, does follow common contemporary ideals of decency, morals and ethics, it has an absolute normative quality which those ideals usually have not (and which explains its higher degree of utility to medical professionals): one is less likely to be socially faulted for following the law, whilst at the same time breaching notions of ethics, than one is for breaking the law in favour of following one's personal idea of what is right. The law therefore not

8 See Chapter 3.

only gives guidance in relation to what might be right or wrong. It also provides the *ex ante* guarantee of exculpation. Responsibility for one's own actions can be transferred to a social normative structure that all have to accept as true and paramount if they want to fully participate in society. All the more disastrous is the situation then when medical professionals are put in a situation where they feel that there is no safe normative legal cushion surrounding them, legitimating their choices. This is a situation where the law has failed to provide for the choices these individuals have to make by necessity on a daily basis: 'In the year or so leading to the tissue bank launch in June 1996, we could find no relevant law in the UK'.[9]

The problem is uniquely pervasive: in almost all areas of medicine where physicians, researchers or nurses deal with human-derived materials, there is considerable doubt as to what is permissible activity in relation to the material and what is not. The law has quite simply failed to provide appropriate guidance for those who regularly have to make choices in relation to such material.

What really is changing, and probably increasing continuously, is the scale on which the human body is now used as a commodity. Choices like the ones referred to are made every day, though, and that leads to the inevitable question of how – in reality – such situations are supposed to be mastered without the support of an appropriate set of laws to indicate which way to go.

> Few would claim that the current law on whether and when the body or its parts can be owned is satisfactory. It is clear that parts of the body and indeed corpses can be property in some circumstances and for some purposes. Complete bodies of living people, it appears, cannot be property. But it is difficult to make a more authoritative statement than that about the English law.[10]

The deficiency of the law is thrown into stark relief when you see the helplessness with which it attempts to prevent negative effects on the source of human material (i.e. the human), caused by the spectre of exploitation or devaluation of the person, whilst at the same time strongly underpinning the socially desirable concept of advancing biomedical research. This is manifested by, and best illustrated using, the fact that the law routinely disenfranchises the source as a matter of course. It provides (whether it is by accident or by design is uncertain) that proprietary entitlements come into existence at some stage during the process of excision, but not before.

> [...] although property does not come into existence until the tissue is removed, the consent to removal ensures that, upon removal, the property becomes vested *in the person removing it.*[11]

9 Womack and Gray 2007, at p. 212.

10 Herring and Chau 2007, at p. 38.

11 Dworkin and Kennedy 1993, at p. 302. Also see Brazier 2002.

Ignoring legal concepts such as *scintilla temporis*,[12] the practical utility of which does not reveal itself in a realistic setting, it becomes clear quite quickly that the point is that the source does not profit, and the person excising the tissue does – even where the whole process is the product of fraud, deception and illegality. Brazier, very accurately, suggests that, if this is indeed the case (which it is), the law is an ass.[13] The question very much is why it is felt that this is the best possible solution to our problem: it manifestly is not. If we can agree on the notion, then, that the source ought to in some way be permitted to profit from an exercise which is not intended to be therapeutically beneficial to the him or herself (D1), we need to see how the law can provide protection to this entitlement prior to the elusive *scintilla* after which we are then so swiftly deprived of it.

12 In this context, the 'fact' is that at some point in time there must be a minute trace of time within which the source must have proprietary interests in order to pass them on as a donation or gift. This is generally thought to be legal fiction and is sometimes used in property law (see, e.g. Sawyer, C. 2001. A World Safe for Mortgagees? Registering a Scintilla of Doubt. In: *Modern Studies in Property Law.* Edited by E. Cooke. Oxford: Hart Publishing, pp. 201- 214 at p. 207). Also see Hoffmann LJ's dictum in *Ingram and Another v. Commissioners of Inland Revenue* [1999] 2 WLR 90, [2000] 1 AC 293, [1999] 1 All ER 297, [1998] UKHL 47: 'For my part, I do not think that a theory based upon the notion of a scintilla temporis can have a very powerful grasp on reality'. (available from http://www.bailii.org/cgi-bin/markup.cgi?doc=/uk/cases/UKHL/1998/47.html, accessed 3 June 2009). Older decisions still deem the scintilla a reality – see *Church of England Building Society v. Piskor* [1954] Ch. 553; [1954] 2 All E.R. 85.

13 Brazier 2002, at p. 563.

Chapter 6
Protecting Entitlements

Introducing Rights and Entitlements

It is necessary to be very clear about some aspects of how law works before embarking on an exploration of how we have tried to normatively capture human tissue so far and before developing new sets of rules for capturing it in the future. This is one particular thematic area where we can see the distinct differences between jurisdictions with the same roots as the English and Welsh system and the more continental traditions. These distinctions become very clear when we attempt to systematically discuss libertarian rights-orientated law and personal rights systems. Legally, we can establish entitlements on the basis of two possible premises:

1. a constitutional or human rights entitlement[1] (e.g. 'the right to vote', 'the right to physical integrity'); or
2. a proprietary entitlement (e.g. ownership, possession, an easement, right to quiet enjoyment).

Having established an initial entitlement, the law can then provide rules which serve to protect the entitlement or provide redress in cases where the entitlement is infringed:

1. criminal law rules endeavouring to deter others from infringing an entitlement;
2. tort law rules endeavouring to prevent others from infringing an entitlement;
3. tort law rules entitling the holder of an infringed entitlement to restitution against a tortfeasor.

Deterrence and Restitution

Both criminal law rules, which provide punishment for an infringement, as well as tort law rules providing for restitution, carry an element of deterrence. In the case

1 Admittedly a very simplified generalized category for a complex area of, often confusing, law as far as the UK is concerned. I will simply ignore the inadequacy of this assertion for the purposes of this illustration, hoping that my point is clear enough without delving deep into questions of UK constitutional law.

of criminal law rules it is the intention to provide for a punishment which is, whilst always proportionate to the crime, also more costly to the offender than the gain he might expect to stand from committing the crime. In the case of tort law norms, they are designed to 'reset the injustice', to put the injured party into a situation as if the tort had not occurred. The reality is such that the exercise generally tends to be more costly to the tortfeasor than the gain yielded by the commission of the tort in the first place.[2]

In order to conduct a sensible debate of any regulatory framework which is to apply to a certain set of circumstances, we therefore need to establish:

a. the basis for the entitlement we intend to protect; and
b. the mechanism we wish to deploy in order to protect the entitlement.

It is not necessary to go into the details of any examples for this – the idea is quite clear. When we speak of entitlement in human tissue, we can see that the law already provides for mechanisms which are sufficient in most cases: the constitutional, human rights and natural justice entitlement to be free from harm is protected by the criminal rules which provide for punishment of offences against the person. Any damage resulting from the infringement is then dealt with by rules of tort, compelling the tortfeasor to remedy the harm done. That is why in cases where a doctor wrongfully goes beyond the consent he has obtained in treating a patient, and causes harm, he faces criminal charges for the battery. He also faces the possibility of a civil claim in relation to any damage sustained by the patient and the non-consensual contact. It is clear that in this context we need not augment the law, nor do we need to introduce questions of proprietary status. Rules of property rather lend themselves as excellent mechanisms where we wish to protect a different kind of entitlement, as we have seen in previous chapters. The kind of entitlement which needs to exist in these cases is simply an individual's better right to a tangible or intangible object.

Where one has the best entitlement to a certain object, there is an initial entitlement cushioned in a proprietary interest. The criminal law provides that no one should deprive us of the full enjoyment of that object, save under exceptional circumstances. If someone else nevertheless removes the object from our possession and excludes us from enjoying it, he faces punishment. If he damages the object, depletes it, passes it on beyond recovery, converts it to something else or mixes it inextricably with something, the civil law provides for an exhaustive arsenal of mechanisms and remedies to aid us in healing as much of the damage resulting from the injustice as is possible and appropriate. It is important to realize at this point that we may not need to make distinctions in individual cases. There will, in all likelihood, have been infringement of both

2 On this basis it is easy enough to see that in the case of Moore, the law failed. The exercise (defrauding Moore of his cells) was less costly for the perpetrators (in legal terms) than it should have been.

kinds of entitlements where something is removed from another's possession forcefully. Systematically distinguishing between these entitlements and their protective mechanisms only makes sense in order to determine the underlying facts of such an infringement.

The Case of Tissues and Cells

Applying what we have determined so far to the case of tissues and cells that belong to an individual, we can see that the current situation is in essence quite similar: there is what has been termed a basic constitutional/human rights entitlement not to be touched and of no part of the body being separated from the individual without lawful excuse. This entitlement is quasi-inalienable (see Chapter 6) save for exceptional circumstances, such as therapeutic surgery and limited instances in which the individual is permitted to manifest his free will as he pleases (get a piercing, get a tattoo, indulge in a boxing match but not, absurdly, ride a motorcycle without a helmet). My consent provides the key to deactivating the legal protection mechanisms in the case of a properly authorized 'injury', and the chain of events stops there. Continuing logically with the assessment, we can determine that where the initial infringement of the entitlement is not healed by appropriate consent, some sort of mechanism needs to be activated to provide punishment for the wrongful act and provide a remedy of restitution for the loss. The law still appears to be sufficient in this regard – a conviction for battery is presumably easily obtained and a claim for compensation for non-consensual contact is also possible. Even damages for the loss of tissue are available: the law has so far not shied away from quantifying the value of body parts, such as a leg, for the purposes of compensation.[3] This is where we ask the question of the status of the separated tissue. Arguably, the law's efficacy stops here and biomedical reality continues in a largely unguided fashion. Legislators and judiciary have unwittingly created a sizeable lacuna, failing to penalize illegal conduct in civil law terms, as profit generated from an unlawful excision will not be the subject of recovery because the source can, so far, not show a proprietary interest. As it currently stands, the source can only show a personal interest which is not quantifiable without showing loss. Is the infringed right therefore only a personal right?

---

3 Cf. Ritchie, R., Norris, W., Aldous, G., Allen, A., Kennedy, J., Lewers, N., Hickey, N., Petts, T. and Rowley, J. (eds) 2005. *Kemp & Kemp: Personal Injury Law, Practice and Procedure*. London: Sweet & Maxwell; *Pettley v. Stridwick* (1988) – PSLA Damages of £33,000; *Re Schembri* (1999) – PSLA Damages of £75,000; *Andrew v. British Railways Board* (1985) – PSLA Damages of £65,000; these were all for loss of a leg above the knee. I do acknowledge that these figures do not only comprise the 'value' of the leg but take other loss into consideration.

Personal Rights or Property Rights?

Rights can traditionally be classified as property rights or personal rights. Property rights define our entitlement to a certain thing (proprietary rights *in rem*) and the law protects this entitlement against the world as a whole. Personal rights are, once again, terminologically ambiguous. To refer to something as a personal right can either mean that it is an entitlement which is enforceable against a specific person or a specific class of persons (rights *in personam*), such as those which result from obligations like liability in tort or contractual entitlements. The term's second meaning is that personal rights can also refer to a class of rights which are personal to us and which make up our status as individuals, such as the right to vote or the right to physical integrity. This latter class of rights is generally not quantifiable whereas the former is. Some rights inhabit an ill-defined area in between classes, such as the personal right to the inviolability of one's own reputation,[4] the loss or infringement of which is nonetheless quantifiable and damages are regularly awarded for an infringement.[5] The three different classes of rights – rights *in rem*, rights *in personam* and personal rights – reflect a certain level of entitlement which is granted a commensurate level of protection by the law.

It is quite clear that entitlements are only ever as good as the protection they enjoy. In the case of entitlements which may arise in relation to human tissue or body products, we may look, again, at the Calabresi model[6] and see a typology of property-based rules and liability-based rules. Taking this idea further, we can resort to personal rights in order to protect entitlements in our bodies – the criminal law generally proscribes interference without consent, the law of torts provides remedies to prevent interference or to compensate in cases where interference has occurred. The law of property on the other hand, licenses alienability of a certain entitlement by usually giving us the ability to transfer the property to others. Returning for one moment to the initial point of the different approaches to protecting entitlements in the human body, it can be argued that these are part of a progressive application of law, not an either-or constellation. Whilst the parts are still connected to the individual's body, they are protected by deterrent criminal and liability rules, seeking to protect his personal right to bodily integrity and providing redress in cases where this integrity has been breached.

---

4 Its 'blurriness' is also mirrored in its conceptual adaptability. Libel can be a tort or a crime; even in tort, civil procedure provides for a trial by jury; barring an action for fraud this is the only instance in civil law where a jury trial is possible. Section 69, Supreme Court Act 1981 (Queen's Bench Division); section 66, County Courts Act 1984 (County Courts); part 26.11 Civil Procedure Rules.

5 Awards for libel being quantified in ostensibly utterly different proportions to, for example, the loss of a limb. Cf. the award of £150,000 for the Scottish MP George Galloway against the *Daily Telegraph* in December 2004, following claims by the newspaper that he had received payment from Saddam Hussein.

6 See Chapter 4.

> The power to consent to physically intrusive activity suggests that we have some control over what others may do to our bodies.[7]

It is possible to consent to the breach of our bodily integrity for certain lawful purposes; some other purposes cannot be consented to.[8] Regardless of how the tissue or material is separated from my body, once the material is separated it is spatially distanced from the body. By virtue of being so distanced, it enters into the realm of what can be best encompassed and protected by property rules. Nozick writes in this context that:

> Property rights are viewed as rights to determine which of a specified range of admissible options concerning something will be realized. Admissible options are those that do not cross another's moral boundary [...].[9]

Nozick's assertion that admissible options are 'those that do not cross another's moral boundary' is not immediately convincing. It should rather be 'those that do not cross another's dominant rights'. Numerous activities are outside the scope of another's moral boundaries, moral boundaries being inherently subjective. The socially motivated consumption of moderate amounts of alcoholic drink or a failure to go to church regularly are likely to cross others' moral boundaries. This does not make these choices inadmissible. The treatment of animals as property will cross quite a few individuals' moral boundaries but, again, this does not result in inadmissibility. Just as the reception of transfusions of blood crosses some people's moral thresholds, so does the giving of blood or sperm.

Whilst one should probably be under a duty to try not to offend others, to restrict the admissibility of the realization of proprietary or personal entitlements to what is morally acceptable to another is evidently inappropriate. The question, here, should therefore be whether excising tissue, parting with it one way or another, and thus subjecting it to the rules of property crosses the threshold of another's dominant rights. If we move on from the question of subjective moral boundaries and for one moment agree that there may be certain things which cross objective moral boundaries, Nozick's assessment is more agreeable: the range of proprietary applicability stops where such an application crosses an objective moral boundary (such as, *inter alia*, slavery, forced labour, forced prostitution).[10] Entitlements such as the freedom from coercion and the right to physical integrity are by and large

---

7 Dworkin and Kennedy 1993, at p. 300.

8 *R v. Brown et al. [1993] 2 All ER 75* where the House of Lords held that *compos mentis* adults were not able to consent to serious harm inflicted during sado-masochistic activities.

9 Nozick, R. 1974. *Anarchy, State and Utopia*. Oxford: Basil Blackwell, at pp. 281-282.

10 The intricate problems of intercultural ethics, particularly the problem of transferring western values to eastern cultures, are acknowledged in this context.

inalienable and cannot be disposed of. This is on the one hand a good moment to indicate that property in living human beings is uniformly legally ruled out.[11] It is clear that the law recognizes no such interest in another human being. Even employer-employee relationships of the most exploitative nature are nothing more than, possibly unfair, contracts for services, not for temporary proprietary transfer of the employee's body. On the other hand it would go well beyond the scope of this text to discuss the question of slavery, prostitution and forced labour in the context of normative proprietary constructions.[12]

Inalienability

> We are not disembodied beings, but complex combinations of intellect, emotion, appetite, spirit and body. Our body has special value because it is the medium through which we express ourselves. Thus, our special value as human beings extends to our bodies.[13]

The principle of inalienability serves an important purpose. Making certain aspects of our lives, certain goods or rights, inalienable, preserves a basic level of individual endowment which represents the necessary minimum equipment in order to participate in society. If, for argument's sake, we had a special class of citizens who did not have the right to vote, this would mean that these citizens could not partake in societal interaction on the same level as others. It would make them less endowed and therefore less powerful and thus by necessity oppressed, as they are forced to subject themselves to the will of others. It follows that there is a generally accepted truth: that of equality, and a corresponding, basic level of endowment with rights.[14]

Cohen, in the quote at the beginning of this section, asserts another purported universal truth, namely that we are inherently special and that this special status is not contingent on any surrounding facts but on our role as members of a community: 'it is not an attribute of isolated individuals, but of individuals who

---

11 See Art. 4 of the European Convention for the Protection of Human Rights and Fundamental Freedoms (Prohibition of slavery and forced labour) and Art. 5 of the Charter of Fundamental Rights of the European Union; also see the non-binding though thoroughly persuasive Art. 4 of the Universal Declaration of Human Rights.

12 See Dickenson, D. 2006. Philosophical Assumptions and Presumptions about Trafficking for Prostitution. In: *Trafficking and Women's Rights*. Edited by C. van den Anker and J. Doemernik. Basingstoke: Palgrave Macmillan, 43-53.

13 Cohen 1999, at p. 291.

14 It is acknowledged, in this context, that there is a convincing philosophical argument that we are simply not all equal but naturally different, with different capabilities and thus different needs. An overarching and unquestioned assumption of equality may not stand up to close scrutiny. 'In its prescriptive usage, "equality" is a loaded and "highly contested" concept'. Entry for 'Equality' in Zalta, E. (ed.). *Stanford Encyclopedia of Philosophy*, available at http://plato.stanford.edu/entries/equality, accessed 3 June 2009.

belong to a community'.[15] She goes on to differentiate between essential and inessential parts of our body, deeming the former to be inalienable and the latter potentially alienable:

> We do not ordinarily consider that hair, spit, or fingernail parings carry human dignity and worth, for these generally function as inessential human bits and pieces unrelated to what it is that makes human beings of special value.[16]

If she in fact suggests that spit and fingernail parings are thus alienable then this can only extend to their tangible attributes, not to the intangible capacity such as inherent genetic information (see the point made on the disposability of familial data above). Nonetheless, the fact that not all entitlements can be subject to property is well established, as is the point that we cannot consent to all kinds of harm for the purposes of financial gain[17] or personal pleasure.[18] It is therefore right to assume that in the realm of the human body and its *bits and pieces* (Cohen) we can stipulate a number of activities which cannot be carried out on the basis that they would represent an undesirable disposal of an inalienable right or good.

15 Cohen 1999, at p. 292.

16 Cohen 1999, at p. 291.

17 Dworkin and Kennedy write that '... in the days of Coke, a person was convicted of a criminal offence when he amputated another's hand, so that he was in a better position to beg, notwithstanding that consent had been given'. *R v. Wright* (1603) in: Dworkin and Kennedy 1993, at p. 299.

18 *R v. Brown et al.* [1993] 2 All ER 75.

Chapter 7
The Common Law Position

The Common Law has had a number of contact points with the question whether human bodies are property capable of being owned. The position taken is that something can either be a person or an object, but not both,[1] which appears to generally be in full agreement with the purported Kantian position illustrated at the outset. The basis for this stance appears to be a rejection of the possibility of a circular property relationship, i.e. the ability to be the *owner* at the same time as the *thing* which is being owned. Consider the following quote:

> Man cannot dispose over himself because he is not a thing; he is not his own property; to say that he is would be self-contradictory; for insofar as he is a person he is a Subject in whom the ownership of things can be vested, and if he were his own property he would be a thing over which he could have ownership. But a person cannot be a property and so cannot be a thing which can be owned, for it is impossible to be a person and a thing, the proprietor and the property.[2]

On the Outright Rejection of Property

Before turning to my main criticism of this line of reasoning, it is sensible to take the opportunity to consider Kant's rejection of the property notion. First, it is clear that there is an assumption that the determination of property and proprietor takes place in a situation where the integrity of the body is intact. His insistence that man *is* not a thing can be distinguished from how one would argue when part of a man has been severed: would, in this case, the argument hold that the proprietor in some way *is* the severed limb? I would submit that it would not. Kant's reflection, though in its product equivalent to the stated Common Law position, can also be criticized in that it does not (and cannot) take into account the contemporary situation. This, whilst affording Kant's deliberations a certain amount of informative value and an excellent starting point for personal explorations of the issues, certainly limits its usefulness in the current context. In particular, there is some doubt as to whether the contextual application of Kantian ethics in a biomedical environment might not lead to a permissive stance on organ giving, possibly even a positive duty to

---

1 See Dickenson, D. 2007. *Property in the Body: Feminist Perspectives*. Cambridge and New York: Cambridge University Press at p. 4.

2 Kant, *Lectures on Ethics*, cited in: Dickenson 2007, at p. 5.

part with one's organs once they are no longer necessary for sustaining life support functions of the body.[3] Further, Munzer draws on Kant's stance as humans as *beings of free will*, closes the description with a negation of the ability to have free will once we are commodified and then leads on to a criticism of this approach:[4]

> Human beings have free will. If they had property rights in parts of their body and exercised those rights, they would lose that freedom. They would move from the level of free human beings to the level of things or objects.[5]

The analysis put forward on behalf of Kant is unconvincing in a twofold fashion:[6] first, the somewhat sportive application of Kant's notions to a context for which they were simply not designed seems to be inappropriate. Kant can be used to argue for the removal of diseased parts of the body as well as the removal of sex organs[7] and the destruction of the entire body[8] as means of punishment and prevention. Kant also rejects transplantation and enhancement practices:

> To deprive oneself of an integral part of an organ (to maim oneself) – for example to give away or sell a tooth to be transplanted into another's mouth, or to have oneself castrated in order to get an easier livelihood as a singer, and so forth – are ways of partially murdering oneself.[9]

The terminology here is ambiguous. The suggestion that to part with body parts does not represent a manifestation of an individual's free will but rather constitutes murder, albeit partial, seems to be a *non sequitur*. It highlights a similar problem to Kant's circular analysis of being owner and owned thing at the same time. Kant, too, appears to argue this point teleologically, seeking to prevent the disposability of the human body by whatever means necessary as it simply does not seem to sit well with his view of the special status of persons.

---

3 See, e.g. Merle, J.-C. 2000. A Kantian Argument for a Duty to Donate One's Own Organs. A Reply to Nicole Gerrand. *Journal of Applied Philosophy*, 17(1), 93-101. It is difficult to envisage how a 'duty to give' can still be described as an act of donation (it smacks more of a compulsory possession construct). This may, however, be just another example of the terminological helplessness I described at the outset.

4 My rephrasing and interpretation.

5 Munzer, S. 1993. Kant and Property Rights in Body Parts. *Canadian Journal of Law and Jurisprudence*, 6(2), 319-341, at p. 322.

6 Though again, I acknowledge that Munzer is criticizing just this aspect of the use of Kant in a modern biomedical and bioethical context in his excellent and in-depth article.

7 Kant, I. 1797. *Doctrine of Right* cited in Merle 2000, at p. 93.

8 Kant, I. 1797. *Doctrine of Right* cited in Merle 2000, at p. 93.

9 Kant, I. 1797. *The Metaphysics of Morals* cited in: Gerrand, N. 1999. The Misuse of Kant in the Debate about a Market for Human Body Parts. *Journal of Applied Philosophy*, 16(1), 59-67 at p. 61.

Crucially, in this portion quoted by Gerrand, Kant clearly makes no distinction between pecuniary advantage and altruistic giving – he is simply against maiming oneself and parting with the component yielded through such an act.[10] This suggests that he would also be against the exercise if it were for the benefit of a sick recipient. It would go too far to explore the question in detail but I would not hesitate to suggest that the change in what is biotechnically possible since Kant's deliberations were formulated renders his premises insufficient. Again, it is simply not of interest what Kant's position would have been had he known about the innovative live organ donation scenarios possible nowadays as his thoughts lack the normative authority to give any more than superficial guidance.

Secondly, it is unconvincing to argue that one is a being of free will and then restrict the reach of this free will by keeping the disposal of one's own body outside what we may control. We are clearly not of free will but of limited will if we are not permitted to do with our shells as we please. A further and more pivotal argument is that of irreversibility: it is unpersuasive that a person, previously endowed with free will (in the limited Kantian sense) who gives away a tooth to be transplanted into a relative's mouth has thereby lost his status as a human of free will and will thenceforth be regarded as a thing or an object. Even on a societal scale – should the practice of giving teeth to relatives assume a generally accepted character – there is no good argument why we should all then be regarded as objects rather than humans. Is my assertion of the extension of my free will to the disposability of my teeth not a demonstration of my larger free will than that of those who adhere to Kant's view?

Consent

> [...] while the importance of consent derives from our concept of the person, its procedural primacy in health care in the UK, the US and some other jurisdictions is owed to the Common Law tradition, which protects individuals from assaults – unlawful touchings. It is consent which makes laying your hands on someone else lawful – hence the importance of obtaining valid consents to all medical procedures which involve interventions which compromise the bodily integrity of patients.[11]

It is interesting that Harris discusses the consent-based orientation of current normative approaches to human tissue in the context of the principle's supremacy in UK and US jurisdictions. It took the English legal system considerably longer to enshrine the departure from the *doctor knows best* maxim. Justice Cardozo

10 In the original passage, Kant goes on to deem the cutting off of hair to be unproblematic, unless it is done for gain.

11 Harris, J. 2002. Law and Regulation of Retained Organs: The Ethical Issues. *Legal Studies*, 22(4), 527-549 at p. 529.

gave the much-cited dictum on patient autonomy in *Schloendorff v. New York Hospital* in 1914: 'Every human being of adult years and sound mind has a right to determine what shall be done with his own body; and a surgeon who performs an operation without his patient's consent, commits an assault'.[12]

At the same time, English courts still underpinned the very paternalistic attitude of primary care and hospital professionals and still did so some 70 years after *Schloendorff*, holding that a practice of not telling patients about certain serious risks involved in by-choice therapy (rather than therapy by necessity) is acceptable – as long as everyone does it.[13] By this point in time, the principle of informed consent had firmly established itself in the context of medical ethics and medical law almost everywhere but the United Kingdom. To moderate the comparison between the US and the UK perspective on consent it is worth noting that the US has qualified its stance in much the same way as the court in *Sidaway* did: 'Disclosure [to obtain informed consent] need not be made beyond that within the medical community'.[14]

Criticizing the basis for the US courts' decision in Moore and analysing its success potential in an English court, Dworkin and Kennedy contend that:

> In English law, it is less likely that a patient would ordinarily have a personal cause of action against a doctor on the same grounds [breach of fiduciary duty]. The doctrine of consent to medical procedures is not so favourable to patients. It is doctor-based and concentrates on what reasonable doctors in the particular circumstances, and in the light of medical practice, might tell a patient rather than on what a reasonable patient would expect to be told.[15]

This appears quite appropriate, as the onus on medical professionals would otherwise be too great to justify. The retreat to what is generally accepted best practice amongst reasonable practitioners provides a considerably more realistic concept than esoteric notions of full informed consent.[16]

> The main trend in biomedical ethics has been patient-centred. This has meant, in effect, a retreat from medical paternalism, but equally a retreat from the paternalism of parents and other relatives in favour of maximising the self determination of patients.[17]

---

12 1914 105 NE 92.

13 *Sidaway v Board of Governors of the Bethlem Royal Hospital* [1985] AC 871.

14 *Cobbs v. Grant* (1972) 8 Cal.3d 229, at p. 246.

15 Dworkin and Kennedy 1993, at p. 308.

16 See pp. 39, 116 as well as Hoppe, N. 2008. Normative Modelle zur regelung der Kommodifikation menschlichen Gewebes in Forschung und Therapie: Fragen der Zustimmung aus der Common Law Perspektive. In: *Kultur und Bioethik. Eigentum am eigenen Körper*. Edited by C. Steineck and O. Döring. Baden-Baden: Nomos, for my criticism of the concept of informed consent.

17 Harris 2002, at p. 528.

Harris cites the cases of *Gillick v. West Norfolk and Wisbech Area Health Authority*[18] and *F v. West Berkshire Health Authority*[19] (*Re F*) as examples of an increase in patient autonomy over medical and family-based heteronomy. In *Gillick*, the question of whether a girl under the age of 16 could consent to contraceptive medical treatment without the knowledge of her parents was put to the test. The House of Lords held in favour of the girl's autonomy:

> Provided the patient, whether a boy or a girl, is capable of understanding what is proposed, and of expressing his or her own wishes, I see no good reason for holding that he or she lacks the capacity to express them validly and effectively and to authorise the medical man to make the examination or give the treatment which he advises.[20]

The case of Re F concerned the non-therapeutic sterilization of a 36-year-old mentally handicapped patient and represents one of the most influential medico-legal cases on the question of consent in the UK.

The mother of the patient had formed the opinion that her daughter's sexual relationship with another patient in the institution created a risk of pregnancy, which she deemed to not be in the best interest of her daughter. A declaration was sought that the procedure, clearly non-therapeutic, would nonetheless be in the patient's best interest and therefore legal. The House of Lords made the declaration after discussing in detail the circumstance under which proceeding without consent would be lawful. In particular, the court expressly stated that a medical professional could proceed with treatment even where there is no consent and the treatment was not for treating a mental disorder, as long as such treatment was in the patient's best interest.[21] We will return to the best interest argument later.

The argument developed in these cases, focusing on questions of administering medical treatment without express consent, concentrated exclusively on issues of autonomy and physical integrity. Where constituents of the patient's body are removed in these circumstances, one could arguably conceive of an issue of property at stake.

> The law has traditionally regarded an interference with a removed part of the body as theft, if anything at all, rather than an offence against the person. In other words, the rights claimed are ones connected to a property model, rather than ones based on a right to bodily [integrity] or autonomy.[22]

18 [1986] 1 AC 112.

19 [1989] 2 All ER 545.

20 *Gillick v. West Norfolk and Wisbech Area Health Authority* [1986] 1 AC 112, per Fraser LJ. Quoted in Mayberry, M. and Mayberry, J. 2003. *Consent in Clinical Practice*. Oxford: Radcliffe Publishing, at p. 28.

21 See Mason and Laurie 2006, at pp. 361-363.

22 Herring and Chau 2007, at p. 38.

This stance was recently reaffirmed in a Court of Appeal judgment.[23] The key concept here appears to be the fact that the interference occurs after the removal of the body part. We have, therefore, issues of autonomy and physical integrity (protected in terms of a prohibition of interference with others in criminal law) prior to the removal of the body part. After the removal, proprietary issues become involved in terms of a prohibition of unlawfully appropriating another's property with the intention of permanently depriving the other of it and civil law remedies in terms of an action for restitution or conversion. If we follow this line of reasoning we still need to address the question of consent for the removal. Harris suggests that we possibly need not ask at all in cases of post-mortem extraction.

> [...] it seems clear that the benefits from cadaver transplants are so great and the reasons for objecting so transparently selfish or superstitious, that we should remove altogether the habit of seeking the consent of either the deceased or relatives.[24]

Much speaks for such an approach and current opt-out regimes in terms of organ procurement to some extent already practise a policy of conscription-by-ignorance. The dividing line appears to fall where one side of the argument views the human body as a Cartesian vehicle which is devoid of personal utility and meaning once the person has died and those who feel that the body is endowed with a higher value. Once it is decided to make the body available for explantation of organs on the basis that the deceased no longer makes any use of them, it is difficult to see where there might be an argument for the unavailability of the body just because this might cross others' moral boundaries.

Necessity

In the interest of completeness, it ought to be discussed briefly that, of course, not all excisions take place within the scope of some degree of consent. A regular occurrence in the context of medical treatment, in particular that of emergency medical treatment, is that of an intervention without the possibility to obtain consent. We can either try to negotiate the pitfalls of treatment without consent by implying a certain level of consent for emergency treatment. The alternative is to determine that the *prima facie* illegality of treatment without consent is healed by an element of necessity.[25] Any tissue or material removed during the course of such a treatment could clearly only be for diagnostic or therapeutic purposes (establishing the cause of a condition or preventing further harm). In the past, the

23 *Yearworth v. North Bristol NHS Trust* [2009] EWCA Civ 37.

24 Harris, J. 1992. *Wonderwoman and Superman: The Ethics of Human Biotechnology*. Oxford: Oxford University Press, at p. 102.

25 See Hoppe 2008, at pp. 52-53.

assumption has been that such materials could then be used for research once their original purpose had been satisfied, as long as the source remained anonymous. The fundamental question of whether material containing DNA could ever be fully anonymous remains largely unanswered in the clinical setting. The Human Tissue Act 2004 currently provides that material taken during the course of medical treatment is surplus tissue and can be treated as 'waste'.[26]

Corpses

The following consideration of the Common Law's position on corpses is in parts, by necessity, anecdotal (but no less informative). The discussion of *property* in corpses is distinguished from that of *possession* in corpses in that the latter is an expression which conveys merely the fact that someone controls the whereabouts of a corpse for a specific purpose. Possession is fairly straightforward and unproblematic – a hospital may initially have lawful possession, and a coroner may[27] and subsequently relatives or the executor of the deceased's estate, may lawfully be in possession for the purposes of arranging an appropriate burial. The relevance of possession in this context flows from the fact that in many cases the subsequent work with corpses or body parts requires lawful possession of the body. Where such work is invested in corpses lawfully in the possession of the individual, something new – capable of being property in the eyes of the law – comes into existence. Prior to such an intervention, corpses have regularly been held to not be capable of property (for example for the purposes of the offence of theft) and the law had to find mechanisms to circumnavigate this defect.

The unlawful disinterment of a corpse has in the past been dealt with by the Common Law as a conspiracy to outrage public decency[28] and it is fairly certain that it would still outrage public decency if corpses were just unearthed. Whilst it seems to be a morally straightforward idea that to disinter bodies without a reasonable excuse is reprehensible, the question remains how the law curbs such behaviour. Initially, it is important to realize that any prohibition of the removal of buried corpses from the grave is not a protective mechanism for the benefit of the deceased. In some jurisdictions, there may be an argument that such disinterment is contrary to the personality rights of the deceased. The actual reasons for requiring a swift burial and prohibiting the subsequent disinterment are those of public order and public health. Historically, there is convincing evidence that the European plague pandemics have changed our perception of corpses and how we should

26 Human Tissue Act 2004, Section 44.

27 *R v. Bristol Coroner ex parte Kerr* [1974] QB 652 – coroners are lawfully in possession of bodies for the purposes of establishing the cause of death.

28 *R v. Lynn* [1788] 2 Durn & E 733.

deal with them – the unregulated handling of corpses has retained its character of being a threat to public health.[29]

For the purposes of regulating the individual handling of corpses, the concept of lawful possession provides convincing mechanisms. The strength of the possessive right some parties may have in a corpse borders on that of a proprietary interest (think of the number of sticks in the bundle). The strong notion of *property in a corpse* suggests that something over and beyond mere possession governs the relationship between the corpse and the possessor or, indeed, between the possessor and third parties (in this case, a strong right of excludability).

Initially, the proprietary interests in corpses were recognized by the courts for the purposes of securing such a corpse for a debt.[30] By the middle of the nineteenth century, the courts had reversed their thinking on the matter and, in one case, granted a mandamus for the release of a body previously sequestered to secure a debt.[31] With the mentioned exception of securing a debt by means of arresting the debtor's body, it has been a firm principle of the Common Law for hundreds of years that there can be 'no property right in corpses' *per se*.[32] This also affects proceedings where a deceased individual has made *ex ante* provisions in relation to dealings with his body – in the absence of a contrary statutory rule, these provisions simply have no legally binding character:

> [...] where a person has directed that his body should be cremated after death, it was held that such a request, though it might be honoured in practice, could not be imposed as a legal obligation upon his executors since he lacked any property rights in his body.[33]

Ex Ante Provisions

Following the expressly property-based ruling in *Williams v. Williams*, an individual therefore has no legal entitlement to have his wishes complied with after death. He has, at most, a strong moral entitlement which may be honoured – depending

---

29 See Bergmann 2004, at pp. 43-65.

30 *Quick v. Coppleton* (1803) 83 ER 349; *R v. Cheere* (1825) 107 ER 1294, cited in Nwabueze 2007, at p. 44.

31 *R v. Fox* (1841) 114 ER 95, ibid., at p. 45.

32 See *Exelby v Handyside* (1749) 2 East PC 652; *R v Sharpe* (1857) Dears & B 160; and Blackstone's Commentaries: 'But though the heir has a property in the monuments and escutcheons of his ancestors, yet he had none in their bodies or ashes; nor can he bring any civil action against such as indecently at least, if not impiously, violate and disturb their remains, when dead and buried'. 2 Bl. Com. 429. (Book II, Chapter 28).

33 *Williams v. Williams* (1882) Ch.D. 659, cited in Dworkin and Kennedy (1993), at p. 294.

on the fortitude of his friends. In most cases, exotic and interesting provisions for what is to be done with one's body will meet with incomprehension, such as Lord Avebury's well-publicized wish to be made into dog food.[34] An example of a successful pre-death wish for post-mortem treatment is that of Jeremy Bentham. The lawyer and philosopher, who died in 1832, had his body embalmed and bequeathed it to University College London, where he is still sitting in a display case. He is reportedly being brought out to attend meetings, featuring as 'present but not voting' in the minutes,[35] going for a drink[36] and, so write Dworkin and Kennedy, also being the subject to misappropriation by students on occasion.[37] Following the ratio in *Kelly* and that in *Doodeward v. Spence*, we would probably conclude that such a misappropriation fulfils all the *actus reus* requirements of a theft offence but not the *mens rea* provision of wanting to permanently deprive the owner of the body of its enjoyment. Despite the successful *ex ante* provisions left by Bentham, the overall conclusion is that in the absence of positive law, legitimating the binding character of such provisions, they will be merely persuasive in nature. At most, they may assist the doctors and others in determining the deceased's presumed intentions.

In the same way that the Alder Hey scandal has led to the introduction of legislation on the retention and storage of human tissue and organs, the misappropriation of bodies has in the past been the reason for introducing similar legislation. In a number of high profile 'body snatching' trials, the courts have had to ascertain whether a corpse can be stolen and thus a taker of a corpse be subject to the charge of theft. One of the more spectacular cases is that of two Irish emigrants Burke and Hare, who perpetrated the Westport murders in Edinburgh in the 1820s. The pair initially supplied bodies of recently deceased individuals to Edinburgh Medical College for anatomical teaching purposes. Realizing the substantial profit that could be made by providing bodies to anatomy departments, they subsequently began to include bodies of individuals they had killed themselves.[38] In the cases of taking corpses after burial, the courts did consider the question of theft. The prosecution was usually adjusted to refer to the theft of collateral items (such as

---

34 See Hoppe 2009, at p. 111, and the author's personal correspondence with Lord Avebury.

35 The UCL Bentham Project, available at http://www.ucl.ac.uk/Bentham-Project/Faqs/auto_icon.htm, accessed 3 June 2009.

36 Vines, P. 2007. The Sacred and the Profane: The Role of Property Concepts in Disputes About Post-Mortem Examination. University of New South Wales Faculty of Law Research Series 13 (19 March 2007): footnote 20, available at http://www.austlii.edu.au/au/journals/UNSWLRS/2007/13.html, accessed 3 June 2009.

37 Dworkin and Kennedy 1993, at p. 294.

38 For an insight into the entertaining tale, see Douglas, H. 1973. *Burke and Hare*. London: Robert Hale.

winding sheets), rather than the theft of the body.[39] This, inevitably, meant that there was no satisfactory answer to the question of property in human bodies.

The weight of the collected case law in this matter suggests that there is indeed no property in a corpse. At the same time, no actual principle of law to this effect seems to have been established by any single case.[40] A study of relevant jurisprudence in this area always returns us to the centennial case of the two-headed foetus in the Australian circus.

> ...sundry contraventions of the strict law as to dead bodies are winked at in the interests of medical science.[41]

These lines originate in the report of the case of *Doodeward v. Spence*. The matter concerned a miscarried two-headed foetus which was on display and had been preserved by a doctor some 40 years previously. The foetus's purported owner was arrested and charged with 'outraging public decency' on account of displaying the foetus as part of a travelling circus.[42] The foetus was confiscated and the defendant successfully convicted. The action here was concerned with his claim to have the foetus delivered after the prosecution as it was, so he claimed, his property.[43] The case will be looked at again when discussing the question of property in body parts (see Chapter 7).

The situation was, and still is, therefore that there is no property in a corpse (notwithstanding future contrary provisions made by Parliament). Corpses and parts of corpses in which skilful work is invested are, by virtue of such work, capable of being subject to property rights. It is worth noting that part of the argument put forward by *Kelly* was the question whether the Royal College of Surgeons was lawfully in possession of the body parts prior to investing the skilful work necessary for them to turn into property. The consequence of the facts of *Kelly* seem to be that prior to turning into property, only those licensed could lawfully be in possession of the body parts.[44] Once skilful work is invested, they turn into

---

39 *Haynes's Case (1614) 12 Co. Rep. 113* is usually cited in this context. The alternative charge of conspiracy to incite public outrage for the disinterment was also used: *R v. Lynn* [1788] 2 Durn & E 733.

40 See, e.g. Dworkin and Kennedy 1993.

41 *Doodeward v. Spence (1908) CLR 406*, per Higgins J, cited in: Dworkin and Kennedy 1993, at p. 296.

42 Not the most recent prosecution in this context: in *R v. Gibson* [1991] 1 All ER 439, the artist Richard Norman Gibson was prosecuted for the Common Law conspiracy offence of outraging public decency. He had mounted an exhibition which featured a model's head (still attached to the model, who was live and well). The model wore earrings made of freeze-dried human foetuses of three to four months gestation. See Lewis, T. (2002). Human Earrings, Human Rights and Public Decency. *Entertainment Law*, 1, 50-71 at p. 53.

43 See Dworkin and Kennedy 1993, at p. 295.

44 Anatomy Acts 1832 and 1984, now the Human Tissue Act 2004.

property and are thus, possibly, subject to all the vicissitudes of the market.[45] The exact point in time when these bodies or body parts in fact do turn into property remains shrouded in mystery. Whilst it is clear that some sort of skilful work must be invested, the level of skill remains vague and undefined.[46]

Property in Body Parts

As discussed above, body parts (meant to include whole organs not for transplantation, limbs, etc.) are regularly retained and stored by hospitals for quality control, teaching and research. Prior to the implementation of the Human Tissue Act, it was legal to retain body parts as long as the relatives or the source did not object to the retention.[47]

In the case of *Kelly*, the court did express the opinion, that the body of precedent dealing with corpses in a non-proprietary fashion did establish such a principle – and that this principle could only be changed by Parliament.

> Hence, the Court of Appeal was correct in that, it is widely accepted in England that a whole corpse cannot be stolen [...]. Nevertheless, even aware of the dubious historical origins of the 'no property' rule for all corpses, the Court of Appeal in Kelly was not prepared to reconsider that rule or contemplate that it should not be applied in principle to parts of dead bodies, stating: 'If that [rule] is now to be changed, in our view, it must be by Parliament...'.[48]

Precedent or Legislation?

The fact that a court refers to an ethically volatile principle that ought to be changed by Parliament, or 'positive law', is by no means a new phenomenon. In *Kelly*, the Court of appeal referred the question of whether body parts can be owned *per se* to Parliament for a decision. In *Somersett's Case*, a case where the courts decided on the admissibility of a claim for *habeas corpus* in relation to a slave, the court

45 A deliberate reference to Marx.

46 It is, however, clear that mere preservation or storage is not sufficient. *Dobson v. North Tyneside Health Authority* [1996] 4 All ER 474 at 479.

47 As long as they were properly informed about the retention. See *AB v Leeds Teaching Hospital NHS Trust* [2004] EWHC 644; [2004] 2 Family Law Reports 365. Parents of three children complained about the removal and retention of organs from their deceased children. The court held that, whilst the parents had no possessory interest in the organs, the consent procedure followed by the hospital was defective.

48 Various 1998. Theft of Body Parts: Property and Dead Bodies. Case Commentary on *R v. Kelly and Lindsay*. *Medical Law Review*, 6, 247-261 at 248.

postulated that the notion of proprietary interests in living humans is so 'odious' that it should be positive law which regulates such a sensitive area of life.

> The state of slavery is of such a nature, that it is incapable of being introduced on any reasons, moral or political, but only by positive law, which preserves its force long after the reasons, occasion, and time itself from whence it was created, is erased from memory. It is so odious, that nothing can be suffered to support it, but positive law. Whatever inconveniences, therefore, may follow from the decision, I cannot say this case is allowed or approved by the law of England; and therefore the black must be discharged.[49]

The point of the claimants argued in this case was close to the one pursued in *Moore v. Regents of the University of California* in that *trover* was invoked (a form of action no longer used assuming that a plaintiff had lost goods and the finder had converted them).

> We pay all due attention to the opinion of sir Philip Yorke, and lord chancellor Talbot, whereby they pledged themselves to the British planters, for all the legal consequences of slaves coming over to this kingdom or being baptized, recognized by lord Hardwicke, sitting as chancellor on the 19th of October, 1749, that trover would lie [...].[50]

The courts were happy to distinguish between live humans and dead ones, in particular only parts of the latter; the rule in *Doodeward v. Spence* is by now so engrained in the judicial mindset that it does, indeed, require positive law to change it. Until such time, the courts will revert to the principle that investing artful work will result in the transformation of *res extra commercium* to *res intra commercium* as if it were water turned into wine. This was only recently illustrated in *Kelly*. In this case, an artist (Kelly) and a junior technician (Lindsay) were convicted for the theft of up to 40 anatomical specimens from the Royal College of Surgeons' anatomical collection. Kelly had paid Lindsay £400 to obtain the specimens and had used them in his artwork (to make casts). He had subsequently interred them in the grounds of his house. The convictions could only be upheld if the requirements for the offence of theft were satisfied. These are:

> 1. Basic definition of theft
>
> (1) A person is guilty of theft if he dishonestly appropriates property belonging to another with the intention of permanently depriving the other of it; and 'theft' and 'steal' shall be construed accordingly.[51]

49 *Somersett's Case* (1771) 20 How. St. Tr. 1, 80-82 (K.B.), per Lord Mansfield.

50 Ibid.

51 Section 1, Theft Act 1968.

In order to convict Kelly of theft, the *actus reus* of the offence needed to be satisfied,[52] in particular that the anatomical specimens were 'property' which was in the lawful possession of the Royal College of Surgeons. The Court of Appeal upheld the convictions and reiterated the principle laid down in *Doodeward v. Spence*[53] and *Dobson v. North Tyneside Health Authority*,[54] which is this: property entitlements in a corpse can arise where artful work is invested, rendering it a different matter to a corpse awaiting burial.

> When a person has by lawful exercise of work or skill so dealt with a human body or part of a human body in his lawful possession that it has acquired some attributes differentiating it from a mere corpse awaiting burial, he acquires a right to retain possession of it, at least as against any person not entitled to have it delivered to him for the purpose of burial, but subject, of course, to any positive law which forbids its retention under the particular circumstances.[55]

Artful Work

Investing work and skill therefore creates something which is 'ownable'. The question very much is whether any work which requires a certain degree of training renders the object property. It is fairly clear that in a clinical setting, excised tissue or expelled body products will usually be treated in a professional and scientific manner, tested, preserved and stored. The question seems to be whether to then speak of property, but not before, is sensible and holds up to closer scrutiny. How does this work in the context of parts of my body which I enhance myself or have enhanced by others as part of a contract (the product of the work clearly being contractually mine)? By the same token as the rules in *Kelly* and *Doodeward v. Spence*, the work I invest in those parts of me, or pay others to invest in parts of me, should give rise to property interests, accruing to none other than me. Crucially, the issue does not pivot on a simple question of statutory interpretation such as in *Hadley and Evans*[56] or *Quintavalle.*[57] In these cases the question was whether a certain kind of expert treatment of embryos constituted *use* for the purposes of the Human Fertilisation and Embryology Act

52 Interestingly, in this case it is clearly easier to prove the *mens rea* than it is to prove the *actus reus*. It underlines the special nature of medico-legal quandaries.

53 (1908) CLR 406.

54 [1996] 4 All ER 474.

55 *Doodeward v. Spence* (1908) CLR 406, per Griffiths CJ at 414.

56 The joined cases of *Evans v. Amicus Healthcare Ltd.* [2003] EWHC 2161, [2004] EWCA (Civ) 727 and *Hadley v. Midland Fertility Services Ltd. and Others* [2003] EWHC 2161.

57 *R (on the application of Quintavalle) v. Human Fertilisation and Embryology Authority* [2003] 3 All ER 257.

1990.[58] Such use would introduce the embryo into a new realm of legal reality and protection-worthiness. For the purposes of our question, the kind of treatment expended must suffice to make something old (which is currently not property) into something new (property).

This particular debate does not stand up to closer scrutiny when viewed in the context of donation: if property comes into existence after I have given away a part of my body, then I do not have the required level of entitlement to gift the part of my body as a donation. This reality underlying the law of gifts was ignored in a number of paradigmatic US cases, which will be the subject of criticism further below.

Property in Body Products

Body products inhabit a very particular place in the spectrum of proprietary considerations. Whilst some products (such as blood) are generally considered to be tissue, other products (such as urine, faeces, seminal fluid and saliva) contain tissue detritus but predominantly consist of other material. The fact that body products are much easier to come by than bodies or body parts means that there is substantially more case law to consider. There have been convictions for the theft of blood[59] and urine,[60] both having been (re-)appropriated by the defendants for the purposes of frustrating a drink-driving charge which the samples were evidence for. Both the materials' *prima facie* status as waste products (or at least in most cases 'non-returnable body products') as well as the public interest[61] in detecting and prosecuting dangerous activities, such as drink-driving, may outweigh the normal desire to controversially debate the law's ability to categorize these materials appropriately.

There is a different perspective where material is provided for the purposes of the giver's own therapy or future treatment. Examples are the case of autologous blood transfusions or the storage of sperm for the purpose of subsequent infertility treatment where there is a risk of infertility resulting from another therapy. In some jurisdictions, the courts do not seem overly hesitant to provide relief in terms of quantified damages in cases where the material was negligently destroyed by the

58 In particular Schedule 3 of the Act.

59 *R v. Rothery* [1976] RTR 550.

60 *R v. Welsh* [1974] RTR 478.

61 Also reflected in the fact that offences committed in relation to driving a vehicle when under the influence of alcoholic drink or drugs is a strict liability offence with no *mens rea* element (ss. 4, 5 Road Traffic Act 1988). Also, the Act's prescription of compulsory specimen provision (involving, in the case of a blood sample, potentially the forceful insertion of a needle into a vein) demonstrates – in the light of proportionality requirements – the intensity of the public interest argument levelled here.

storage facility, though (until recently[62] not on proprietary bases.[63] In the Australian case of *Roche v. Douglas*,[64] it was decided that stored sperm was 'property' in the sense that civil procedure related to entitlements to have property delivered to the parties applied to it. In *Hecht v. Kane*,[65] the same held true for sperm in order to subject it to probate law and thus render it disposable property. The application of certain procedural law as well as aspects of battery (compromising the person's autonomy or physical integrity) seem to be less problematic than the application of pure property law in the contexts described. The reason may be the body's *sui generis* status, entailing the necessity to develop new rules, akin to property but outside its traditional remit.[66]

---

62 The recent case of *Yearworth v. North Bristol NHS Trust* [2009] EWCA Civ 37 will be discussed below.

63 Notably in Germany. See the Bundesgerichtshof's opinion in a case where a cryogenically preserved sperm sample of a cancer patient was negligently destroyed by the storage facility, rendering him unable to obtain infertility treatment with his partner (BGHZ 124, 52 (9 November 1993)). But also see the decision of the OLG Frankfurt a.M. which provided relief for a patient who had not been informed of the possibility of such storage prior to chemotherapy likely to lead to infertility in the first place (OLG Frankfurt a.M. 2002, 183 (26 April 2002)). Contrasting both decisions, it becomes obvious that there is not a proprietary issue here in terms of the destruction of property, but a *loss of amenities* point instead, founded on the legal basis of a battery.

64 [2000] WAR 331.

65 16 Cal App 4th 836 (1993). For both *Roche v. Douglas* and *Hecht v. Kane*, I gratefully acknowledge Mason and Laurie (2006), at p. 514.

66 The enterprise underlying the third part of this text.

Chapter 8
Legislation

> There are still many immoral acts which do not amount to torts, and the law has not yet enacted the golden rule.[1]

In 1995 the Nuffield Council on Bioethics published a report entitled *Human Tissue: Ethical and Legal Issues*.[2] In this report, the Council sought to identify problems in the current treatment of human tissue by the legal system. The Council expressly voted against the establishment of property rights in the human body. It ostensibly did so out of the same motivation which inspired the judges in the case of *John Moore* (see Chapter 9 below) – the fear that individuals may maximize their benefit when parting with tissue:

> It was concerned [comments McHale] as to the potential consequences were property law rights to be recognized, for example the need for patient waivers to allow use of tissue and the prospect of bargaining by patients over commercial tissue rights, etc.[3]

McHale very helpfully outlines some of the recommendations of the Council:

1. Where tissue is removed, with consent, for treatment, the tissue should be treated as abandoned by the patient and thus available for research.
2. Where tissue is removed, with consent, for purposes other than treatment, the tissue should be treated as a gift.
3. Where tissue is removed, with consent, for the purposes benefiting the patient, the tissue should belong to the patient.

Despite using terms such as *belong*, the idea seems to be to foot potential legal action in relation to excised tissue not in property, but in tort. A lack of consent would constitute a battery, for which the victim only has to show the unwanted contact by the tortfeasor. A substantial body of case law relating to consent has shown that an action for battery is easier to bring and prove than one for negligence. In negligence, a quantification of actual harm has to be undertaken, this then being the subject of restitution. In much the same way, an action for damages in relation to trespass to property (where we declare excised tissue as property) would falter when put to the test of quantification. Asking any court to

1 *Wallis v Smith 2001 NMCA 17*, as per Alarid J at para. 26.
2 Nuffield Council on Bioethics 1995. *Human Tissue - Ethical and Legal Aspects.*
3 McHale 2000, at p. 125. Also see Nuffield Council on Bioethics 1995, para. 9.13.

put a figure on the value of portions of tissue could be suggested to be only a step shy of asking it to quantify the value of the whole body. In the context of trespass to the person, a battery as the result of a lack of consent would circumnavigate the question of property. The patient need only show that there was no consent for the procedure in question. This approach also features one of the advantages addressed in our discussion of Equity below: the lack of a need to quantify value before clawing back profit. Before turning to alternative solutions, it is necessary to discuss the current English legislative model in more detail.

The Human Tissue Act 2004

The Human Tissue Act 2004 is an attempt at dealing with some of the fall-out of Alder Hey. One of the conclusions of Alder Hey (see Chapter 3) was that there was a lack of clear legal guidance on the issues at stake. The taking and storing of tissue samples and organs forms an important part of clinical life – for example for quality control or training purposes and for establishing the cause of death or of a certain disease. What was clearly underestimated in the Alder Hey setting was the need to obtain proper consent for any subsequent use of retained materials.[4] The miscalculation of the requirements for proper organ and tissue retention was, to a large extent, caused by the obscurity of the relevant law at that time. Interestingly, the Human Tissue Act 2004 tries to unite rules which were previously contained in an array of other legislation[5] in order to reduce complexity and increase the legislation's usefulness to practitioners. This is of particular interest because, in the wake of the European Union's regulatory activity, countries such as Germany responded by breaking up the regulations into a number of different Acts[6] rather than containing them in one text. This leads to a confusing fragmentation, which was rectified in

4 The retention protocols of Dick van Velzen at Alder Hey did, admittedly, go over and beyond sensible collection practices and are deserving of criticism. They are, this much appears clear, in no way representative of the general practice of retention in pathology departments.

5 Such as, *inter alia*, the Human Tissue Act 1961, the Anatomy Act 1984, the Corneal Tissue Act 1986 and the Human Organ Transplants Act 1989.

6 The *Gewebegesetz* (Tissue Act) is a so-called *Mantelgesetz* (mantle act). Its contents are incorporated into, and amend, existing legislation upon enactment rather than representing stand-alone legislation. The acts amended by the Gewebegesetz are: (1) *Transplantationsgesetz* (Transplantation Act), (2) *Arzneimittelgesetz* (Medicines Act), (3) *Transfusionsgesetz* (Transfusion Act), (4) *Apothekenbetriebsordnung* (operating regulations for pharmacies), (5) *Betriebsverordnung für Arzneimittelgroßhandelsbetriebe* (operating regulations for wholesale medicines merchants), (6) *Infektionsschutzgesetz* (Infection Prevention Act), (7) *Strafgesetzbuch* (Criminal Code) and (8) *Sozialgesetzbuch* (Social Security Act). The fragmentation is evident.

England as part of the lessons learnt from Alder Hey: the law needed change and consolidation.

> The existing law on retention and use of organs and tissue was reviewed following public inquiries into events at Bristol Royal Infirmary and the Royal Liverpool Children's Hospital (Alder Hey). These inquiries, together with the Isaacs Report, which focused on the retention of adult brains following coroners' post mortems, showed that storage and use of organs and tissue without proper consent after people had died were commonplace.[7]

The obvious response was an item of legislation which would unite all aspects of dealing with human tissue under its mantle. The government drafted a paper outlining the changes that were deemed to be desirable.[8] The proposal sets a number of basic criteria as a starting point for legislation, which are set out and commented upon below. It becomes clear that, whilst the Human Tissue Act 2004 has not included these criteria, it has provided the legitimization for the inclusion of these proposals in the Authority's guidelines:[9]

1. ***Respect*** *(for people who have died and their families) – Treating the person who has died and their families with dignity and respect.* The concept of respect for the deceased and the relatives is a constitutive component of natural law. Enshrining a respect for people who have died to the extent that they are holders of rights post-mortem would represent an express convergence with continental notions of enduring personality rights – and this would certainly be an interesting development from an international perspective. The idea of the dignity of the deceased can be found in its most expressive form in the Human Tissue Authority's Codes of Practice, twice in relation to the reconstruction of the donor's body. The first is in Code of Practice 2 (Donation of organs, tissue and cells for transplantation):

   > The removal of tissue from a donor after death must be undertaken by staff who are trained in tissue retrieval and in reconstructing the body to appear as normal as possible, in a manner similar to that in surgical reconstruction taking place after theatre operations. This

7 Department of Health 2005. The Human Tissue Act 2004 – New legislation on human organs and tissue, p. 1. Available at: http://www.dh.gov.uk/en/Publicationsandstatistics/Publications/PublicationsLegislation/DH_4109578, accessed 3 June 2009.

8 Department of Health 2002.

9 From Department of Health 2002, at pp. 6-7, 14. I consolidated the two lists and introduced the numbering and italicization for ease of reference. The comments not in italics are my own and refer to whether the recommendations have percolated into legislation or regulations.

> will help to minimise the distress to relatives wishing to view the body. It also maintains the dignity of the deceased donor.[10]

The second mention can be found in Code of Practice 5 (Removal, storage and disposal of human organs and tissue): 'Procedures for conducting post mortems, and for the removal and storage of organs or tissue for examination, must always maintain the dignity of the deceased person'.[11] The fundamental principle of dignity as found in the Act is cited in the code of practice on public display of bodies and body parts.[12] A somewhat superficial series of references to the general dignity accorded to human bodies, body parts and tissues can also be found in the code of practice relating to the import and export of bodies:[13]

2. ***Understanding*** *(that love and feelings of responsibility remain after death) – Realizing that to many parents and families, their love and feelings of responsibility for the person who has died are as strong as they were in life.* Similar to the notion of respect and dignity, this criterion is difficult to find in the Act. The details of dealings with the family are regulated by the appropriate code of practice of the Human Tissue Authority.[14]

3. ***Informed Consent*** *(enabling fully informed choices to be made) – Ensuring that permission is sought and given on the basis that a person is exercising fully informed choice; consent is a process, not a 'one off' event.* Both the Act as well as the relevant guidance produced by the Human Tissue Authority give detailed advice on the question of consent.[15] It is worth noting that neither the Act nor the guidance makes a single reference to the *terminus technicus* 'informed consent'. The guidance refers to the making of an informed choice as a continuing process and therefore mirrors the Department of Health's terminology well – apart

10 Human Tissue Authority, Code of Practice 2, at p. 26, para. 111. I will refer to the Human Tissue Authority's Codes of Practice as 'COP' and their number from now on.

11 COP 5, p. 8, para. 29.

12 COP 7, p. 4, para. 8. The Department for Culture, Media and Sports (DCMS) has also issued guidance in relation to existing collections of human remains in museums ('Guidance for the Care of Human Remains in Museums', October 2005). The DCMS guidance notes, interestingly, that research value seems to play a role in granting dignity protection to human remains: 'This part of the document [...] is based on the concept that human remains have a unique status, are often of high research value, and should be treated with dignity and respect'. DCMS Guidance for the Care of Human Remains in Museums, at p. 16.

13 COP 8, at pp. 8, 9 and 13.

14 In particular COP 1 on consent where sensitivity in the treatment of relatives is shown to be paramount, pp. 9, 19.

15 See Part 1, ss. 1,2 of the Human Tissue Act 2004; COP 1 on consent.

from shying away from using the terminology of informed consent.[16,17]

4. ***Time and Space*** *(to consider what decisions to make) – Recognizing that a family member may need time to consider whether to agree to a post mortem examination and to consider donation of tissue and organs and will not wish to feel under pressure to agree in the moments after death.* The guidance makes express reference to the requirement of a sensible amount of time and privacy for making decisions.[18] The ability to make a decision without undue influence and duress, which can convincingly be argued to include being put under undue time pressure, has been a facet of the law in relation to consent prior to these guidelines. While there is considerable extraneous time pressure in relation to procuring organs for the purposes of transplantation, no similar time pressure exists in relation to tissue samples, which results in an adequate time setting for making a decision.

3. ***Skill and Sensitivity*** *(in dealing with those close to a patient or deceased person) – NHS staff must be sensitive to the need of the relatives of someone who has died and sufficient staff skilled in bereavement counselling must be available.* The guidelines issued by the Human Tissue Authority make reference to health care professionals and other staff being suitably qualified in bereavement management to deal with relatives in the context of obtaining consent.[19]

4. ***Information*** *(to improve understanding and decision-making) – Much better information is required, both generally by the public and specifically for relatives who are recently bereaved, about post mortems and the use of tissue after death. Relatives may also require information about the progress of research involving donated material.* The public communication of issues in relation to material donation is of major importance throughout Europe. It is accepted fact in the literature that the public support of the concept of organ donation far outstrips actual donation activity.[20] This discrepancy is said to be the result of a lack of information. Adequate and factual information on issues surrounding the

16 COP 1, p. 16, para. 68.

17 Though the guidance states as its key principles that 'consent need not always be given in writing to be appropriate and informed'. (Ibid., p. 20, para. 90).

18 COP 1, p. 19, para. 84.

19 COP 1, p. 16, paras 71, 72; p. 17, para. 76. COP 3, p. 6, para. 17; p. 19, paras. 81-83. COP 5, p. 10, paras. 40-41.

20 See Kerridge, I.H., Saul, P., Lowe, M., McPhee, J. and Williams, D. 2002. Death, Dying and Donation: Organ Transplantation and the Diagnosis of Death. *Journal of Medical Ethics*, 28, 89-94 at p. 89.

importance of organ and tissue donation are a vital step in ensuring that a transparent and voluntary system of giving can succeed.

5. ***Cultural Competence*** *(ensuring that different attitudes to post mortems, burial and use of organs and tissue are recognised) – Attitudes to post mortem examination, burial, and the use of organs and tissues after death differ greatly between different religions and cultural groups; health professionals need to be aware of these factors and respond to them with sensitivity.* The Authority's guidance documents contain extensive material on sensitivity in relation to religious, cultural and language issues.[21] The responsibility for training staff appropriately rests with the NHS trusts and other establishments subject to the rules.

6. ***A Gift Relationship*** *(shifting the emphasis from organ retention to organ donation) – The emphasis in all present legislation and guidance is on 'taking' and 'retaining'. The balance should be shifted to 'donation', so that tissue or organs are given as a gift to help others and recognized as deserving of gratitude to those making donations.* The Act does refer to material as being stored, used and donated rather than to use the *retention* terminology tainted by Alder Hey. It does not, however, clarify the exact mode of transfer. The spirit of this criterion, as well as of no. 6 above, can, however, be found in the relevant later EU Directive 2004/23/EC: 'It is necessary to promote information and awareness campaigns at national and European level on the donation of tissues, cells and organs based on the theme "we are all potential donors"'.[22] The idea of altruistic giving in this context is defined in the guidelines in a very narrow fashion as:

> **Altruistic non-directed donation** A form of non-directed living donation, where an organ or part organ is donated by a healthy person who does not have a relationship with the recipient and who is not informed of whom the recipient will be.

The list reminds one slightly of the elevated list of criteria established by the 1994 British Medical Association conference.[23] Points three and six overlap to the extent that in order to obtain informed consent, 'much better information is required'. Given that English case law has not developed a track record of granting patients the right to give fully informed consent,[24] the suggestion that such a level of consent should

21 COP 1, p. 17, paras. 74-76.

22 Directive 2004/23/EC, preamble, para. (3).

23 Discussed in BMA 2004. *Medical Ethics Today*, at p. 17: competence, caring, commitment, integrity, compassion, responsibility, confidentiality, spirit of enquiry and advocacy.

24 See Chapter 7.

form the basis of the legislation on tissue retention is surprising but, in the context of research, certainly not unwelcome. The overriding question is whether this level of consent has made it into the legislation – if it has then it is clearly in the disguise of the idea of 'appropriate consent'.[25]

The Human Tissue Act 2004, as a result of the retention scandals and the government consultation, structurally reminds one of the Human Fertilisation and Embryology Act 1990.[26] It does not contain provisions in relation to the extraction of the material on the basis that the criminal law and tort law provide sufficient protection to deal with cases of unlawful extraction. The Act is concerned primarily with storage and use of excised tissue. It excludes reproductive tissue, such as gametes or embryos, narrowly defines which purposes it applies to and does not affect the way the coroners' system works.[27]

The activities for which the Act legislates and stipulates general consent provisions are:[28]

1. anatomical examination;
2. determining the cause of death;
3. establishing after a person's death the efficacy of any drug or other treatment administered to him;
4. obtaining scientific or medical information about a living or deceased person which may be relevant to any other person (including a future person);
5. public display;
6. research in connection with disorders, or the functioning of the human body, and
7. transplantation.

The Act further contains provisions for material from a deceased person for the following purposes:

8. clinical audit;
9. education or training relating to human health;
10. performance assessment;
11. public health monitoring; and
12. quality assurance.

---

25 See Chapter 8.

26 Which, itself, was not without inherent problems when it touched on medical reality (which tends to always surprise us with constellations we just cannot foresee). See *R v. Human Fertilisation and Embryology Authority, ex parte Blood* [1997] 2 All ER 687, [1997] 2 WLR 806 where the Act was shown to have failed to take into account situations where the semen donor is dead at the time of conception and the corresponding Authority (the Human Fertilisation and Embryology Authority) was ill equipped to deal with the case.

27 Cf. Human Tissue Act 2004, ss. 9, 11. Also see Herring 2006, at p. 346.

28 Human Tissue Act 2004, Schedule 1, Part 1-2.

From this list it appears that the aim of the exercise is to provide overall consent provisions for the vast majority of purposes human tissue is needed for in research. As far as therapy is concerned, number six in the list above (research in connection with disorders, or the functioning, of the human body) very much appears to be a catch-all provision.

The Act provides that it is lawful to store or use an entire human body, store or use material from living people and remove, store or use material from a deceased person provided that the consent provisions are satisfied and the purpose was one that can be found in Schedule 1 of the Act (see the list above).[29] Herring outlines the provisions of the Act in relation to activities which can be carried out without direct consent:[30]

- *Education, training and audit* – material taken from a live patient can be used for these purposes without specific consent being obtained. The rationale behind this is that audit, in particular, is a purpose with a high degree of significance for public health.
- *Where the source is unknown* – the Human Tissue Authority can 'deem consent' in situations where the source of the material cannot be identified but its use may benefit another.
- *Pursuant to a court order* – an appropriate court can order the use of tissue for the purposes of no. 6 above.
- *Research* – material can be stored for research purposes (no. 6) provided that the research is ethically approved and the material is anonymous. The material can be used despite possible or actual objections by the source.
- *Disposal of surplus material* – where material was taken, stored and used for a lawful purpose, the appropriate consent for such an initial use also includes consent for the disposal of the tissue as waste afterwards.
- *Imported material* – where material is imported from another country, it is up to the originating country to ascertain compliance with domestic laws. The Human Tissue Act does not apply in these cases.
- *Existing collections* – any collection of materials, organs or bodies in existence before the Act came into force is exempt from its provisions.
- *Coroners* – the lawful activities of a coroner are not touched by the provisions of the Act.

The Act, similar to the provisions of the Human Fertilisation and Embryology Act 1992 further provides for the creation of the Human Tissue Authority to oversee and regulate the activities subject to the Act. The Authority is tasked with providing information to the general public and the government on issues which are within

29 Also see Herring 2006, at p. 347.

30 Herring 2006, at pp. 350-351.

the remit of the Act. It further issues codes of practice and guidance documents, currently comprising:[31]

- Code of Practice 1: Consent;
- Code of Practice 2: Donation of organs, tissue and cells for transplantation;
- Code of Practice 3: Post mortem examination;
- Code of Practice 4: Anatomical examination;
- Code of Practice 5: Removal, storage and disposal of human organs and tissue;
- Code of Practice 6: Donation of allogeneic bone marrow and peripheral blood stem cells for transplantation;
- Guidance 7: Public display; and
- Code of Practice 8: Import and export of human bodies, body parts and tissue.

A number of the activities subject to the Act are only permitted when carried out by licensed persons or institutions. The Authority issues such licences and inspects licensed institutions to ensure compliance with the Act. Where the stipulations are not complied with, the Act provides for a number of criminal offences:

- Failure to obtain appropriate consent;
- false representation of consent;
- failure to obtain a death certificate;
- use or storage of material for improper purposes;
- analysis of DNA without consent;
- trafficking; and
- unlicensed activities.

Looking at the offences created by the Act, it becomes evident that one of the main criticisms of the provisions of the Act is that the focus appears to rest on the kinds of activities it does not prohibit rather than those it does prohibit. Bell cites from Hansard and reflects the stance of the government of underpinning the aspect of residual rights in relation to treatment of tissues and organs: '[..] the minister of state before the standing committee, who declared such interventions "lawful because there is no law against it. ... Just as embalming is lawful, so is cold perfusion"'.[32]

Gearing legislation specifically towards those things it does not prohibit appears to be a somewhat indirect way to positively legalize certain activities

31 See http://www.hta.gov.uk/guidance/codes_of_practice.cfm, accessed 3 June 2009.

32 Bell, M. 2006. The UK Human Tissue Act and Consent: Surrendering a Fundamental Principle to Transplantation Needs? *Journal of Medical Ethics*, 32, 283-286, at p. 283. (Sic.) The Human Tissue Act does not apply to Scotland. References in this text to 'UK Human Tissue Act' are references to Bell's article.

without exposing the legislation to critical assessment. The Human Tissue Act received Royal Assent on 15 November 2004 and has been gradually implemented from April 2005. It remains to be seen whether the Act is suitable for preventing the kind of incidents which prompted its introduction in the first place. It does appear to give the English system an edge over other European Member States in terms of implementing EU legislation which came after the drafting of the bill.

The Directive

As a highly relevant example of supranational attempts of regulating the use of human tissue, it is sensible to briefly discuss some of the European Union's legislative activity. Currently, the European Commission lists ten normative documents in relation to the treatment of human tissues and cells in the European Union:[33]

1. Commission Directive 2006/86/EC implementing Directive 2004/23/EC of the European Parliament and of the Council as regards traceability requirements, notification of serious adverse reactions and events and certain technical requirements for the coding, processing, preservation, storage and distribution of human tissues and cells;
2. Commission Directive 2006/17/EC implementing Directive 2004/23/EC of the European Parliament and of the Council as regards certain technical requirements for the donation, procurement and testing of human tissues and cells;
3. Directive 2004/23/EC of the European Parliament and of the Council of 31 March 2004 on setting standards of quality and safety for the donation, procurement, testing, processing, preservation, storage and distribution of human tissues and cells;
4. Opinion of the Commission of 5 February 2004 on the European Parliament's amendments to the Council's common position regarding the proposal for a Directive of the European Parliament and of the Council on setting standards of quality and safety for the donation, procurement, testing, processing, storage, and distribution of human tissues and cells;
5. European Parliament legislative resolution of 16 December 2003 on the Council common position adopting a European Parliament and Council directive on setting standards of quality and safety for the donation, procurement, testing, processing, preservation, storage and distribution of human tissues and cells;
6. Communication from the Commission to the European Parliament of 18 August 2003 concerning the common position of the Council on the

33 Available at http://ec.europa.eu/health/ph_threats/human_substance/legal_tissues_cells_en.htm, accessed 3 June 2009.

adoption of a Directive of the European Parliament and of the Council on setting standards of quality and safety for the donation, procurement, testing, processing, storage, and distribution of human tissues and cells;

7. Common Position (EC) No 50/2003 of 22 July 2003 of the Council with a view to adopting a directive of the European Parliament and of the Council on setting standards of quality and safety for the donation, procurement, testing, processing, preservation, storage and distribution of human tissues and cells;
8. Amended Proposal of the Commission of 28 May 2003 for a directive of the European Parliament and of the Council on setting standards of quality and safety for the donation, procurement, testing, processing, storage, and distribution of human tissues and cells;
9. Opinion of the European Economic and Social Committee of 8 April 2003 on the 'Proposal for a Directive of the European Parliament and of the Council setting standards of quality and safety for the donation, procurement, testing, processing, storage, and distribution of human tissues and cells';
10. Proposal of 19 June 2002 for a directive of the European Parliament and of the Council on setting standards of quality and safety for the donation, procurement, testing, processing, storage, and distribution of human tissues and cells.

It is clear that these documents either form a part of the genesis of the Human Tissue Directive[34] (the Directive) or are instruments implementing the requirements of the same directive. It is therefore time to briefly look at the provisions of the Directive before progressing to some fundamental issues raised by case law in relation to the focus of this text.[35]

The Directive, published on 31 March 2004, seeks to provide a quality control framework in terms of donation, procurement, testing, processing, preservation, storage and distribution of human tissues and cells. The European Union is lacking Treaty authority to intervene directly in Member States' health policy and thus, health-related policy on a European level tends to come in the disguise of public health or consumer protection instruments. The Directive bases its authority on the EU's regulatory powers in relation to the protection of public health.[36] The Directive requires Member States to implement an accreditation system for organizations undertaking any of the activities in relation to tissue outlined, as

34 2004/23/EC.

35 A substantial European Union funded project, entitled Tiss.EU, is currently investigating the legal and ethical culture medium in the Member States for the implementation of the Directive's requirements. See http://www.tisseu.uni-hannover.de., accessed.

36 Article 152(4)a of the Treaty on European Union and of the Treaty Establishing the European Community.

well as an adverse incident reporting system.[37] Interestingly, the Directive covers tissue and cells used for therapeutic and to some extent cosmetic purposes but not for research. The extension of its application to testing tissue and cells for human application begs the question whether such testing might include research or is merely intended to denote the kind of quality tests necessary to ascertain the material's fitness for purpose.

There is a strong emphasis on donation and altruism throughout the Directive, even extending to a mention of the slogan-like 'we are all potential donors' in the preamble[38] and the quality of donated tissue is directly linked to the voluntariness and gratuitous altruistic character of the giving.[39] In the following, a brief descriptive overview of the Directive's regulatory content will be given to provide background information on the state of play at EU level.

Accountability: Accreditation, Supervision, Reports

Together with its adjunct instruments, the Directive creates a detailed framework of regulations in relation to the quality of institutions and persons involved in the handling of human tissue.[40] The procurement and testing of tissue must only be done in appropriate surroundings by suitably qualified staff,[41] the appropriateness of the surroundings being ascertained by Member States which are required to accredit certain establishments.[42] The accreditation is subject to regular change where the make-up of the establishment in question changes and can be revoked if this is considered appropriate.[43]

Further, the Member States are required to establish a national authority to oversee the compliance of establishments with the provisions of the Directive, as well as to carry out inspections of accredited premises.[44] This requirement also extends to non-accredited third parties with whom accredited establishments have an agreement. Inspections are to be carried out at least every two years but in any case when a serious adverse incident is reported.[45] The flow of information

37 Gassner, U.M. 2007. Legal Aspects of Tissue Banking. *Pathobiology,* 74, 270-274, at p. 274.

38 2004/23/EC, preamble, para. (3).

39 Ibid., para. (19).

40 The Directive distinguishes between 'tissues and cells'. I shall use the term 'tissue' as being inclusive of cells and having the same meaning as in the Directive.

41 Directive 2004/23/EC, Article 5.

42 The technical requirements of the accreditation process can be found in Article 3 and Annex I of Commission Directive 2006/86/EC, which implements provisions of Articles 8, 11 and 28 of Directive 2004/23/EC.

43 Directive 2004/23/EC, Article 6.

44 Ibid., Article 7.

45 Adverse incident reporting is stipulated in Articles 5, 6 and 8, Directive 2006/86/EC.

between Member States in relation to adverse incidents is ensured by Article 7(7) and Article 8 of Directive 2006/86/EC, which provides that national authorities are to communicate information amongst each other and with the Commission to ensure adequate responses.

Interestingly, Article 7 of the Directive also contains, in paragraph 5, distinct instructions for the creation of guidelines in terms of inspections and the training and qualification of personnel involved to reach a consistent (harmonized) level of quality in the EU. As far as the traceability of tangible tissue and data in relation to the tissue is concerned, the Directive stipulates that such data should be kept for at least 30 years.[46] The data to be kept includes tracking information from the donor to the recipient and vice versa, as well as information in relation to all products and substances that have come into contact with the tissue. It further provides for the creation of a donor identification system and the attribution of a unique code for each donation and each product associated with it. The tissue sample itself is to be marked with a label which contains sufficient identifying information.[47]

Article 10 of the Directive enshrines the requirement of a register of tissue establishments and details the reporting obligations of the establishments and the Member States and envisages the creation of a publicly accessible register of tissue establishments in each Member State as well as a networked resource showing establishments throughout Europe.

In terms of quality management, the Directive envisages a system based on prevailing standards of good practice, based on Community standards established by the Commission. Minimum requirements for such a system are established in the Directive, with the potential of more detailed technical stipulations being released under Article 28 of the Directive. Accredited establishments must have all relevant documentation ready for inspection and keep data in relation to the tracing of tissue for at least 30 years.[48]

Finally, the Directive requires the nomination of a responsible person who is trained to university degree level in biology or medicine and who holds at least two years of experience in a relevant field. This person is responsible for overseeing the implementation of the requirements of the Directive[49] in his or her institution and reports to the Member States' competent authority. The responsible person, and any changes to the identity of the responsible person, must be reported to the national authority. The Directive establishes a system of reporting from the responsible person to the national authority[50] and from the national authority of

46 Directive 2004/23/EC, Article 8. Also see Article 9 of Directive 2006/86/EC.

47 Article 8, Directive 2004/23/EC. The detailed technical requirements for documentation and records in relation to the tissue and cells can be found in Annex I of Commission Directive 2006/86/EC.

48 Ibid., Article 16.

49 In particular Articles 7, 10, 11, 15, 16, 18-24 thereof.

50 Ibid., Article 17(2) b.

each Member State[51] to the Commission.[52] The Commission, in turn, reports to the European Parliament, the Council, the European Economic and Social Committee and the Committee of Regions.[53]

Freedom of Movement: Storing and Transferring Tissue

The Directive makes provisions in relation to the import of tissues and cells into the Community, as well as the export of tissues and cells from the Community to third countries. All imports of tissues and cells into the Community from third countries must be undertaken by licensed establishments and that all tracing and quality requirements of the Directive are satisfied.[54] Material which has particular therapeutic relevance, or which is deemed to be of an urgent nature, can be imported or exported directly following authorization by the competent authority.[55] When tissue establishments receive material, they must ensure that the material is tested according to the provisions of the Directive.[56] The establishments are further required to document the quality of tissues and cells they receive and the related documentation. Where the material or the documentation fall short of the expected standard, the establishments are required to discard the material.[57] Until the appropriate quality of the material is established, the tissue and cells are to be quarantined.[58]

Treatment and storage of tissues and cells must be undertaken using standard operating procedures which are commensurate with the requirements of the Directive.[59] Further, these procedures must provide for a safe procedure for discarding unsuitable material and to safeguard the quality of the remaining material.[60] Article 21 of the Directive stipulates conditions for the storage of material. The conditions for storage are to be documented in the standard operating procedures of the tissue establishment.[61] The distribution of tissues and cells is prohibited unless all the requirements of the Directive have been met.[62] Where a tissue establishment ceases to carry out licensed activities, agreements are to be put in place by the Member States to ensure that material is transferred to another licensed establishment.[63] In relation to labelling and distribution of tissues and cells, the Directive refers to separate technical documents, in particular Commission Directive 2006/86/EC.

51 Ibid., Article 4(1).
52 Ibid., Article 26(1).
53 Ibid., Article 26(2).
54 Ibid., Article 9(1).
55 Ibid., Article 9(3) a. and b.
56 Ibid., Article 19(1).
57 Ibid., Articles 19(3), 19(4) and 19(5).
58 Ibid., Article 19(6).
59 Ibid., Article 20(1) and 20(2).
60 Ibid., Article 20(3).
61 Ibid., Article 21(1).
62 Ibid., Article 21(4).
63 Ibid., Article 21(5).

Procurement: Altruism and Consent

The primary principle of procurement, laid down in Article 12(1) of the Directive, is that donation of the material must be voluntary and unpaid. Compensation is available to cover disbursements and inconvenience only. Member States are required to report the compensation modalities to the Commission which may then adapt the requirements, as needed. The notion of financial gain for tissue giving is further restricted in Article 12(2) where Member States are required to create restrictions on advertising for tissue donation. Additionally, not only the giving of the material is to be unpaid: the procurement process itself is to be on a non-profit basis.[64]

Interestingly, the consent requirements are limited to those already in existence in the Member State.[65] The Annex of the Directive provides that living donors are to be told:[66]

- the purpose and nature of the procurement;
- consequences and risks;
- the nature of the tests carried out on the material;
- the kind of data about the individual which is to be recorded;
- the therapeutic purpose and benefits; and
- the measures taken to protect the donor.

As far as post mortem tissue procurement is concerned, the Directive refers only to legislation already in force in the Member States.[67] Donor procurement is to be carried out safeguarding the principles of safety and quality set out in the Directive[68] and all results are to be documented.[69]

Failures: Adverse Incidents

The Member States are required to document, report and investigate serious adverse incidents in relation to all aspects of the use of the material from procurement to application.[70] Such incidents are to be reported by the tissue establishments to the competent authorities, following procedures laid down by the Commission.[71] Appropriate measures for a rapid recall of affected materials must be in place.[72]

64 Ibid., Article 12(2).
65 Ibid., Article 13(1).
66 Ibid., Article 13(2) and Annex, para. A.
67 Ibid., Annex, para. B.
68 Ibid., Article 15(1), 15(2) and 15(4).
69 Ibid., Article 15(3).
70 Ibid., Article 11(1) and 11(2).
71 Ibid., Article 11(3) and 11(4).
72 Ibid., Article 11(5).

Data: Protection and Confidentiality

The tissue establishments are required to keep a detailed record of their activities and make these reports available to the competent authority in the Member State as well as the general public.[73] Each Member State is required to create a register of tissue establishments and network these registers on EU level.[74]

Data, which is accessible by third parties, must be anonymous.[75] The tracing and coding[76] requirements of the Directive effectively mean that a pseudonym is to take the place of data which travels outside the sphere of influence of protagonists named in the Directive. The safety and integrity of the data is to be safeguarded.

Discussion

The Directive goes to surprising lengths in order to harmonize conditions throughout the European Union in the area of procurement, storage and transfer of tissues and cells for therapy. The level of harmonizing ambition is surprising because the Directive fails to address the core issues which underlie some of the problematic discussions in relation to the area in which it seeks to legislate: questions of consent and procurement from post-mortem donors are merely referred to provisions already in force in the Member States. Whilst it is difficult to envisage how the EU could have tried to legislate in this intricate setting, it is also quite clear that the Directive amounts to not much more than a supranational impetus for the creation of national legislation (the quality and extent of which varies to a degree negating all possible notions of harmonization or convergence in the EU).[77] It also provides for a better flow of information and for the creation of a network of information on quality and failure issues, which is both useful and necessary and will aid the comparability of national systems at a later stage; the near impossibility of the task and the impotence of the means used, however, becomes clear when considering that, at the time of writing, the reporting requirements in the Directive have not been met by the Member States[78] and the Commission.[79]

---

73 Ibid., Article 10(1).

74 Ibid., Article 10(2) and 10(3).

75 Ibid., Article 14.

76 Ibid., Article 25(1).

77 Compare, in this context, the Human Tissue Act 2004 and the German *Gewebegesetz*.

78 Directive 2004/23/EC, Article 12(1), 26(1).

79 Ibid., Article 26(2), 26(3).

Chapter 9
A Look at Paradigmatic Case Law

When it comes to detailed case law and the quality of the subsequent discussion, the United States has been comparatively active in the past 20 years. Three particularly interesting cases have met with intense interest in the medico-legal and bioethical research communities: the case of the missing spleen of John Moore, that of a failure to exercise benefit sharing in genetic research and, finally, the question who is the owner of tangible tissue samples. All three will briefly be introduced here. A discussion of the recent *Yearworth* case will conclude this chapter with a glimpse of how the law is beginning to change.

Moore v. The Regents of the University of California

> [...] but how actions must be done and distributions effected in order to be just, to know this is a greater achievement than knowing what is good for the health.[1]

Having referred to this case on numerous occasions above and below, it is time to outline the case of *John Moore*[2] in all brevity.[3] Moore was being treated for a rare form of leukaemia[4] at the University of California, Los Angeles. The doctor treating him, Dr Golde, said that he 'had reason to fear for his life, and that the proposed splenectomy operation [...] was necessary to slow down the progress of his disease'.[5]

The operation not only slowed down the progress of the disease, but also yielded highly valuable material. Moore's spleen possessed characteristics which would, together with further samples, lead to a patent[6] estimated by some to be worth up to US$3.01 billon.[7] What is certain, is that Moore was coaxed back from his

---

1 Aristotle, Nicomachean Ethics, Bk V, § 13 [1137a].

2 *Moore v. Regents of the University of California* 793 P 2d 479 (Cal, 1990).

3 An early version of this chapter appeared as part of Hoppe (2008b).

4 Hairy cell leukaemia. The Leukemia and Lymphoma Society estimates that only between 500 and 800 people in the US develop hairy cell leukaemia out of an expected 40,440 people developing leukaemia in 2007 (only 1.2-2 per cent). See http://www.leukemia-lymphoma.org/all_page?item_id=8507, accessed 3 June 2009.

5 *Moore v. Regents of the University of California* 793 P 2d 479 (Cal, 1990), at p. 481.

6 US Patent No. 4,438,032 of 20 March 1984.

7 The court cited the figure from Moore's written pleadings: *Moore v. Regents of the University of California* 793 P 2d 479 (Cal, 1990), at p. 482; also see Merz, B. (1990). Biotechnology: Spleen Rights. *The Economist*, 11 August 1990 at p. 30.

home town of Seattle to the University of California's Medical Centre[8] regularly for some seven years (between November 1976 and September 1983). Golde and his researcher Quan, extracted blood, blood serum, skin, bone marrow aspirate and sperm,[9] making Moore believe that he was in fact enjoying aftercare for his condition as opposed to being the unwitting participant of cutting-edge cancer research. Regardless of whether we subscribe to the fantastic figure of US$3 billion above, it is certain that Golde and Quan benefited financially – personally and substantially – from the development of the patent[10] which was the result of the sustained and unlawful extraction of cells from Moore.

Moore attempted to gain access to some of the pecuniary benefits paid to Golde, Quan and the Regents of the University of California through the courts; the obvious illegality of the acquisition of his cells, he believed, morally entitled him to a share of the substantial commercial value of the end product. The court agreed with him on this particular point: it morally sided with him and suggested he retry by claiming a breach of fiduciary duty on the part of the doctors treating him. Legally, sided with the defendants and, in order to not shackle the progress of science, his claim was dismissed for conversion, leaving him without the windfall he had hoped for.

The question of the conversion of property and the act of mixing or converting the material beyond recognition or recovery is one which leads us to what I have in the past described as the *sublimation of the entitlement.*[11] Following this theorem, an entitlement in tangible property should sublimate to an entitlement in intangible property when, as in the *Moore* case, the downstream profit and the aim of the entire exercise lies not on the sustained storage and work with the tangible material, but the intangible information it contains as a type of medium. This is made necessary by the particular characteristics of the genetic information stored within our cells; the cells merely function as a medium for transport and the aim of the procurement of the cells is in some cases only to obtain access to that information – much like the value of a cheque is not the value of the paper it is printed on but of the *chose in action* it represents. Where, as in the *Moore* case, the appropriation is illegal, we need to ask whether the source can legitimately be said to have waived his entitlement in the cells or – by sublimation – the information contained therein. The theory revolves around the simple question (1) whether there are two distinct types of property, namely the cells and subsequently the new and distinct property in the data; or (2) a single property entitlement in the cells which merely subsequently sublimates into a property entitlement in the data.

8 Well over 1,000 miles.

9 *Moore v. Regents of the University of California* 793 P 2d 479 (Cal, 1990), at p. 481.

10 US Patent No. 4,438,032 (20 March 1984).

11 Hoppe, N. 2007. Bioequity: Applying the Principles of Equity to Resolve Conflicting Interests in Human Tissue. Paper presented at the PropEur Final Conference, University of Birmingham, 22 September 2007.

This, to some extent, follows the notion of the tort of conversion, which Moore pleaded as part of his claim:

> The tort of wrongfully dealing with a person's goods in a way that constitutes a denial of the owner's rights or an assertion of rights inconsistent with the owner's. Wrongfully taking possession of goods, disposing of them, destroying them, or refusing to give them back are acts of conversion.[12]

Moore was quite right in that there was certainly a wrongful interference of Golde and Quan with his body. The acquisition of samples from Moore for the purposes of research, outside the ambit of his original consent, certainly constituted a tortious interference with the person, so why not a tortious interference with property? Interestingly, Moore needed not to be the outright owner to bring his claim for conversion but merely have been in lawful possession of the converted chattel. This fits in neatly with the notion of not turning to the concept of ownership for the purposes of this text and concentrating on possession instead. Regrettably, the claimant needs to show that what was converted was a chattel and establish a reasonable market value for it – it is simply too much to ask the court to take the first steps towards a quantification of the value the human body.[13] Even if the value of his cells were to be established – did the value he was after not relate to the genetic information encoded in the cells (locked away for him prior to the artful intervention of Golde and Quan)? Moore's claim for conversion failed, foreseeably, because the legal mechanism he chose was unsuitable for the ethical and medical realities he tried to respond to. It is also clear that recent statute law does not come to the aid of English plaintiffs in the same situation as Moore either:

> None of the various protections the [Human Tissue] Act introduces apply to human cell lines by virtue of section 54(7) which excludes material 'created outside the human body'. [...] This is surprising since cell lines can be immortal clones of the donor's tissue and are widely used in research and traded for profit.[14]

The question thus remains unanswered. Below, there will be an attempt to solve the dilemma in the case of *Moore* using alternative mechanisms.[15] *Moore* does, however, raise a number of noteworthy points – besides being the first case of this kind to be looked at in this kind of detail. It was quite clear from the detailed pleadings in *Moore* that proprietary causes of action (such as conversion) and

12 Extract of the entry for 'conversion' in the (1997) *Oxford Dictionary of Law* 4th Edition, Oxford: Oxford University Press, at p. 107.

13 Even if such quantification routinely takes place where the result of an accident is the loss of a limb. See, e.g. D.A. Kemp (ed.) 2000. *Kemp and Kemp: The Quantum of Damages*. London: Sweet & Maxwell.

14 Liddell and Hall 2005, at p. 202.

15 See Chapter 12 below.

the associated remedies appeared to be quite suitable to achieve what everyone (including the bench) felt was morally justified. To point John Moore to an action for breach of fiduciary duty did not amount to much though, as Moore wanted to participate in the enormous profit gleaned from the obvious trespass. Recognizing that the law is wanting in that it denies remedies in cases where remedies ought to be available, should provide sufficient impulse to rectify the lacuna. Instead it produced precedent which amounted to a fresh, modern and universally applicable 'no-property' rule in modern biomedical research – licensing researchers to act dishonestly and disenfranchising the patient or research participant.

Greenberg v. Miami Children's Hospital Res. Inst.

The substantive difference between *Moore* and *Greenberg* could be argued to be one of deception. In Greenberg, a researcher – at the request of an afflicted family – directed his research focus to an autosomal recessive genetic disorder called Canavan disease.[16] In such disease, the parents are generally unaffected by the disease but carriers of the causal gene.[17] The disease affects predominantly Ashkenazi Jews and afflicted children rarely make it into their teens before succumbing to the disease. By means of carrier (i.e. parent) screening as well as prenatal screening of the foetus's DNA, would-be parents can identify the risk of having an afflicted child. The Greenbergs had had two children, both of whom were sufferers of the disease. Their first-born, Jonathan, succumbed to the disease and the Greenbergs – for lack of appropriate diagnostic methods – decided to take the risk and tried to have another child. Their second-born, Amy, was also a sufferer. Jonathan died aged 11; Amy died aged 16.[18] The Greenbergs decided to dedicate a sizeable proportion of their time and resources, together with a number of non-profit organizations, to the procurement of samples and encouragement of potential participants. The result was a registry containing epidemiological information and the availability of tissue which substantially assisted the researcher in finally identifying the relevant gene in 1993. Without the knowledge of the Greenbergs and the others, the researchers registered a patent in 1997 and proceeded to dictate licensing terms and conditions in a manner which was not commensurate with the

---

16 See Kaul, R., Gao, G., Aloya, M., Balamurugan, K., Petrosky, A., Michals, K. and Matalon, R. 1994. Canavan Disease: Mutations among Jewish and Non-Jewish Patients. *American Journal of Human Genetics,* 55(1), 34-41. Matalon was one of the defendants in the lawsuit and the researcher persuaded by the Greenbergs to focus on Canavan rather than a related disorder, Tay-Sachs disease.

17 Kumar, P. and Clark, M. 1998. *Clinical Medicine*. Edinburgh: W.B. Saunders, at pp. 146-147.

18 Gillis, J. 2000. The Human Blueprint: Patenting Life? *Washington Post*, 30 December, available at http://www.canavanfoundation.org/news/12-00_humanblueprint.php, accessed 3 June 2009.

wishes of the Greenbergs.[19] Greenberg and the others claimed on the basis of six causes of action, including – as did Moore – on the basis of conversion, as well as on the basis of unjust enrichment.

The defendants predictably argued that the claims must fail on the basis of the *Moorean* 'no-property' rule. The court could not identify a property interest in the tissue which was given to the defendants[20] but essentially failed to provide a convincing logic for their decision: they asserted the legal character of the transaction from donor to researcher as a donation but still negated property interests. This is a *non sequitur*, as, simply put, I cannot give as a gift what I do not own. The decision seems to underscore the utilitarian approach to reaching such decisions. The undesirable outcome of affording sources some sort of property interest is to be avoided, but the positive disposability aspects of giving property interests to the researchers are welcome.

This is, essentially, also the substantive gist of *Greenberg*. The courts had moved on slightly from the barefaced neglect of basic elements of justice in *Moore* and attempted to find some sort of solution in accord with the situation. Nonetheless, they too went over and beyond what could be described as common sense when they attempted to construct a legal gift relationship whilst at the same time denying any sort of property interest. The case of *Catalona*, which will be described in detail now, hinged on very much the same faulty logic.

Washington University v. Catalona

The *Catalona* case concerned a prostrate cancer researcher, William Catalona, who had undertaken research work for Washington University (WU) since 1976.[21] From 1983 on, he collected cancerous tissue from prostrate cancer patients, as well as tissue from healthy male relatives of patients for the purposes of accumulating these in a WU biorepository for research. The repository contained samples from some 2,500-3,000 patients who could be directly attributed to Catalona. The patients had all signed consent forms of varying quality and content, some waiving any proprietary entitlements they may have, some not. An important issue of the case of *Catalona* is that of an unfortunate mixing of samples procured by Catalona and those procured by others: the repository contained samples of up to 30,000 patients, only approximately 1/10 of which appeared to be from work done by Catalona.

---

19 US Patent No. 5,679,635 of 21.10.1997; now replaced by US Patent No. 7,217,547 of 15 May 2007.

20 Nwabueze, R. 2008. Donated Organs, Property Rights and the Remedial Quagmire. *Medical Law Review*, 16(2), 201-224, at p. 20.

21 The description of the case is from the judgment of the District Court of Missouri (*Washington University v. Catalona* 437 F.Supp.2d 985) and from Nwabueze (2008).

In 2003, Catalona left WU to take up a research post at Northwestern University. He wrote to all patients featured in the biorepository who had had contact with one of Catalona's research undertakings to inform them of his departure and to request that they consent to their samples being transferred to Catalona's new research university. Catalona himself states that he thought that up to 60,000 relevant individuals received his letter. Approximately 6,000 recipients of the letter returned the enclosed mandate for the release of their samples. Washington University resisted the release of the samples on the basis that the patients had no proprietary interest in their tissues that they might dispose of in this fashion. Even if they had such a proprietary interest, they had waived it in favour of WU by gifting the samples to WU.

The consent forms used by WU contained a proviso that research participants could ask for their samples to be withdrawn from the research and destroyed, stored but not used or made anonymous. There were no provisions, however, that meant that the research participant or patient had retained a right to request the transfer of the tissue. The question posed to the court was whether there were any property rights which the source could relinquish in the first place. The court did not go quite that far but concluded that the patients or participants had 'parted with any semblance of ownership rights once their biological material had been excised for medical research'.[22] On the basis that all relevant requirements of a valid *inter vivos* gift were present, the court decided that the material had been gifted to WU and that WU was the sole owner of the samples. Catalona and some of the patients appealed the decision to the US Supreme Court: the court's order list of 22 January 2008 shows that *a certiorari*[23] it was denied in both cases.

Again, the flaw in the court's logic, much the same as in *Greenberg*, becomes immediately apparent. Asserting strenuously that all legal requirements for a valid *inter vivos* gift[24] are present simply does not amount to changing the law of gifts: there still needs to be property to deliver to the donee and the donor must have some sort of entitlement to pass. Further, the entitlement to be passed on cannot be worth more than the entitlement in the hands of the donor.[25] The idea that the courts can simply apply the law of gifts to the transfer of entitlements in human tissue thus does not stand. If we see entitlements in human tissue from the perspective of Equity, as we shall see below, the idea shifts to one of assigning entitlements, possibly in a chose in action, to an assignee and the law of gifts appears to be even less suitable in the way it was applied by the courts in *Greenberg* and *Catalona*. The decisions have a clear objective: to achieve a certain outcome,

---

22 Nwabueze 2008, at p. 19.

23 Quashing order.

24 Property, intention to transfer the property, delivery of the property, acceptance of the property. See *Re Cole* [1964] 1 Ch 175 and *Bowman v. Secular Society Ltd.* [1917] AC 406.

25 See Treitel, G. 1995. *An Outline of the Law of Contract*. London: Butterworths, at p. 263.

namely a certain degree of justice and systematicity whilst under no circumstances shackling biomedical research. The application of the law of gifts is merely a weak pretense of legal validity: the courts have shied away from addressing the property question adequately. The Court of Appeal's judgment in the case of *Yearworth* is a very recent and most notable exception and will be outlined in all brevity here.

Yearworth v. North Bristol NHS Trust

This case concerned six men[26] who were advised to undergo chemotherapy treatment. They were told that their fertility might be impaired by the treatment and the treating physicians offered the possibility of storing the men's sperm for subsequent artificial insemination, should their fertility not recover. After accepting the sperm for storage but before it could be used for an artificial insemination procedure, the NHS Trust negligently failed to maintain equipment that was necessary to keep the sperm frozen.

The six men were told about the loss of the sperm and were, understandably, shocked. Five out of the six claimed compensation on the basis that they had suffered a nervous shock. They also claimed that they were entitled to compensation under either one of two alternative headings:

1. that the damage to the sperm constituted a personal injury and that they were entitled to damages as a result of this injury; or
2. that the sperm was the men's property and they were entitled to damages for the loss of the property.

The first instance court, Exeter County Court, considered that the sperm was neither property nor did its deterioration constitute personal injury. On appeal, the Court of Appeal was also asked to consider whether liability for the loss of the sperm might also result from contract or bailment.

The first issue which the court addressed was whether damaging the sperm constituted personal injury. Counsel for the appellants was unable to provide domestic or common law authority for this assertion, but relied instead on a paradigmatic German case[27] with virtually indistinguishable facts. The Court of Appeal distinguished this case on the basis of the difference in legal systems, namely that the German court had no choice but to find that there was personal injury. In order to recover damages, the claimant had to show personal injury, deprivation of liberty or economic loss. The Lord Chief Justice, Lord Judge, concluded that '[a]s this judgment will proceed to show, we have concluded that we labour under no such constraint'.[28]

---

26 To be accurate: five men and the administratrix of the sixth man's estate.

27 9 November 1993, BGHZ 124, 52.

28 *Yearworth and others v. North Bristol NHS Trust* [2009] EWCA Civ 37, at para. 22.

The court proceeded to reject the notion of personal injury in this context on the basis that it was unconvincing that damage to a severed or expelled part or product of the body could still – by virtue of nexus to the original organism – be thought to be an integral part of that body.

The part of the judgment which is of particular interest to the issues discussed here is that of damage to property. The court was asked to consider whether 'a substance such as sperm, generated by the body but removed from it, [is] capable at common law of being owned?'.[29]

The court considered the question in the light of Honoré's theory of bundles, briefly discussed above. The cardinal feature of the notion of ownership is convincingly argued to be the right or liberty to use at one's discretion. The court found that neither the common law, nor statute removed the right to use to a degree sufficient to negate a property interest. After lucidly and in detail considering all relevant authority on this question, the Court of Appeal concluded that the men's power of control over the sperm amounted to a property right – they retained sufficient sticks of the bundle to constitute property. The court continued in its analysis and found that the law of bailment was also applicable – that the Trust was the gratuitous bailee of the sperm, providing the basis for a duty of care in bailment. Having already established sufficient property rights for the purposes of an action in tort, it followed that the appellants had sufficient rights in relation to the sperm to render it capable of bailment – and the damages for a breach of a duty in bailment are closer to those in contract and therefore preferable to those in tort.

> In summary, the breach of bailment here was a breach not just for the duty owed by every gratuitous bailee but of a specific promise extended by the Trust to the men. The law of bailment provides them with a remedy under which, in principle, they are entitled to compensation for any psychiatric injury (or actionable distress) foreseeably consequent upon the breach.[30]

In conclusion, the court held that the sperm was the property of the men for the purposes of their action in the tort of negligence and for their action in bailment.

The Court of Appeal, in this excellent and lucid judgment, overcomes the disenfranchisement barrier established in *Moore*. Hypothetically altering the facts of *Yearworth* towards a more *Mooreian* scenario, it is conceivable that, had the sperm been used for research leading to a subsequent profit without consent, the rationale behind their Lordships dictum would have provided a starting point for a non-disenfranchised claw-back of at least some of the profit. The court's criticism of reverting to the principles identified in *Doodeward v. Spence*[31]

29 Ibid., at para. 26 (a).

30 Ibid., at para. 58.

31 Ibid., at paras. 45(c)-(d).

mirrors perfectly the criticism contained in this book and it is clear from this judgment that the courts' doors are opening for a contemporary, modern and appropriate analysis of property rights in relation to human tissues, cells and body products.

Chapter 10
The Law, Systematically

The following section follows the structure of the matrix introduced above (see Chapter 2). The legal issues in relation to the different components of a possible retention scenario will be discussed in detail. Where appropriate, the term *patient* will be used, though it will be clear from the context that in most circumstances this also includes *research participant* in its definition.

Source

The source is in most cases a patient, sometimes a research participant. The character of the source is important in relation to the permitted activities. The nature of the source (for example, whether the source is competent or incompetent) is inextricably tied in with a subsequent consideration of consent issues, which in turn often hinges on the nature of the motivation for the taking of the tissue.

The Competent, Adult Patient

> Every human being of adult years and sound mind has a right to determine what shall be done with his own body; and a surgeon who performs an operation without his patient's consent, commits an assault...[1]

Competent, adult patients can consent to medical treatment either expressly or by an advance directive. Where they are able to express their wishes, these wishes must be followed. This rule is paramount in cases of refusing medical treatment, but not necessarily in electing a certain kind of treatment.

> Where a competent patient makes it clear that he does not wish to receive treatment which is, objectively, in his best medical interests, it is unlawful for doctors to administer that treatment. Personal autonomy or the right of self-determination prevails. [...] The corollary does not, however, follow, at least as a general proposition. Autonomy and the right of self-determination do not entitle the patient to insist on receiving a particular medical treatment regardless of the nature of the treatment.[2]

---

1 *Schloendorff v. NY Hospital* (1914) 105 NE 92 per Cardozo J.
2 *R (on the application of Burke) v. GMC* [2005] 3 FCR 169, paras 30-31.

This is where the tie-in to questions of the type of tissue and impact occurs: not all kinds of activity can be consented to and this will be discussed in detail below.

The Incompetent Patient, Children

The English law only recognizes by-proxy consent (consent on behalf of incompetent or incapacitated patients) where the *incapax* has made appropriate arrangements, giving express authority to third parties to decide on his behalf. In the absence of such express authorization, consent on behalf of others is only admissible where the law explicitly provides for such consent, for example in circumstances of guardianship.[3] Where a child does not fulfil the conditions for a *Gillick* competence, the parents may take treatment decisions on behalf of the child.[4] The reach of by-proxy consent generally does not extend to the refusal of life-saving treatment on behalf of someone else and it may in fact be a breach of an *incapax's* human right to physical integrity and life for a trust hospital not to try to enforce treatment against the wishes of the guardian.[5] Nor does the notion of others consenting on behalf of someone who is unable to consent him or herself usually extend to procedures which are non-therapeutic. Where there is no possibility to reliably reconstruct the incapacitated patient's presumed wishes, the procedure to be carried out must satisfy the *best interest* criteria as laid out in *Bolam*[6] and *Re F*.[7]

Post Mortem Organ Retention

We have seen already that once the source has died, there are no enduring legal interests which the source may have in him or herself. Any *ex ante* provisions in relation to the disposal of the body only represent a morally binding wish rather than a legally binding decree.[8] The reason for this, so Harris argues convincingly, lies in the fact that whilst there may be weak enduring interests, the person to whom harm could be done (which the law would see as its duty to prevent) no longer exists. Sperling raises these very issues in the introduction to his book *Posthumous Interests: Legal and Ethical Perspectives*:

3 See, e.g. the Mental Capacity Act 2005; Adults with Incapacity (Scotland) Act 2000.

4 *Gillick v. West Norfolk and Wisbech Area Health Authority* [1986] 1 AC 112.

5 *Glass v. UK* [2004] 1 FLR 1019.

6 *Bolam v. Friern Hospital Management Committee* [1957] 2 All ER 118. For a discussion on the shift away from the traditional concepts in Bolam, see the excellent Brazier, M. and Miola, J. 2000. Bye-bye Bolam: A Medical Litigation Revolution. *Medical Law Review*, 8(1), pp. 85-114.

7 *Re F* [1990] 2 AC 1

8 Cf. Harris 2002, at p. 537; also see the provisions of the Human Tissue Act in relation to *ex ante* provisions.

> When subjected to these non-consenting procedures are the dead being harmed? Are they wronged? And if so, in what sense? Assuming that there is such harm would entail not only that the dead, who are now being harmed, *exist* as subjects to be harmed, but also that they are *the same* persons or subjects they were before their death.[9]

Continental legal traditions pursue a notion of an enduring entitlement to human dignity.[10] The question whether in the case of a post-mortem retention of organs, any enduring interest (proprietary or otherwise) of the deceased are touched upon deserves as much attention as the question whether relatives have entitlements which may be infringed.

Anonymous or Pseudonymous Sources

One mechanism for circumventing problems in relation to an individual's rights in material and the information encoded thereon is that of using pseudonyms or anonymous material. Anonymity entails the irreversible removal of any information which may lead to the identification of the original source, whilst pseudonyms represent a reversible process of anonymity – a so-called coding where there is a key which allows for the identification of the source, usually held by a third party custodian.

Given that on the one hand, for epidemiological purposes, some data such as age and gender as well as the originating institution and other collateral information are known, the question whether the sum of all of the data may mean that there is no such thing as anonymity or use of pseudonyms is justified. On the other hand, the fact that most of the material in question here will contain identifying genetic data which may not only enable us to track an individual (possibly through cross-linking of other databases, such as a sex offender's register, military personnel databases, unsolved crimes registers or insurance databanks)[11] but also reveals in-depth and highly private information on the individual's and his family's genetic make-up. The Human Tissue Act 2004 is silent on notions of anonymity and pseudonyms in relation to tissue and a consequent potential for loss of a right to interfere in the material's use for the source. The analysis of DNA on the basis of procured tissue is prohibited unless qualified consent is obtained.[12] This requirement can be

---

9 Sperling, D. 2008. *Posthumous Interests: Legal and Ethical Perspectives*. Cambridge: Cambridge University Press, at p. 8. Emphasis from the original.

10 In some cases for a considerable amount of time (such as some thirty years after a person's death: see the decision of the German Bundesgerichtshof (Federal Supreme Court) of 8 June 1989 (I ZR 135/87)). The court held that the deceased's personal rights fade at the same rate as our memory of them.

11 Also see the controversy around the UK's National DNA Database. Wallace, H. 2006. *The UK National DNA Database*. EMBO reports 7:S26-S30.

12 Section 45, Human Tissue Act 2004.

derogated from on the basis of a large number of excepted purposes, contained in one of the Schedules to the Act.[13]

Consent

General Consent Issues

The quality of consent in the biomedical setting has seen a change from the grateful recipient of ostensibly wondrous cures merely holding still, acquiescing, to the curative intervention – to the enlightened patient, consumer of therapeutic services, demanding a full *ex ante* scientific explanation of surgery. This change has been gradual, underpinned by a number of well argued and incisive decisions over the years, some of which have been discussed already.[14]

Deutsch and Spickhoff recount an interesting anecdotal memory of Bismarck when discussing the origins of patient autonomy and consent in the wake of the discovery of the German prince regent's laryngeal carcinoma:

> At the end of May 1887, the physicians had decided that they were going to make the prince regent unconscious and completely remove his larynx without telling him that this was what they were going to do. I objected and demanded that they should not proceed without obtaining the patient's consent and, since we were dealing with the heir to the throne, also the consent of the head of the family. Having informed the Kaiser, he prohibited the procedure unless his son gave his consent.[15]

Despite the overwhelming acceptance of the concept of full informed consent, there are still some persuasive arguments in favour of a good degree of paternalism in the medical context. From respecting a 'right not to know' to actively lying at the patient's bedside on the assumption that the lie might make the patient better, or at least represents the lesser of two evils, is a thin line. For many years, the basic assumption was that a patient would always be happier, better off, if he received the best possible treatment available. The notion that patients would willingly choose to not receive treatment, possibly life-saving or life-prolonging treatment, was not considered seriously. Yet there are many convincing scenarios in which such a decision might occur: the elderly patient who opts against chemotherapy in order to avoid suffering from crippling side-effects for a long time, in favour of

---

13 Schedule 4, Part 2, Section 5, Human Tissue Act 2004. Excepted purposes in this section are, *inter alia*, prevention or detection of crime, prosecution, national security and on the order of a court, including courts outside the UK.

14 See Chapter 7.

15 Bismarck, quoted in Deutsch, E. and Spickhoff, A. 2008. *Medizinrecht*. Heidelberg: Springer, at p. 164. My translation.

relishing maximum interaction with his family for a short time is but one realistic example.

The general consensus is that in order to respect the individual's autonomy as fully as possible, we must let the individual take all decisions he or she is able to take. The gold standard for making sure that this is the case is therefore informed consent.

Informed Consent

Neither the classic Hippocratic Oath nor the modern version contain provisions in relation to consent. It could be argued that the physician's overriding duty to treat the sick by whatever means necessary might well outweigh any contrary considerations of the patient in a paternalistic fashion: 'I will apply, for the benefit of the sick, all measures [that] are required [...]'.[16]

The value of assessing differing versions of the Hippocratic Oath is dubious as is any assertion that the Oath may possess any legally binding character. It rather allows a glimpse of the task physicians set themselves when embarking on careers in their profession and of their self-conception. A detailed outline and criticism of informed consent, both in the therapeutic as well as in the research setting, can be found above.[17]

Liability, for failing to obtain appropriate consent may be limited to a simple but-for test: would the patient have consented to the procedure but for the missing information? If this is indeed the case, the value of informed consent hangs in the balance as the consideration of whether an individual may still have agreed to a certain procedure if given certain information can never give sufficient weight to the autonomous (and possibly irrational) decision-making processes of the individual.[18] Mason and Laurie outline the case of *Chester v. Ashfar*[19] in their contemplation of what extent of information is necessary to protect the physician from incurring liability and they quite rightly ponder that all involved parties must have been oddly reminded of *Sidaway*: the facts are virtually identical. A young woman underwent spinal surgery and the physician failed to warn her of a 1-2 per cent risk of serious harm. The harm materialized and she claimed against the physician in negligence. Her claim was rejected by two out of five judges on the basis that she had failed to show that, had she known about the risk, she would have rejected the procedure – she therefore did not leap the '*but-for*' hurdle. The majority found in favour of the appellant on public policy grounds.

16 Modern version of the Hippocratic Oath by Louis Lasagna (1964), now used in most medical schools.

17 See Chapters 7 and 10.

18 For a discussion of this element of informed consent, see Mason and Laurie (2006), at pp. 407 and 308.

19 [2005] 1 AC 134, [2004] 4 All ER 587, [2004] 3 WLR 927.

Informed consent as a concept goes further than these '*but-for*' considerations – which admittedly flow not from a theoretical assessment of informed consent but from the realities of tort law in litigation practice. Informed consent requires not the satisfaction of a '*but-for*' test but the adherence to the principle that the opportunity to make a treatment decision must be given, not the *ex post* assessment of whether not giving information made a causal difference.[20] Lord Steyn gives a solid explanation of the benefits expected from obtaining fully informed consent from patients:

> A rule requiring a doctor to abstain from performing an operation without the informed consent of a patient serves two purposes. It tends to avoid the occurrence of the particular physical injury, the risk of which a patient is not prepared to accept. It also ensures that due respect is given to the autonomy and dignity of each patient.[21]

His explanation of the rationale behind informed consent is particularly noteworthy as it reflects a brief departure from the flak-jacket argument so often cited.

In summary, it ostensibly amounts to a fluid quality of consent depending entirely on the quantity and quality of the information given, the individual's ability to comprehend the information and – on an evidential basis – the physician's ability to accurately record the decision-making process. As informed consent is, as already outlined, a highly individualized product of the interaction and intellectual capacity of several involved parties, there is no distinct level which can be defined as acceptable or unacceptable in all cases.

Impact

The category 'impact' plays an important role in our assessment. It is intended to denote the quality of a certain interaction: is the intervention in question merely the retention of material, which was obtained under the guise of appropriately sought consent for a reasonable therapeutic procedure and merely left over, or was the procurement of the tissue itself the reason for breaking the source's skin? Are we speaking of a saliva swab or a splenectomy?

One of the principal underlying rationales of justice is the dogma of proportionality. The law's interference will only extend to a proportionate interference.

---

20 For an excellent discussion of the problem of informed consent in the clinical setting, see O'Neill, O. 2003. Some limits of informed consent. *Journal of Medical Ethics*, 29, 4-7.

21 *Chester v. Afshar* [2004] UKHL 41, per Lord Steyn at para 18, cited in Herring 2006, at p. 83.

Criminal Law Aspects of Invasive Medical Treatment

Adverse consequences of medical treatment are usually restricted to the realm of civil law, in actions in tort for negligence or battery. The courts are hesitant to permit regular prosecutions of doctors for fear of increasing the onus on the medical practitioner to an intolerable level, thereby stultifying the profession.[22]

> There are [...] certain circumstances in which the law does not permit a defendant to rely [...] on the victim's consent. The victim's consent to being killed would provide no excuse for the killer. Where the assault to which consent is given involves permanent injury or maiming – e.g. the severing of a limb – there is no dispute that the victim's consent is immaterial.[23]

We have seen above[24] that the law of theft has failed to get a firm footing in many situations in relation to tissue taking: seeing property as coming into existence after the unlawful taking takes place removes the criminal law's ability to sanction ostensibly illegal conduct outside the realm of an assault.[25] In the past, the criminal law has managed to react to self-created lacunae. When the notion of simple theft[26] was unable to capture the idea of culprits filling their vehicles' fuel tanks at petrol stations or failing to pay at the end of a night out in a restaurant (by reason of the *actus reus* of 'appropriation' not concurring in time with the *mens rea* of the appropriation being 'dishonest'), the law reacted appropriately and provided for the offence of *making off without payment*.[27]

Aspects in Relation to Non-invasive Interference

Where the impact of a medical intervention is such that no physical contact is made, there is nevertheless the possibility of subsequent harm. In the case of Alder Hey and other similar circumstances, it is reasonable to assume that the relatives of those whose organs were retained may well have suffered from nervous shock or some other kind of psychiatric harm. The harm is, therefore, independent of touching. The courts have been reluctant, however, to accord the same value to psychiatric harm as they have done to physical harm and there was considerable doubt for quite some time as to the definition of 'nervous shock' in the first place:[28]

---

22 Though Mason and Laurie cite a spate of prosecutions in the 1990s: see Mason and Laurie 2006, at p. 344.

23 Dworkin and Kennedy 1993, at p. 299.

24 See Chapter 7.

25 Such as a theft offence.

26 Section 1, Theft Act 1968, as amended.

27 Section 3, Theft Act 1968, as amended.

28 *See Attia v. British Gas plc* [1988] QB 304; *Page v. Smith* [1994] 4 All ER 522.

for example nervous shock 'involves the sudden appreciation by sight or sound of a terrifying event which violently agitates the mind'.[29]

In its consequence, the shock must be of a quality to cause 'positive psychiatric illness', i.e. a medically accepted condition as a result.[30] In the case of *Alcock*, cited above, the resulting condition was post-traumatic stress disorder as a result of the Hillsborough football stadium catastrophe, where almost 100 fans were crushed to death.

What is decisive in our context is that on the one hand, the harm is not directed at the subsequent victim (such as the patient's relatives) and on the other hand we will not have a situation where such a terrifying event is caused wilfully, as required by the notion of the intentional infliction of nervous shock. Rather, the doctors can at best be said to be negligent about the terror that they may cause to third parties by their acts. Where we have a third party to an act we need to look at a more restrictive judicial approach to the idea of nervous shock. Primarily, it is clear that there must be an individual, identifiable shock which leads to the condition – the accumulation of bad news to a degree where a subsequent condition is evident is simply not sufficient. Returning to our context, the relative of the child whose organs were retained must, as a secondary victim, establish that the defendant caused the death, injury or imperilment of a loved one and the proximity in terms of space and time is sufficiently close.[31]

Further, the damage must be foreseeable. In the Alder Hey context,[32] it is submitted that where organs of young children are retained, it is quite foreseeable that even a parent of normal psychiatric fortitude[33] would suffer distress as a consequence. As far as establishing the close personal proximity required to constitute the 'close tie of love and affection',[34] a detailed discussion here is superfluous – again, it can safely be assumed that such a tie exists between parents and children.

Motive

As we have already seen, human biological material holds considerable promise

29 *Alcock v. Chief Constable of South Yorkshire Police* (1992) 1 AC 310, per Ackner, LJ at p. 401.

30 *McLoughlin v. O'Brian* [1983] AC 410, per Bridge LJ at p. 431.

31 A detailed discussion of the current law of liability for psychiatric injury would be outside the remit of this text. A very good outline can be found in the Law Commission's Report. 'Liability for Psychiatric Injury' (No. 249, 1998).

32 Which, admittedly, concerns outrageous circumstances likely to be suitable to cause distress.

33 *Bourhill v. Young* [1943] AC 92.

34 *Alcock v. Chief Constable of South Yorkshire Police* [1992] 1 AC 310. Parents and children are indeed one of the express classes of people named for the purposes of establishing love and affection in law. See Wilberforce LJ in *McLoughlin v. O'Brian* [1983] AC 410.

for a number of applications. It is used for research, teaching, therapy and cosmetics and thus sought after by research institutions, teaching hospitals and pharmaceutical companies alike. This leads to inevitable, and quite justified, questions on whether the ultimate purpose of taking the tissue has, in some way, a bearing on the admissibility of the procedure as a whole. Harris seems to take precisely this stance and suggests that it is the objective usefulness of the excised tissue which justifies the taking of the tissue in the first place:

> Absent the good moral reasons for organ and tissue examination and retention, either because nothing useful can be learnt from them, or because they have been retained in a way which prevents such beneficial use, there is no justification for either taking or retaining tissue and organs.[35]

Somewhat disappointingly, Harris includes in his very sensible formula a caveat ('...or because they have been retained in a way which prevents such beneficial use...') in order to encompass scenarios in which consent requirements, for example, are infringed.

> There is a lot of hypocrisy about the ethics of buying and selling organs and indeed any other body products and services – for example, surrogacy and gametes. What it usually means is that everyone is paid but the donor. The surgeons and medical team are paid, the transplant coordinator does not go unremunerated, and the recipient received an important benefit in kind. Only the unfortunate and heroic donor is supposed to put up with the insult of no reward, to add to the injury of the operation.[36]

There is, therefore, an at least superficial question of whether the ultimate destination of the material can make a difference in terms of the lawfulness of the overall procedure. Such arguments seem to be, *prima facie*, not in evidence but the different concepts ought to be discussed nonetheless.

Therapy

Tissue and cells used for research hold an isolated place in this debate. The EU's Human Tissue Directive[37] is one example of a normative instrument which concerns itself solely with therapeutic aspects ('human application'), as does the German implementation, the *Gewebegesetz*.

35 Harris 2002, at p. 528.
36 Erin and Harris 2003, at p. 137.
37 2004/23/EC.

Research

The history of biomedical research has displayed an accelerated development in the recent past. Research used to be an arena within which the research subject was often the unwitting participant, either unaware that he was undergoing experimental treatment or fully disenfranchised as the inmate of an institution designed to be a conduit of poor people to research.[38] Following on from the Nuremberg trials after the Second World War, detailed attention was given to the interaction between researchers and research participants, resulting, *inter alia*, in today's Declaration of Helsinki. Whereas the relationship between doctor and patient is one which tends to be guided by a desire to be helped and a desire to help for the benefit of a defined individual, the stakeholders and motives in the research setting are not always this clearly defined.

This has resulted in a dense network of ethical and legal guidelines, some within the realm of medical self-regulation and some in a legislative arena.[39] The distinct line between medical care and research are notoriously difficult to draw and a certain amount of overlap, for example in the context of experimental medical treatment, is inevitable.

Other Motives

The use of human bodies and body parts does not stop at categories such as therapy and research. Cosmetic or enhancing use of human body products – such as the use of human-derived hormone preparations – are widespread. Auditory ossicles are fashioned from the bones of deceased donors. The use of human bodies and body parts in the arts is also well documented.[40]

Discussion

Having shown the three categories of application above it is time to ask whether the kind of category makes a difference to the lawfulness of the excision. When looking at the provisions in relation to organ donation, in particular the question of conditional organ donation (i.e. whether an organ can be donated specifically for a certain purpose or recipient or not) it appears that the ability to decree the destination or application of such a donation is limited.[41] Nwabueze (2008)

---

38 See Bergmann 2004, p. 240.

39 See, e.g. the guidelines issued by the Medical Research Council or the Council of Europe's Convention on Human Rights and Biomedicine, Oviedo 1997.

40 See, e.g. Schneede, M. (ed.) 2002. *Mit Haut und Haaren – Der Körper in der Zeitgenössischen Kunst*. Cologne: Dumont.

41 Nwabueze cites the case of an attempt to restrict the circle of recipients of a post mortem organ to 'white people only'. Nwabueze 2008, at footnote 13. In this case the authorities refused the donation rather than accept the donation and deal with it in other

outlines that in many states of the US, directed donation is possible and the UK has, to a somewhat limited extent, also similar provisions.[42] The decisive element in the debate appears to be the fact that where consent for the removal is sought for one particular purpose (such as therapy), this purpose must also be the only discernible motive for the actual act of procurement. If the possible use of the tissue changes subsequently (such as in terms of leftovers after diagnostic measures), the provisions of Section 44 of the Human Tissue Act 2004 are applicable: the material is regarded as waste.

Where an excision is planned in relation to a subsequent use for industrial purposes, our capacity to consent to such harm is severely limited. As discussed above, the giving of regenerative tissue and body products involving a low level of harm is deemed possible, and serious harm in relation to such giving is unacceptable.[43] Consenting to serious harm for the therapeutic benefit of another, specific or unspecific, person such as in the case of live organ[44] and blood donation[45] is expressly mandated by law.

Type of Tissue

Differences in the type of tissue bear legal relevance where the tissue type determines which kind of legal framework finds application. Where a complete organ is concerned, the legal requirements for organ transplantation are applicable, including but not limited to the prohibition of commercial transactions.[46] Where tissue or body product or fluid samples are concerned, other stipulations are relevant.[47] It could be argued that the redundancy or replaceability of a certain body part tends to determine the legal status of the treatment of that particular part. Whilst this probably stands up to scrutiny in terms of the assessment of the seriousness of the harm (as we are able to consent to a haircut but not to a non-therapeutic amputation) this seems to have less to do with the type of tissue and more with the seriousness and permanence of the harm caused.

---

ways than demanded, so the presented logic may not hold as no assignment, donation or gift occurred – based on the refusal to accept the conditions attached.

42 Nwabueze 2008, at pp. 3-4.

43 See the discussion of *R v. Brown* above.

44 Human Tissue Act 2004, Section 33.

45 See, e.g. The Blood Safety and Quality Regulations 2005 (S.I. 50/2005).

46 Human Tissue Act 2004, Section 32.

47 In particular the regulations in relation to blood safety and quality on a domestic (see no. 45 above) and European level: Directive 2002/98/EC; Directive 2005/61/EC; Directive 2005/62/EC.

Appropriation

In the context of theft offences, the term *appropriation* refers to the taking of something from the control of another. In the context of human tissue and cells, the term procurement is often used, though it describes the whole process from donor acquisition to the actual taking of the tissue. The use of the term *appropriation* in this context is deliberate, as it denotes both the moment in time where possessive control of material changes as well as the active role taken by the person procuring the tissue.

Criminal Law Consequences of Dishonest Appropriation

Looking at appropriation from the viewpoint of the source, the criminal law does not sanction the illegal taking of the tissue over and beyond simple aspects of assault. Where the material is procured and stored legally, and a commensurate level of skill is expended on the material, the criminal law of theft applies when the material is illegally appropriated from an entity or person lawfully in possession of the material.[48] US cases, such as *Greenberg* and *Catalona*, assert that the law of gifts find application and thus see proprietary entitlements for the purposes of civil law for the source, capable of being assigned to third parties during the course of a donation. For the purposes of criminal law, no such entitlements seem to exist.

The idea behind introducing proprietary entitlements for the purposes of criminal law is to ensure that the dishonest appropriation of tissue from another does not remain without consequences. In criminal law terms, nothing speaks against an application of the law of theft in these circumstances (though this is not the object of this text). In particular, there are no convincing arguments why and how there can be property in the eyes of civil law for gifts, but not simultaneously also in the eyes of the criminal law for theft.

Civil Law Consequences of Dishonest Appropriation

Even within the construct of the civil law, a similar divide seems to be deployed. For the purposes of assigning my entitlement without remuneration (as a donation or gift) the civil law concedes the existence of a proprietary entitlement.[49] This is not so for the purposes of assigning the entitlement for a return value.[50] Where an appropriation is unlawful, the source should have the ability to require the return of the tissue and the fact that the tissue may no longer be of any actual use to the source is irrelevant

48 *R v. Kelly* (1998) 3 All ER 741.

49 See *Washington University v. Catalona* 437 F.Supp.2d 985 (2006) and *Greenberg v. Miami Children's Hospital Res. Inst.* 264 F. Supp.2d 1064 (2003); also see *Doodeward v. Spence* (1908) CLR 406 and *R v. Kelly* (1998) 3 All ER 741.

50 Which, in fact, is made explicitly illegal: Human Tissue Act 2004, Section 32.

in this context. It is this particular civil aspect of the question which will be redressed in the final part of this book.

Agency

Parts, and to some extent products of the body (see above) are regularly removed from the live patient in order to facilitate therapy. In the very same way, samples are taken from the dead patient for the purposes of establishing the cause of death and for quality control reasons. After establishing the current legal situation in relation to these and other scenarios in terms of the removal of parts and products, an issue ought to very quickly be raised which we will not have the opportunity to delve into deeper as part of this text but which is nonetheless of great interest in this context: where these tissues are removed as part of therapy at the bidding of the patient, the question of agency must be resolved. The hospital and its employees are, in most circumstances, acting within the scope of a contractual relationship with the patient. Tissues are taken by the hospital for the purposes of procuring a cure or establishing the condition in question in the same way as one would give faulty parts of a car to a garage for the diagnosis of the reasons behind the part's failure. There can be no suggestion that the garage obtains anything more than a transient possessory interest in the parts: why would they suddenly be the owner of such parts? Applied to our question – why is, by and large in all debates, the assumption that the hospital or the doctors become owners merely by the patient handing over control of the tissue to them? This may be of particular interest in relation to the patents mentioned above in the cases of *Moore* and *Greenberg* and finds affirmation in the dictum in *Yearworth*.

Pecuniary Aspects

Commercial dealings with human material for transplantation purposes are prohibited.[51] Material which is subject to property due to the application of human skill (see p. 82 above) is an exception to this rule.[52] As the use and storage of other tissues and cells, not intended for transplantation, is subject to the Act's licensing requirements,[53] the contravention of which is penalized,[54] any dealings with human tissue are subject to strict regulation. Nonetheless, the Act does not proscribe commercial dealings with tissue.

The prohibitive stipulations in relation to the sale of transplantable organs are the same as in most other countries.[55] Sale simply is prohibited and penalized. The

51 Human Tissue Act 2004, section 32.

52 Ibid., section 32(9) c.

53 Ibid., section 16.

54 Ibid., section 25.

55 The notable exceptions being Iran and Pakistan: for a critique of legalized organ sale, see Mor, E. and Boas, H. (2005). Organ Trafficking: Scope and Ethical Dilemma. *Current Diabetes Reports*, 5(4), 294-299, particularly at pp. 294 and 298.

issue of transplantable organ sale appears to be ethically more volatile than that of, for example, gamete sale.[56] Friedman and Friedman quite plausibly criticize this discrepancy: '[...] commercialization of semen and ova is more morally questionable than organ sale because those cells might create entirely new human beings'.[57]

The qualitative difference between organs and reproductive material is already reflected in the systematic structure introduced in the matrix.[58] In this structure, the column representing the idea of a pecuniary value denotes the special consideration which is given where a pecuniary commercialization takes place. In the first part, we have already established that donation is fine, but sale is not:[59] the question why this is and whether the law mirrors this attitude, needs to be asked. Before we do that, the idea of money needs to be reflected on a conceptual basis.

The use of money as a representation of value is technically merely an assistance mechanism to ensure an efficient economic exchange. Where something is of distinct value, subjectively, this value can be translated into the required amount of money. Some things may have a value over and beyond a pecuniary value. An example may be that a certain item has emotional value, such as a wedding ring. The ring may have an objective value and a more or less equivalent subjective value to third parties. To the individual whose wedding ring it is, the overall value, or the amount of money offered when the individual's indifference whether to sell or not to sell is exceeded in favour of sale, may outstrip any realistically available money. This threshold is, however, a decision for the individual. Where an individual decides that there is a price which would convince him to part with his wedding ring, there is not much we can sensibly say to criticize that over and beyond '*I would not do the same*' or '*I would not do the same for the same*'. The same goes, technically for parts of a human body and body products (notwithstanding the law's intervention in preventing harm and risk to an individual despite consensual participation) – and why not? The proverb *pecunia non olet* ('money does not smell') has its roots, oddly, in the commercialization of body products:

> Censured by his son Titus for devising a tax on urine, [Vespasian] held to his son's nose a coin from the first money received, asking him whether the odour

---

56 A metasearch on the National Library of Medicine's *Medical Literature Analysis and Retrieval System* (3 June 2009) reveals 120 sources featuring the non-parenthesized key words 'organ sale', the British Medical Journal's *Journal of Medical Ethics* literature search returns 775. The equally un-parenthesized key words 'gamete sale' return 31 references and the *Journal of Medical Ethics* returns 254. This is obviously no suitable expression of the ethical volatility of either concept as some or all of the references returned might praise the process rather than criticize it.

57 Friedman, E.A. and Friedman, A.L. 2006. Payment for Donor Kidneys: Pros and Cons. *Kidney International*, 69, 960-962 at pp. 961-962.

58 See the matrix in Chapter 2.

59 See Chapter 10.

was offensive. The latter responded in the negative. 'Yet', Vespasian answered, 'it's made from urine' [Atqui ... e lotio est].[60]

Though Titus clearly seems to feel that body products ought not be commercialized, it is difficult to reconstruct whether this is due to his respect for the body (and, clearly, its waste products) or whether he was merely disgusted at this kind of extortionate tax.[61] It appears to be clear that the notion of money as a reward for giving up parts of our bodies seems repulsive, whereas giving up parts of our bodies in exchange for better health care, peace of mind or the approval and well-being of our families appears to be at worst more acceptable and at best worthy of applaud.

In terms of contract law, no substantial difference is made between money paid or property transferred.[62] Where property passes or services are provided for value, the law is indifferent whether this is in exchange for other property or services or for money. The substantial difference seems to be where money is unlawfully appropriated or kept. The court can require that interest be paid in relation to sums where they are not repaid by the time an action for the money has begun.[63] Technically, the difference between being party to a bargain where, upon receipt of a cadaver heart plus lung transplantation, one's own healthy heart is transplanted into another appears to be merely a system of trade-offs. The clear difference made by the law in these contexts is that there must be no commercialization of the bargain.[64] This results in a clear prohibition of sale for money, even despite the admissibility of giving an organ to strangers in the Human Tissue Act 2004. It does not, however, give sufficient weight to the positive effects believed by some to be the result of compensated organ donation. Becker and Elias have concluded that a regulated system of financial compensation for organ giving increases the number of organs on supply whilst having no appreciable effect on the price of organ transplantation.[65] They also criticize the current system's failure to take into

60 Suetonius (1979). *Divus Vespasianus*. Cambridge MA: Harvard University Press, at 23.2, cited in DiPiero, T. (1988). Buying into fiction. Diacritics, 18(2), 2-14 at p. 2.

61 Some sources point to the latter: Choi, J.P. and Thum, M. (2004). The Economics of Repeated Extortion. *The RAND Journal of Economics*, 35(2), 203-233, at p. 219.

62 See, e.g. *Scott v. Brown* [1892] 2 QB 724 where it was held that money paid or property transferred under an illegal contract could not be recovered.

63 See, e.g. Supreme Court Act 1981, s. 35A; Part 40, Rule 8, Civil Procedure Rules.

64 Some sources suggest that the reason might be that when it comes to money, every person involved has an inherent conflict of interest. See, e.g. the submission of Andrew Lansley during the reading of the Human Tissue Bill, MP for South Cambridgeshire in: Standing Committee G, House of Commons, 3.2.2003, column 148 (Hansard).

65 Becker, G.S. and Elias, J.J. 2003. Introducing Incentives in the Market for Live and Cadaveric Organ Donation. University of Chicago, 16 May 2003, available at http://home.uchicago.edu/~gbecker/MarketforLiveandCadavericOrgan.Donations_Becker_Elias.pdf, accessed 6 September 2009. Becker and Elias conclude that a price of US$15,200 per kidney

account the fact that an exchange for money may well be ethically more acceptable than a free exchange following emotional pressure exerted by relatives.[66]

Discussion

It appears evident that a number of variables need to be given in order to establish that a certain activity is legally admissible, such as voluntariness, ability to consent to the activity and the lawfulness of the activity itself. There is a certain kind of overlap with notions of what may or may not be morally acceptable, but certainly no one hundred per cent match of these two spheres. In particular, the law would not be unable to encompass notions of remuneration in relation to human tissue whilst this is generally deemed to be morally questionable.

Conclusion

This part must inevitably end with a criticism. After investigating the different mechanisms at our disposal to define and defend entitlements abstractly, the common law approaches of the past were outlined. Almost exactly 90 years passed between the two leading cases in relation to the question of ownership in body parts, *Doodeward v. Spence* and *R v. Kelly*, and it is safe to say that biomedical reality has made giant steps in those 90 years. From the development of organ transplantation to the use of the human body as a repository of information and material which helps us understand some of yesterday's and today's most devastating diseases, the human body has become a priceless resource of material. This material is doubtless used in the same way that other commodities are used in the market. Blood is traded, human growth hormone is sold, and bones are bought and made into implants. Art exhibitions filled with plastinated human bodies generate phenomenal income. Life has, therefore, changed and so has public perception. The outrage felt at the first organ transplantation has given way to a disinterested acquiescence to the everyday transfer of hearts and lungs from one person to another. On the other hand, the disinterested and reverential acquiescence to the paternalistic conduct of physicians and researchers has given way to the enabled, educated and easily outraged purchaser of medical services. The law should have at least tried to keep pace with these developments and it is evident that it has not.

R v. Kelly is only one illustration of this. The Human Tissue Act 2004, as a result of the outrage caused by the Alder Hey affair and similar incidents, shows

is reasonable in relation to the average cost of a transplantation in the US of US$160,000 (at pp. 10, 13). The cost of the transplantation would increase by less than ten per cent in exchange for a transition from zero market elasticity to full market elasticity (at p. 15).

66 Becker and Elias 2003, at p. 8.

– and so does the section of this text above – that many, if not all, of the normative attempts made today in relation to this topic follow either one of two disappointing motives. They are either intended to provide a flak jacket against liability and public relations disasters (such as the Human Tissue Act) or they are toothless instruments of information networking and quality control which do nothing to solve the intricate problems of the day (such as the EU's regulatory attempts) as they delegate questions of consent.

In other settings, the law has denied the existence of property and the associated civil remedies where an aspect of financial compensation for the source is concerned. In the same breath it has acknowledged the existence of property for the *scintilla* necessary to assign the property as a gift or donation to medical research or therapeutic application. All criminal law perspectives of property which flow from the acknowledgment of this *scintilla* are, absurdly, simultaneously denied and only come to effect where the assignee has then expended, possibly quite superficial, artful work. At this point, the rules of *Doodeward v. Spence* and *R. v. Kelly* can be said to be applicable again: the assignee having expended this work has made it into property: his property. It can now be the subject of a disposition for money's worth and to the law of theft.

The reasoning is this: we do not want to give individuals property rights in their bodies or parts thereof because we fear the spectre of exploitation discussed earlier. At the same time we realize that we need their bodies and the parts thereof to progress medical research and help others get well. Whilst the way this legal framework is achieved in terms of twisting – and probably breaking – the law of gifts is questionable, the motive is not. It is one defensible way of achieving a transferability of tissue for research whilst excluding transferability for money or money's worth for the individual him or herself. The flaw of this system becomes eminently apparent when we look at it in terms of the facts of the *Moore* case discussed above: where the taking of the tissue (*appropriation*) is dishonest and the result is a financial gain for the wrongdoer (*pecuniary*), the law has nothing at its disposal to remedy this most undesirable of situations: that of true exploitation, not merely self-exploitation.

In the following, final, part of the text we are going to look at some of the elements of the Law of Equity which may give interesting impulses in terms of resolving just this kind of *Moorean* dilemma.

PART III
Bioequity

Chapter 11
Equity

Introduction

The previous two chapters have served an important purpose. Initially, it was necessary to identify some of the problems which generally affect the debate on this and similar topics. In particular, we needed to underscore the differences between genuine legal and ethical disagreements and those which merely take place in a terminological dimension. After selecting those issues which played a significant role in the assessment of qualitative differences in terms of procuring human tissue, the data was displayed in a matrix and subsequently assessed on a conceptual level in Part I and in a legal context in Part II.

The outcome very much is that there is a twofold problem: terminology is applied in a flawed and prejudicial fashion and law is applied in a flawed and prejudicial fashion. Human tissue and body products are already being treated in a proprietary fashion and property rights are granted to those who take the tissue but not those who possess the tissue initially. As far as those who possess the tissue initially (the source) are concerned, the law is inconsequential and insufficient in the protection of their interests. It conclusively acknowledges property rights where the legal construct of a donation is to be satisfied and, in the same breath, denies the existence of the very same rights where the legal construct of a contract for sale is contemplated. In *Moore*, *Greenberg* and *Catalona* and the provisions of the Human Tissue Act 2004 we have seen a manifest helplessness on the part of the judiciary and the legislator in framing the issue in a way that it can be resolved in a fair and just manner for all parties involved. In particular – and this is the main criticism – the law as it stands currently misapplies existing property law in order to disenfranchise the source of the material for fear of self-exploitation of the source. This leads to the possibility of exploitation by others, which in turn remains unsanctioned because the initial refusal to grant property rights to the source means that no civil remedies are available and no criminal sanctions in relation to the dishonest appropriation are possible. '"The law", says Hobbes, "is the public conscience"'.[1]

The law, however, is not as inflexible and as blind to reality as it appears in this context. It has in the past evidently managed to adapt and evolve in ways which will seem surprising to most who contemplate them. It is the intention behind this third part of the text to show how the evolution of English law bears a facet which

1 Thomas Hobbes in 'Leviathan', cited in: Munger, R. 1915. A Glance at Equity. *The Yale Law Journal*, 25(1), 42-57, at p. 56.

in the present context may well be eminently useful in resolving the problems we have encountered in the first two parts: that of *epikeia*, or *Equity*. Initially introducing the idea of *epikeia* on a conceptual level, its manifestation as *Equity* in the English legal system will be described. This chapter can, by necessity, not provide a full account of the genesis and workings of the Law of Equity. There are many excellent texts already doing so.[2] A very brief history of the development of Equity and the common law will be followed by an illustration of how Equity has been used in the past to create new property classes which the common law did not know and how these property classes have subsequently filtered into the common law.

Dworkin and Kennedy exclaimed in exasperation that, surely, in an English court, John Moore would have had the assistance of Equity.[3] It is submitted that this observation may well have been right and, following on from this introductory part, a suggestion will be made for a third way in terms of property classes: that of *Bioequity* or *property in biomaterial*. The idea will be set against facts borrowed from the case of *Moore* to demonstrate their workability. This part of the text will culminate in a discussion of the advantages, disadvantages and the potential of Bioequity.

The Concept of *Epikeia*

Epikeia, as the ethical originator of Equity, has its roots in the notion that abstract norms are inherently flawed. The idea of *epikeia* is to give relief in situations where the application of the law leads to a manifestly unfair result because of this abstract character. The kind of systemic unfairness described here is not at all unusual: all legal systems thrive on abstraction. In order to find a comprehensive set of rules regulating everyday conduct, one needs to deal with abstract, general rules which indicate appropriate and inappropriate behaviour in similar situations. The capacity for failure in individual cases is inherent in such a system when the facts lie in a way that the legislator could not foresee. A sound legal system therefore needs to contain mechanisms for 'self-healing', notions of deviating from the strict rule in order to satisfy an overriding requirement for justice in individual cases rather than a dogged adherence to the letter of the law.

The notion of a concept, such as Equity, as a safety valve within the legal system is certainly not unique to the English system. The roots of Equity can be seen in legal philosophical writings from Aristotle via Thomas Aquinas to

2 See, for example, Martin, J. 2005. *Hanbury and Martin: Modern Equity*. London: Sweet & Maxwell; and Watt, G. 2006. *Trusts and Equity*. Oxford: Oxford University Press.

3 See Chapter 12.

Blackstone.[4] The idea behind it is simply that the abstract nature of laws cannot, by necessity, foresee all individual cases and provide for justice in these individual cases. Aristotle writes:

> Hence whenever the law makes a universal rule, but in this particular case what happens violates the [intended scope of] the universal rule, here the legislator falls short, and has made an error by making an unconditional rule. Then it is correct to rectify the deficiency; this is what the legislator would have said himself if he had been present there and what he would prescribed, had he known, in his legislation.[5]

The aim is, therefore, to give effect to the presumed intention of the legislator by means of substituting positive law for a decision based on fairness. It is, in its objective, a similar mechanism to the *mischief rule* in statutory interpretation in that the system intends to give coherence to what the legislator would have wished to achieve had he envisaged this particular situation. Over and beyond the uncertainty of the court's choice of mechanism in statutory interpretation, the Law of Equity seeks to establish sets of rules which are certain and can be relied on to unfold the normative character of precedent, in keeping with the concept of Common Law traditions.[6] These systems of rules, overriding the strict application of general law, were accorded special status because of their specific reference to moral justice.

> The law of God or of nature or of reason must be obeyed; and these laws require, and, through the agency of conscience, enable abstract justice to be done in each individual case, even at the cost of dispensing (if necessary) with the law of the state.[7]

As will be seen below, the workings of Equity experienced a distinct shift away from the notions of Canon law to an adherence to principles of natural justice in the wake of Henry VIII's reformation of England. The overlap between Canon law and the rules of natural justice was, however, sizeable. We can find evidence of Equity's derivation from *epikeia* in the writings of Thomas Aquinas:

---

4 See Blackstone, W. 1765. *Commentaries on the Laws of England.* Book 3 (On Private Wrongs), Chapter 4 (Of the Public Courts of Common Law and Equity) and Aquinas, T., Leftow, B. et al. 2006. *Summa Theologiae: Questions on God.* Cambridge; New York: Cambridge University Press.

5 Aristotle, Dirlmeier, F. et al. 1969. *Nikomachische Ethik.* Stuttgart: Reclam. Book V (1138a).

6 It should be noted that a codification of equitable doctrine to a certain quality of *lex scripta* occurred very late in the development of Equity.

7 Holdsworth, W. 1915. The Early History of Equity. *Michigan Law Review*, 13(4), 293-301, at p. 295.

> Legislators in framing laws attend to what commonly happens: although if the law be applied to certain cases it will frustrate the equality of justice and be injurious to the common good, which the law has in view. Thus the law requires deposits to be restored, because in the majority of cases this is just. Yet it happens sometimes to be injurious – for instance, if a madman were to put his sword in deposit, and demand its delivery while in a state of madness, or if a man were to seek the return of his deposit in order to fight against his country. *On these and like cases it is bad to follow the law, and it is good to set aside the letter of the law and to follow the dictates of justice and the common good. This is the object of 'epikeia' which we call Equity.*[8]

Equity has many faces and mechanisms such as doctrines of public morals, decency and public interest, which serve to unhinge the law where it threatens to procure undesirable results. The Law of Equity in the English and Welsh legal system has – over the years – developed into more than an individual mechanism, however. In the following section, a brief overview of some of the main issues related to *epikeia* and Equity in the English legal system will be given before we turn to a detailed account of the evolution of Equity.

Epikeia's transition to Equity: Distinctions between *Common Law*, *common law* and *Equity*

> the Chancery, the Pretorian power for mitigating the rigor of the common law in case of extremity by the conscience of a good man.[9]

The legal systems generally referred to as *Common Law Systems* all have their roots in the English legal system. One of the aspects of this common heritage is a facet which is fairly unknown to outsiders (and possibly also to numerous insiders): the term *Common Law system* itself is misleading. Within these systems,[10] two distinct legal systems coexist: the common law and the law of Equity.[11] Common Law, in this context, therefore describes the general set of norms and regulations making up the legal system of England and Wales. It therefore has a number of different meanings, depending on its context. In its distinction as set against statute law, custom and royal prerogative, common law has denoted, since the time of Edward I (b. 1239, d 1307, r. 1272-1307) that part of the law which is not enacted, particularly the decisions recorded in precedent. Where the term is set

8 Aquinas, T., Leftow, B. et al. 2006.

9 Sir Francis Bacon, cited in: Munger 1915, at p. 50.

10 At least within some of them; not all have retained the distinction.

11 It is worth noting that, whilst the influence of the Law of Equity has been immense in all common law jurisdictions, it only applies in the form argued here in England and Wales.

side by side with the notion of Equity, common law describes the principles of English law developed in the common law courts as opposed to those developed in the courts of the chancery, admiralty and ecclesiasy.[12] The *Law of Equity*, on the other hand, is a body of rules and regulations which has developed largely independently and has a very special function: to redress injustice in cases such as the ones described above. Initially developed by the *Curia Regis* to provide relief where the common law failed to do so and developed by a long line of active Chancellors, the principles of the Law of Equity disembogued into a fully fledged legal system within the legal system.[13]

Equity's institutional justification, being enshrined in the function of the king and his court,[14] stems from fundamental notions of the duties and prerogatives of the sovereign:[15]

> [...] the original justification of the right of equitable interference, the supreme duty of the king to secure justice to all, as carried out by the royal prerogative, continued as the chief justification of equitable interference [...].[16]

The king had supreme authority to overrule the findings of his courts of law and exercised this authority in order to achieve justice in individual cases: '[...] it falls within the function of the equity court to enforce the rules of reason and of conscience'.[17]

Common law and Equity coexist, more or less peacefully within the English legal system. In cases of conflict between the common law and Equity, Equity prevails. The law of Equity, the common law's virtuous twin, can be described as a mechanism of self-healing. In cases where the strict application of the common law leads to manifestly unfair – and thus undesirable – results, the Law of Equity steps in as a counterweight and takes control, based on the superiority of its moral motivation.

> Thus, in Roman legal history praetorian or equitable law overcame the strict law of the Twelve Tables, which supposedly remained invulnerable and dominant. In English legal history Equity overcame the strict Common Law, which supposedly remained dominant. [...] in both instances, the hegemony of negative Equity was

---

12 The description of the distinction of the term Common Law can be found in Hood Phillips, O. and Hudson, A.H. 1988. *O. Hood Phillips First Book of English Law*. London: Sweet & Maxwell, at p. 9.

13 Hood Phillips and Hudson 1988, at pp. 12-13.

14 For the purposes of this discussion, the male version 'king' tends to be used.

15 The same basis which grants the sovereign the right to bounty: to pardon convicted criminals.

16 Adams, G. 1917. The Continuity of English Equity. *The Yale Law Journal*, 26(7), 550-563 at pp. 558-559.

17 Adams 1917, at p. 560.

> justified on ideological grounds, which for historical reasons were regarded as hierarchically superior to the positive law.[18]

The Roman Law's praetor was, in the English legal system, the Chancellor: the functionary who developed Equity, eventually took on predecessors' rules and added his own.[19] The specific significance of Equity in this context is that it can be used to go diametrically against the common law in order to achieve what the common law cannot achieve: justice in keeping with the common good, natural law and the individual's moral entitlements. Whilst the Law of Equity is an add-on to the common law, fixing its deficiencies but more or less unable to stand on its own,[20] its contributions to the English and Welsh legal system have been nothing short of superb, including *trusts*, *restrictive covenants*, *redemption* and its range of formidable remedies.[21] Before turning to these contributions in and directing them at our dilemma, an outline of the evolution of Equity in England and Wales is helpful to understand Equity's place in the legal system.

A History of Equity in England

Recent developments of Equity in England are well documented and largely undisputed. Prior to the Judicature Acts of the late nineteenth century, however, the structural development of Equity is subject to some disagreement. It appears from the literature that, whilst the facts themselves do not seem to be in dispute, the interpretation of these facts split scholars into two possible categories: those who feel that the development of early Equity was *discontinuous* and those who feel it was *continuous*. In the following, the two different views will be presented in outline. The developments of the nineteenth century will follow on in a third section before a conclusion is drawn.

Discontinuous Evolution

Holdsworth describes that the development of the Law of Equity can be distinguished from that of the common law in that the common law developed continuously whereas the Law of Equity did not.[22] What is meant here is the fact that whilst both systems have common roots in the customary law and natural

---

18 Franklin, M. 1951. A New Conception of the Relation between Law and Equity. *Philosophy and Phenomenological Research*, 11(4), 474-488 at p. 474.

19 Austin, J. 2005. *Lectures on Jurisprudence, Or, the Philosophy of Positive Law*. New Jersey: The Lawbook Exchange, at pp. 615-616.

20 Hood Phillips and Hudson 1988, at pp. 12-13.

21 Which will be discussed in more detail below.

22 Holdsworth, W.S. 1915. The Early History of Equity. *Michigan Law Review,* 13(4), 293-301 at p. 293.

justice dispensed by the common law courts after the Norman Conquest in 1066, the Law of Equity has broken away from the rest of the legal system on a number of occasions and during these breaks renewed and reinvented itself and has thus failed to retain continuity.

Tradition has it that English Equity then came into its prime as a product of the crusades in the twelfth century.[23] Crusaders would convey their feudal estates to trusted friends in order to circumnavigate highly detrimental taxes in the event of their death during the crusade. The understanding would have been that the trusted friend manages the land during the crusader's absence and makes sure that the family was well looked after from the proceeds of the estate. In the event of the crusader's death, the land was to be conveyed to an appropriate person in the family of the knight or continuously held 'on trust' for them. Upon the safe return of the knight from the Holy Land, the property was to be conveyed back to him. The idea was to avoid losing part of the estate in inheritance tax if the knight should die during the crusade, and therefore to get around the statutory provisions to that effect. The aim was therefore explicitly to circumnavigate the law, overriding its provisions by superimposing moral obligations on a friend. The common law only recognized the transfer of property from the crusader to the trusted friend. The moral obligation on the friend to comply with the crusader's wishes at a later stage was in no way legally binding and, so the tale has it, more often than not, knights returned from the crusades to find their estates squandered and a trusted friend unwilling to convey the property back to the original owner. The common law sided with the friend (who was by now presumably no longer trusted). The promise to convey the estate back to the crusader was therefore not held to be binding.[24] The outcome of all of this was, of course, an incredible injustice which the common law did nothing to mend as it simply could not.[25] The only way to seek redress for this injustice was to petition the king to overturn the common law in each individual case and decide according to his conscience. These decisions following petitions to the king would be taken, in general, by the King's Council, the *Curia Regis*.[26] The King encouraged such petitions actively, particularly in cases involving high-profile land disputes between gentry and the Crown, in order to further his authority and extend his control of the fragmented country. Holdsworth sees this as the first break, or phase, in the development of Equity.[27]

Such distinct problems giving rise to equitable intervention, often used to explain the emergence of Equity as an autonomous jurisdiction, are not, however, the most plausible evolutionary explanation. A more feasible exegesis of the evolution of Equity is achieved by viewing the very slow and gradual change as

---

23 Worthington 2006, at p. 63.

24 Worthington 2006, at pp. 63-64.

25 Compare, in this context, the incredible injustice done to Moore where the law also failed to intervene.

26 Cf. Hoppe 2008, pp. 57-59.

27 Holdsworth 1915, at p. 249.

Royal petitions were the plaintiff's only possible response to an unsatisfactory rigidity of the common law. Towards the end of the thirteenth century, the common law had in all of its procedural facets started to become enormously inflexible.[28] A finite number of writs had been fixed by the Provisions of Oxford in 1258 and a rigid system of law had emerged.[29] Failure to use these writs accurately, and choose the right one, would lead to a failure of the claim on procedural grounds.[30] As described above, here too the only way to prevent the enforcement of a common law judgment would be to petition the *Curia Regis* to rectify the injustices perpetrated by failures of this inflexible system. These petitions would later be directed at the Lord Chancellor, the King's spiritual advisor, who initially considered the petitions alone[31] and later established the Court of Chancery. This delegation from direct decisions by the monarch, to decisions made by the *Curia* in its large or small constitution to decisions reached by an individual, sitting as the Court of Chancery, is seen as a second break in the continuous development of Equity.

The common law courts continued in much the same way as before and, through the sheer number of petitions directed at the *Curia*, two systems developed. These two systems operated side by side, with Equity intended to have '*exclusive jurisdiction*' in cases where the common law saw no rights, '*concurrent jurisdiction*' where the common law saw rights but provided no relief and '*auxiliary jurisdiction*' where new procedures were required to strengthen available remedies. A succession of chancellors built an impressive reserve of rules and instruments which were applied in individual cases, in particular a number of doctrines which underscore the elements of fairness and justice (such as '*he who seeks Equity must come with clean hands*', meaning that a wrongdoer cannot rely on the protection of Equity; 'Equity looks on that as done which ought to be done',[32] Equity presumes that the parties act in accordance with principles of fairness and assumes that ordinarily expectable acts are done, even before they actually are). In the first half of the sixteenth century, the long line of ecclesiastic Lord Chancellors broke with the end of the term of office of Cardinal Wolsey in 1529[33] and, with Sir Thomas

28 Holdsworth argued that this hardening of the common law did not come about until the late fourteenth, early fifteenth century. See Holdsworth 1915, at p. 294.

29 In 1258 a number of powerful barons assembled at Oxford to effectively take power from the monarch (Henry III) and give it to Parliament. During the course of these reforms, they decreed that no new forms of writ could be created, essentially rendering the courts powerless in situations where the common law procured unfair results. Maddicott, J.R. 1996. *Simon de Montfort*. Cambridge: Cambridge University Press, at p. 158.

30 von Bernstorff, C. 2000. *Einführung in das Englische Recht*. Munich: C.H. Beck, at p. 5.

31 'As early as 1349, under Edward II., the Chancellor was holding court alone'. Munger 1915, at p. 49.

32 As an illustration, see *Walsh v. Lonsdale* (1882) 21 Ch.D. 9 where the courts held that an agreement to execute a deed for property was held to be specifically enforceable in Equity.

33 He died a year later, under a charge of treason. See Gairdner, J. 1899. The Fall of Cardinal Wolsey. *Transactions of the Royal Historical Society*, 13, 75-102.

More, a lawyer took over as chancellor. This represents the third break in the continuity of Equity: rules of Canon law were disposed of and replaced by notions of natural justice. The lack of codification during the reign of the Church in the Chancery was subsequently remedied by extensive scripture from 1529 onwards and, it is argued, none of the previous precent were retained: on the one hand for lack of codification by the Church and on the other for lack of comprehension from the side of the lawyer Chancellors.

Continuous Development

Another interpretation of the evolution of Equity is that of a continuous evolution throughout the lifetime of the English legal system. Munger persuasively gives a structure for his assessment of this kind of development: 'Legal history regarded as a whole is a history of institutions as well as of doctrines'.[34]

The institution we need to focus our attention on for the purposes of the assessment of the development of Equity is merely the King's Council, the *Curia Regis*, which may have changed in terms of name, composition and jurisdiction over the years but the basis has remained the same. We will look initially at the different stages of development of the *Curia* up to today before considering questions of continuity of doctrine.

From the middle of the eleventh century, the Norman Conquest, onwards, justice was principally dispensed by the Crown. The King's Council, and in particular the Lord Chancellor decided individual petitions on the basis of the common law and principles of *epikeia* or natural justice. Whilst the previously existing doctrines of the law of the land were wisely left unchanged by the conquerors, the influence of Roman law was a feature of the control wielded by the Chancellor as a high representative of the Catholic Church.

> We see the early Chancellors, Churchmen all of them, not lawyers, adopting sometime precepts of the Roman law in the exercise of their extraordinary jurisdiction [...].[35]

The *Curia* subsequently appointed royal commissioners[36] and itinerant justices[37] who travelled the country to decide disputes in accordance with local customs[38] and natural justice. The dispensation of justice thus flowed directly from the Crown to the people. Adams argues that at this point in time, common law and

34 Adams 1917, at p. 552.

35 Munger 1915, at p. 45.

36 See Adams 1917, at p. 554.

37 See Putnam, B. 1913. 'Early Records of the Justices of the Peace'. *The English Historical Review*, 28(110), 321-330.

38 These could be quite different regionally.

Equity were 'undistinguished and indistinguishable'.[39] Between 1170 and 1300, the courts of common pleas and the itinerant justices – under judicial changes implemented by Henry II – administered both common law and equity as distinct and separate jurisdictions in the same court.[40] Prerogative action on behalf of the Crown still rested with the *Curia Regis*, who supervised the regional courts accordingly. Important and difficult cases remained the exclusive jurisdiction of the *Curia*, which could also be directly petitioned.[41] These regional courts began codifying their procedure and developed it into a strong but inflexible normative framework, the intricate workings of which were inaccessible to the lay person. This led to an organic progress of unsatisfactory decisions inevitably reviewed by the supervisory body, still the *Curia*. Institutionally speaking, the equitable infrastructure simply had not changed. The Chancellor obtained an increasing amount of power from the *Curia Regis* to decide these petitions. He subsequently established a Court of Chancery which dealt with these petitions, still power delegated from the *Curia*. Munger comments that '[u]nder Richard II, we find the Chancery certainly established as a separate court [...]'.[42]

The friction between Chancery and common law became ever more tangible. During the reign of Edward IV, in 1483, the Chancery issued an injunction to restrain a plaintiff from obtaining judgment in the King's Bench. The King's Bench, in particular the Chief Justice,[43] was so incensed at this obvious interference by the Crown that he issued a statement saying that the plaintiffs should obtain judgment and that if the Chancellor were to imprison them for disregard of the injunction, the King's Bench would issue a writ of *habeas corpus* to release them immediately.[44] This fragile state of affairs continued and developed until, as described above, there was indeed an abrupt change in the development of Equity, which nonetheless does not constitute an interruption in terms of continuity. After Cardinal Wolsey and as part of Henry VIII's English Reformation, Sir Thomas More became Lord Chancellor. This was the germ cell of the development of a long line of legally trained chancellors, taking over the office from the previous incumbents, the spiritually and ecclesiastically minded Cardinals and Bishops.

> [...] the common lawyers of the thirteenth and early fourteenth centuries used equity in a wide sense and included under the term such ideas as justice and analogy. The ecclesiastical chancellors, on the other hand, based the equity which they administered upon reason and conscience. Conscience must decide

39 Adams 1917, at p. 550.
40 Adams 1917, at p. 554.
41 Adams 1917, at p. 555.
42 Munger, 1915, at p. 49.
43 William Huse.
44 Munger 1915, at p. 45.

> how and when the injustice caused by the generality of the rules of law is to be cured.[45]

Far from representing a Holdsworthian break in the continuity of Equity, the new style of chancellorship led to a codification of the rules and decisions applied in the Court of Chancery. Legally educated Chancellors were immediately recognized as a threat to the autonomy of the common law courts and every decision or injunction (prohibiting the enforcement of a judgment from a common law court) was seen as a direct attack on the judiciary. Much resistance developed amongst the common law judges and some suggested that the decisions of the Chancery should be ignored. Many accused the Chancellor of arbitrariness and of subversiveness.

> The judges charge the chancellor with attempts to subvert the whole law of England, with the practice of substituting conscience for definite rule.[46]

The first legally educated Chancellor, More, attempted to reconcile the Chancery and the common law courts but failed. The tale is reproduced in the biography of Thomas More, written by his son-in-law William Roper. More had his clerk draw up a list of the different causes in which he had to intervene and the decisions he had taken – a testament to the well-documented equitable *lex scripta* which was about to develop under the auspices of the new breed of Chancellor.

> Which done, he invited all the judges to dine with him in the council chamber at Westminster: where after dinner, when he had broken with them what complaints he had heard of his injunctions, and moreover showed them both the number and causes of every one of them, in order so plainly that, upon full debating of these matters, they were all enforced to confess that they, in like case, could have done no otherwise themselves. Then offered he this unto them; that if the justices of every court unto whom the reformation of the rigour of the law, by reason of their office, most specially appertained, would upon reasonable considerations by their own discretions, as they were, as he thought, in conscience bound, mitigate and reform the rigour of the law themselves, there should from thenceforth by him no more injunctions be granted. Whereunto, when they refused to condescend, then, said he unto them, Forasmuch as yourselves, my lords, drive me to the necessity for awarding out injunctions to relieve the people's injury, you cannot hereafter any more justly blame me.[47]

More had offered them Equity as a bounty, literally on a silver platter: if the judges had agreed to his suggestion, and had from that point on implemented the rules

---

45 Holdsworth 1915, at pp. 294-295.

46 Munger 1915, at p. 45.

47 Roper, W. [1626] Singer, S. (ed.) 1822. *The Life of Sir Thomas More*. London: R. Triphook at p. 43. Also cited in another version in Munger (1915), at pp. 53-54.

of Equity in their common law courts, the exclusive jurisdiction of the Chancery and the Chancellor would have ended there and then. Their refusal resulted in friction and conflict for another 300 years. The interim climax of this dispute was the clash between Edward Coke and Sir Francis Bacon at the beginning of the seventeenth century. Coke, a staunch defender of the common law as the 'perfection of reason'[48] had indicated that he would, as Lord Chief Justice, ensure that every injunction issued by the Chancellor would be resisted by the common law courts. Eventually, the conflict had to be decided by the King who came down on the side of the Chancellor – a predictable choice as any removal of power from the Chancellor would, by its direct connection to the power of the *Curia Regis*, mean a diminishing of the power of the Crown.[49]

> The case was referred to the law officers who, under the leadership of [Sir Francis] Bacon, sustained the Chancellor and he in turn was upheld by the King. [...] But scarcely could [James I] act otherwise than in defence of his Chancellor, for in doing so he was defending his own authority.[50]

This led to the final resolution of the conflict: the common law had lost. It resulted in the firm establishment of the Court of Chancery as a law court proper, working alongside the common law courts and overruling or stopping them when necessary. The supremacy of Equity and the superiority of equitable principles had been finally confirmed and fixed in the common law systems.

Recent Developments

The conflict having been more or less settled, matters progressed quietly (given the relative upheaval in English politics in the second half of the seventeenth century). By the second half of the nineteenth century, both systems, that of Common Law and that of Equity, had again become rigid, contradictory and consequently inconsistent; both systems simply worked in an unsatisfactory fashion. Parliament recognized a need for reform and instructed the Judicature Commission to draft appropriate proposals. The Commission concluded that: 'The evils of this double system of judicature and the confusion and conflict of jurisdiction to which it has led, have been long known and acknowledged'.[51]

One result were the Judicature Acts of 1873 and 1875 which represent a notable reform of court procedure. They removed the separate equitable court structure of the Chancery and created a joint system, compelling the common law courts to

48 Munger 1915, at p. 45.

49 Holdsworth 1915, at p. 297.

50 Munger 1915, at p. 46.

51 Judicature Commission. Need for Further Reform: First Report of the Judicature Commission (1868-1874). Reprinted in: Douglas, D., Young, G. and Handcock, W. (eds) 1996 *English Historical Documents*. London: Routledge, at p. 534.

apply both Common Law and Equity and stipulating that, in cases of conflict, the Law of Equity prevailed.[52] Sir Thomas Moore's idea for reconciliation, amicably presented over a dinner to the judges of the common law courts three hundred years previously, was finally made into a statutory reality by Parliament. Munger comments: 'In all this long history of development there is no more significant thing in modern times, than the English Judicature Act and the abolition it carried of all distinction in form between law and equity'.[53]

The Law of Equity had, in the course of 800 years, developed strong normative concepts based on what is fair, just and reasonable and these were to now be applied in every case in every court in the country without a need to petition the Chancery separately.[54] It still took a good century for the system to recover from the forced fusion.

> The innate conservatism of English lawyers may have made them slow to recognise that by the Supreme Court of Judicature Act 1873, the two systems of substantive and adjectival Law formerly administered by the courts of law and Courts of Chancery [...] were fused.[55]

The provisions of the Judicature Acts are now contained in the text of the Supreme Court of Judicature Act 1981 and still have validity. Equity still has superiority over the provisions of the common law:

> Subject to the provisions of this or any other Act, every court exercising jurisdiction in England or Wales in any civil cause or matter shall continue to administer law and Equity on the basis that, wherever there is any conflict or variance between the rules of Equity and the rules of the Common Law with reference to the same matter, *the rules of Equity shall prevail*.[56]

---

52 Section 25, Supreme Court of Judicature Act 1873.

53 Munger 1915, at p. 44.

54 See *Creswell v. Potter* [1978] 1 WLR 255 at 257 (per Megarry J): '[...] it is for the defendant to prove that the transaction was fair, just and reasonable'.

55 Lord Diplock in *United Scientific Holdings Ltd. v. Burnley BC* [1978] AC 904, at p. 925, quoted in Akuffo, K. 2006. Equity in Colonial West Africa: A Paradigm of Juridical Dislocation. *Journal of African Law*, 50(2), 132-144, at p. 133.

56 Section 49(1), Supreme Courts Act 1981 (my emphasis). Similar rules can be found in the Law and Equity Act 1996 (British Columbia, Canada) and the Judicature Act 2000 (Alberta, Canada). Charity law in Malaysia still applies Equity over Common Law in cases of conflict. See George, M. 2001. An Overview of Issues in Charity Litigation in Malaysia. *International Journal of Not-for-Profit Law*, 4(1), available at http://www.icnl.org/knowledge/ijnl/vol4iss1/index.htm, accessed 3 June 2009.

Discussion

This short history of the development of Equity serves two purposes. Initially, it was necessary to put the idea of Equity into a legalistic context. In its ordinary use of the word, it merely denotes 'justice' or 'fairness'. Here, we needed to show that it in fact represents a concrete, solid jurisdiction which has developed organically, if not exactly peacefully, over the last 800 years in England and Wales. Secondly, it was important to show its supremacy in the English legal system. In cases of conflict between common law and Equity, modern-day English courts are required to apply the Law of Equity to achieve a fair and just result. The advantage in our context is evident: the Common Law system provides a range of rules and mechanisms which are superior to the common law and specifically designed to deal with property questions, as we shall see shortly. These mechanisms are not legal fiction but tried and tested in 800 years of litigation. Nonetheless, these principles have so far not been looked at when discussing the question of proprietary treatment of the human body. It is time this is done.

Chapter 12
Developing New Property Classes

Introduction

'Possession is nine tenths of the law', goes the mantra instilled in budding law students from the very start of property law classes. The law of recognizing and enforcing property is of utmost importance in the context of keeping society, based on entitlements, alive. The previous section has shown, with some examples, that Equity has predominantly occupied itself with questions of property: estates adversely possessed by friends with a moral obligation they failed to recognize. Other examples include the moral entitlement of a spouse in the property bought and developed during the course of a marriage in the name of the other spouse – the wife, who gives up her work to classically look after the house and the children enjoyed Equity's full protection in times of divorce. This equitable protection has now filtered into statutory provisions as part of the 1925 property law reform in England and Wales. On the one hand it is inevitable that Equity should concern itself with property questions. On the other, the rules of Equity are eminently suitable for protecting moral entitlements in property or such *choses* as the common law fails to see as property so far: 'It is sufficient to remark that [equity] has directly or indirectly claimed cognizanze of almost every other matter that respects property [...]'.[1]

Jeremy Bentham suggested that property is but a creature of the law, not an object but the expectation of enjoyment of an object.[2] As a formalist legalistic concept, the idea of property can therefore be amended or redefined correspondingly: can the law not, by the stroke of a judge's pen, create a new proprietary entitlement? Whilst the common law firmly adhered to traditional concepts of property, the Law of Equity has been deft to develop new property concepts, often going directly against traditional concepts used by the common law. The common law then inevitably chose to follow Equity and enshrined formerly equitable property concepts in its sources.[3] Where the common law does not do so, Equity usually provides a range of formidable remedies to achieve what is just and fair, potentially

1 Zephaniah Swift, cited in: Munger 1915, at p. 49.

2 Bentham, J. 1843. *Principles of the Civil Code. The Works of Jeremy Bentham*. London: J. Bowring. Chapter 8: On Property.

3 Such as in section 1 of the Law of Property Act 1925 (legal estates and equitable interests) or the recognition of intangible property rights, or the transferability of debt. The common law was, for a long time, struggling to come to terms with proprietary interests in ideas and works of art. See *Millar v. Taylor* (1769) 4 Burr. 2303 and *Donaldson v. Beckett*

going entirely against the grain of the common law. Adams states that '[...] the remedies provided are an interference with the ordinary system of justice'.[4]

One of the remedies will be illustrated when looking at a possible equitable solution to Moore's dilemma below. Despite such remedies certainly being a gross interference in the administration of the common law, this is simply the nature of Equity. It is merely a mechanism for helping the common law on its way in terms of encompassing the latest developments in society without the impetus of parliamentary legislation. In the following, we will criticize the dogged inflexibility of the common law before showing the flexibility of the appropriate remedy in Equity.

The Dilemma of Stare Decisis

> In the development of our law, two principles have striven for mastery. The first is for the protection of property; no one can give better title than he himself possesses. The second is for the protection of commercial transactions: the person who takes in good faith and for value without notice should get a better title. The first principle has held sway for a long time, but it has been modified by the common law itself and by statute so as to meet the needs of our times.[5]

Lord Denning, quoted above, is a source to be treated with utmost respect. His ratios, and even his *obiter dicta*, particularly in ground-breaking cases such as *High Trees House*,[6] have developed the law of England and Wales in a way which has not been matched and is unlikely to ever be matched. In this quote he underscores the difficulty encountered in the realm of common law decisions that old decisions must be adhered to in the interests of legal certainty (the doctrine of *stare decisis*). He does advocate the possibility of developing normative proprietary approaches in a fashion which meets 'the needs of our times'. In as far as that interpretation of his statement goes, many if not all would be in accord with him. However, if his statement goes as far as suggesting that one can give better title than one has, we must disagree with Denning. A *bona fide* purchaser for value without notice ('Equity's darling') can receive better title than the purported giver of the title in that the law protects him on the basis of his innocence in the transaction; one can certainly not give better title than one has – this would be against the principles of Equity altogether. In this regard, the common law principle of property cannot

(1774) 4 Burr. 2408 where the House of Lords held that, at common law, a book becomes public property as soon as it is published.

4 Adams 1917, at p. 559.

5 *Bishopsgate Motor Finance Corp. v. Transport Brakes Ltd.* [1949] 1 KB 332, per Denning LJ.

6 *Central London Property Trust Ltd. v. High Trees House Ltd.* [1947] KB 130. [1956] 1 All ER 256.

change.[7] What is to be done then, when the common law has well defined property principles and *stare decisis* is preventing progress? The doctrine is not immune to the intervention of Equity or the progress of society.

> When rights of property have become fixed stare decisis must stand. But precedent must be the servant, not the master of law. There come times when responsibility passes beyond the branch of the legislature.[8]

To satisfy the doctrine of precedent, respect must be paid to *stare decisis* at the same time as maintaining a degree of flexibility to react to changes in public perception. It has been discussed already that much of what needs to be addressed in the biomedical context is a direct result of procedures that have become a possibility where they were impossible before and an ethical assessment of these procedures which goes diametrically against the ethical assessment of the past. In the very same way, the law will have to look at certain entitlements coming into existence where none were before and other entitlements ceasing to exist, where they existed before. Not all that long ago – in historical terms – slaves and married women were the subject of property norms. This is, in most countries and, arguably, in all civilizations, no longer the case.

If we look at certain rights being made into property rights, we can see that it is the question of transferability of a certain right which moves it into the realm of property. If something is not transferable – such as the right to vote – it will not be classed as property. This does not, however, mean that rights which are at one stage regarded as non-transferable, i.e. inalienable, remain in this state forever. Public perception of a certain right may change or pure commercial necessity may make it desirable for a right to be transferable.

Equity as a Solution

Equity can deal with these kinds of questions in a twofold fashion: it can use its *concurrent* jurisdiction and take the bundle of rights which the common law regards as property, pick the sticks in the bundle apart and grant proprietary entitlements in the same thing to more than one individual.

The second way Equity can deal with property is to use its *exclusive* jurisdiction where no common law property interest exists and designate that, which was not property in the eyes of the law, to be equitable property. As an illustration may serve that, in the past, the law regarded debts as non-transferable entitlements. Equity changed this and treated debts as transferable entitlements, contrary to the common law, and thereby created a new proprietary concept.[9] *Choses in*

7 As Equity would intervene, as a shield, protecting the original proprietor.
8 Munger 1915, at p. 56.
9 Worthington 2006, at p. 59.

action (such as debts) and intellectual property were recognized as 'tradeable' entitlements by the law of Equity well before the common law caught up with the idea. This willingness to treat as property that which was not treated as property before neither stops at the human body, nor does it tolerate the generation of profits from ill-gotten property. He who has obtained property by deception can be made to account for all the profit generated from the wrongful use of the property.[10]

A case which is of particular interest in the context of applying the law of Equity to the questions raised by *Moore* is that of *Herring v. Walround:*[11] the defendant was given a loan of Siamese twins in order to exhibit them in his show 'for the life of the twins'. The children died within a month and the defendant had them embalmed and displayed them as a 'monster'[12] in his circus. The twins' father argued, invoking rules of Equity, that this was a wrongful use of the body and succeeded: the plaintiff had to account for all profit generated. In this case, the subject of the claim is quite clear – the Siamese twins. In other cases, and arguably those which involve the largest degree of pecuniary profit, it is no longer easy to put a finger on something and say 'this is what was taken from me'. Where the subject matter of the claim has moved, we need to find it and identify it to recover it or its conversion chattel.

It is unnecessary and inappropriate to criticize the decision from the high horse of our twenty-first century moral perspective. Equity encompassed the fair and just expectations of both parties by seeing that the loan was for the life of the twins. Despite being unenforceable at common law, Equity recognized the agreement and provided a remedy: Walround had to account for all of his profits. This is the action and the remedy referred to above: *tracing in Equity* and *accounting*.

Equity developed the notion of tracing in relation to dealing with delinquent trustees of trust property.[13] The claimant had to (1) show that he was the equitable owner of the property in question and (2) that the defendant who misappropriated the property owed him a *fiduciary relationship*.[14] The claimant can then trace his property in Equity and subsequently claim: 'Tracing is simply the technique for identifying new forms of property that can legitimately be regarded as substitutes for the claimant's initial asset'.[15]

---

10 Because Equity treats the wrongdoer as a trustee for the benefit of the source of the ill-gotten property, the assumption is that it was invested for the benefit of the source and thus the trust property plus the profit are to be the sources. See Worthington (2006), at p. 99.

11 (1682) 22 ER 870; [1681] 2 Chan Cas 110.

12 Terminology used in the judgment.

13 Worthington 2006, at pp. 100-102

14 *Re Diplock's Estate* [1948] Ch 465, confirmed by *Ministry of Health v. Simpson* [1951] AC 251.

15 Worthington 2006, at p. 101.

The technique was developed in a way to dispense with the requirement of all individuals in the tracing chain having to have had a fiduciary duty towards the claimant. By now it was only important for one of the individuals to have had such a duty. Critically, the mechanism of tracing is only an evidentiary process of showing that an initial asset was transformed into a new asset. It does not concern the question whether the claimant's initial entitlement was frustrated by the conversion. Once the tracing chain was established, the claimant thus needed to claim his entitlement in the converted asset. Equity presumed that the individual with a fiduciary duty acted as a trustee and invested the trust property. The conversion is thus seen as the investment of the trust property and the equitable entitlement of the claimant must extend to both the value of the original trust property as well as to the profit generated from the investment.[16]

Bioequity: Developing a New Property Class for Human Material

> To look forward we must look back.[17]

In this section we will outline the case for a new property model in relation to human biological material. In order to do this, we will use the past principles of Equity to create a future property framework.

John Moore based his claim against the defendants[18] on 13 causes of action.[19] The Superior Court only addressed the issues arising from the first allegation, that of the tort of conversion. The assumption was that the remainder of the allegations hinged on the success of the first. The Court of Appeal later directed the Superior Court to address all issues, the allegation of conversion and that of breach of fiduciary duty surviving this second assessment. The Supreme Court finally held that the action for conversion must fail but that there was a breach of disclosure obligations on the part of the physicians. Whilst this gave the impression of justice for Moore, it disenfranchised him in terms of participating in the highly lucrative commercialization of his cells.

---

16 Worthington 2006, at pp. 312-313.

17 Munger 1915, at p. 44.

18 David Golde (his treating physician), The Regents of the University of California, Shirley Quan (a researcher), Genetics Institute Inc. and Sandoz Pharmaceuticals Corporation.

19 (1) The tort of conversion, (2) lack of informed consent, (3) breach of fiduciary duty, (4) fraud and deceit, (5) unjust enrichment, (6) quasi-contract, (7) bad faith breach of the implied covenant of good faith and fair dealing, (8) intentional infliction of emotional distress, (9) negligent misrepresentation, (10) intentional interference with prospective advantageous economic relationships, (11) slander of title, (12) accounting and (13) declaratory relief.

His claim for conversion would have had to satisfy a number of preliminary aspects. Moore would have to prove that (1) he was lawfully in possession of (2) goods and that these goods are (3) permanently lost to him following (4) the defendant's unlawful conduct.

Dworkin and Kennedy exclaimed, quite rightly, in 1993 that had the case of *Moore* happened within the jurisdiction of England and Wales, he would have had the support of Equity.

> In any event, it is likely that an English court would be prepared to employ equitable principles in support of the patient: Moore surely must come somewhere within the equitable principles relating to 'fraud, duress or undue influence' to receive the support of equity. Moore would have the right to avoid the transaction and be free to pursue a conversion action, in addition to any other cause of action that may be available.[20]

Equity's exclusive jurisdiction in this context arises from the fact that there is no appropriate remedy in common law to achieve a fair and justiciable result. 'Equity,' says Holland, 'springs from old rules becoming too narrow, or out of harmony with advancing civilization [...]'.[21] *Stare decisis* with the common law, as outlined above, ought to take priority in cases where the solution provided is appropriate and sufficient. Where this is not the case, we must use Equity to facilitate progress.

'On the one side is made an appeal to progress, on the other to precedent', says Munger.[22] Equity represents progress, common law represents precedent. The common law, due to its clear principle of *stare decisis*, contains more potential for desirable legal certainty. The point is this: as shown above, the Law of Equity has more than once developed new concepts on the basis of its roots: fairness and justice. The common law has then followed these new concepts and taken them in when appropriate. Further, it is simply Equity's duty to intervene in situations such as the one of *Moore*.

> It enabled the equity court to insist that faith should be kept in cases where the common-law courts could not act from lack of some condition which they regarded as essential, as of a formal agreement, or of some other necessary evidence. *It enabled [the equity court] to insist that unjust advantage should not be taken of ignorance or folly; that fraud should not succeed because mere forms were on its side, or because the common law had not provided an exact remedy.*[23]

---

20 Dworkin and Kennedy 1993, at p. 312.

21 Holland, T. 1900. *Elements of Jurisprudence*, at p. 67, cited in: Munger 1915, at p. 48.

22 Munger 1915, at p. 54.

23 Adams 1917, at p. 560 (my emphasis).

Equity protects the fool and the ignorant and recognizes concurrent entitlements, one enjoying stronger protection whilst the other one enjoys the, *prima facie* less complicated, texture of legal ownership. This means that a certain thing can be legally owned by one party whilst the equitable entitlement rests with another. Equity recognizes that the legal owner can use the semblance of outright entitlement to dishonestly divest the property and has developed strategies to protect the person with the equitable entitlement. Applying the ailing legal concept of proprietary interests arising *ex post* (as in the cases of *Moore v. The Regents of the University of California*, *R v. Kelly* and *Doodeward v. Spence*), we acknowledge that Golde and Quan have acquired a legal entitlement in Moore's biological material.

Let us assume that Moore retains the equitable entitlement: Golde and Quan have obtained the material on the condition that they use it to further his health and well-being. They are quasi-trustees of his cells and the information they contain. If they go ahead and sell the material or the information derived from investing the material in research, Sandoz can only be protected from Moore's claim if they were *bona fide* purchasers for value without notice.[24] It is suggested that in the case of intellectual property derived clearly from genetic information, it is prudent and reasonable to expect Sandoz to realize that there is a source involved, whose equitable entitlement has to be waived before the property is free to be used commercially. Had Golde and Quan been straightforward and honest with Moore, he may have waived his entitlement. The illegality of the acquisition results in a number of possible remedies in Equity for Moore. In particular, he may be able to trace his entitlement in Equity, resulting in a full recovery of the unlawful profit accumulated by Golde, Quan, the University of California and Sandoz. It is therefore the illegality of the act which prejudices the accrual of financial benefits to the researchers, not the notion of medical research – the progress of science would continue unshackled if the protagonists only obtain sufficient consent for their actions. This is more than in line with current standards of informed consent in relation to patient autonomy and research subjects' rights.[25]

Using the assessment of tracing and claiming introduced above, we can easily see how it may be argued – terminologically and legally – that Moore had an equitable (moral) interest in his body parts and products. Golde and Quan owed him a fiduciary duty as his physicians – he was, after all, not a willing research participant but for all intents and purposes a patient receiving medical treatment. They misappropriated his body products and invested them in research. The direct causal result was a patent which was licensed to others for considerable profit. Using Equity, Golde and Quan would have had to account to Moore for all of the profits generated from the unlawful acquisition and investment of Moore's equitable interest.

---

24 Even Worthington suggests that these are 'rare people'. Worthington 2006, at p. 65.

25 Even if we are to hold that Moore was a research subject as opposed to a patient, which – I would argue – is difficult.

Despite the somewhat spectacular character of the facts of *Moore* and the possibly naïve, but instructive, legal attempts at resolving them,[26] the ideas we might gather from *Moore* have, it seems, not fully found entry into current law. There is still a situation in which there is an invisible, intangible dividing line between the beneficiary and the trustee, or: between the patient and the physician. The original aim of Equity, to develop and encompass new fields of action coming into existence from an expansion of the complexity of our social life, is suited to resolving these problems.

> The growing complexity of the business life of the community, especially the wide extension of the practice of uses, created new legal needs which equity supplied by corresponding extensions of its fundamental principles, extensions always in harmony with the old though made by the help of doctrines borrowed from without and leading into new and larger fields of action.[27]

Nonetheless, the lessons we still might learn from *Moore* are valuable: if we permit the Law of Equity to intervene in such cases (should they happen in England or Wales) or in modelling possible normative attempts on the virtues shown in the last 800 years in the development of Equity.

Conclusion

The development of the Law of Equity, as outlined above, gives an insight into the workings of the English legal system. Equity, as an overriding principle of justice and fairness – and specialized in questions of property – is intended to intervene in cases where the application of the common law leads to unfair results or is simply insufficient for its purposes. It is not Equity's intention to reinvent property, but to add to that which is already there in the interests of providing for new fields of application.

> Large new fields were opened but they were added to the old, not put in place of them, and both old and new have continued to be diligently cultivated together to the present day.[28]

Since the settlement of conflict between Equity and common law by the introduction of the Judicature Acts, the development of equitable principles has taken on a disciplined and structured manner.[29] Their application in the current context to

---

26 I do acknowledge the benefit of hindsight in this context.

27 Adams 1917, at p. 563.

28 Ibid.

29 See the doctrine of *equitable estoppel*, developed by Denning J, as he was then, in High Trees House. The common law simply had no possibility to enforce the formally

procure a fair and reasonable state of affairs in situations where the appropriation of tissue is clearly illegal seems only appropriate. The common law's current practice of disenfranchising the source of the material, even in situations where the taking was illegal, is inequitable. A consistent application of the law of property, including the Law of Equity, would yield far more desirable results in terms of justice, fairness and legal consistency.

lacking agreement. Denning's *obiter* provided for a distinct amount of certainty in cases where parties sought to renege agreements with formal errors *ex post*.

Chapter 13
Concluding Thoughts

> It is an evil to be compelled to acknowledge a mistake in recent decisions, but it is a greater evil to be compelled to repeat time after time a statement which we, in common with all professions, know is not true [...].[1]

This text has shown a number of things: in the first part, the complexity of the thematic area we are dealing with was outlined and the many different concepts and issues at stake were differentiated. The second part has looked at the legal and ethical status quo of each of the issues identified previously. Finally, the third part has provided an impetus for a possible solution based on equitable proprietary aspects. The result is a different approach to the question of property rights in the human body. Instead of merely outlining traditional common law approaches to the idea, some important aspects were highlighted and lifted from the mass of arguments and notions and then transferred to the setting of developing new property approaches by using a flexible and justice-based equitable approach.

In the first part, the emotionally charged terminology was criticized, as well as the conceptual blending of ideas which leads to a Gordian knot of argumentative lines. To cut this knot, a matrix was deployed to visualize the differences that each nuance makes in debate. This matrix provided the structure for the subsequent analysis of the problem. The remaining chapters of the first part then proceeded to explain the different concepts hiding behind the matrix's columns and rows. The agility of the matrix became apparent when it was illustrated that it is able to differentiate between reproductive tissue and non-reproductive tissue in a considerably more efficient manner than previous approaches. Via the exploration of different tissue types and the uses this tissue may be put to, the investigation focused on large-scale incidents in the recent past, such as the scandal at Alder Hey where a considerable amount of tissue was retained. One of the reasons for the unquestionably reckless conduct of those responsible for the Alder Hey scandal was argued to be the different stance clinicians and pathologists have in relation to human tissue. In particular, the views taken by practitioners on consent issues in this context were looked at and it became clear that consent is largely seen as a legalistic necessity and a wise public relations manoeuvre – a flak jacket against liability – rather than a nucleic feature of medical reality. This part culminates in a criticism of informed consent, the realistic chances of which in clinical reality is questioned and its unaltered application in a research setting doubted. Finally, it addresses a number of different important concepts in order to provide a setting for the second part of the text: a model for the assessment

1 Hamersley J. in *Tingler v. Chamberlain* (1899) 71 Conn. 566, cited in Munger (1915), at p. 55.

and apportionment of entitlements is chosen and applied, notions of ownership versus possession explored, the use of force to dispossess discussed and philosophical viewpoints of property as a bundle of sticks introduced.

The second part opens with a view of normative approaches in the past and a description of the pivotal concept of the autonomous participant (otherwise known as patient or research participant). It goes on to explore the mechanisms used in law to describe and enforce rights and entitlements in criminal and civil law. The notion of inalienability of certain rights is discussed in the context of rights in the human body before turning to the concrete common law position in relation to property in the human body: a distinction is drawn between UK and other common law jurisdictions. The extent and limits of consent are assessed and ideas of proceeding without consent in terms of necessity are detailed. The attention then turns to the question of how the law has dealt with the questions posed here in the past. Notions of dealing with property in corpses, body parts and body products are looked at and the incapacity of the law of theft to criminally sanction obvious moral transgressions is highlighted. As a continuance to the discussion of the incident at Alder Hey in the first part, the next section focused on the genesis of the Human Tissue Act to counter such practices. A detailed analysis of the Act provided an insight into its workings and limitations. An equally detailed analysis of the EU's Human Tissue Directive provides a rounded picture of primary legislative norms in relation to human tissue persuasively in force at this time. Then, three paradigmatic cases from the United States are described and discussed: *Moore*, *Catalona* and *Greenberg*, each serving to illustrate some of the practical issues of a non-consequential application of existing norms, before a look at the case of *Yearworth*, illustrating recent developments. This provides the backdrop to the deployment of the system introduced by means of the matrix – a systematic workup of the law using the same structure: source, consent, impact, motive, type of tissue, appropriation *mens rea* and pecuniarity. In particular, the matrix's last aspect leads on to issues addressed in the penultimate part of this text: Equity.

The third part of the text was intended to achieve two things: first, it needed to provide an outline of the development of Equity which is so far lacking in the contemporary literature. This was necessary to show Equity's supremacy and positioning in the English and Welsh system as well as its underlying rationale, in order to show why it is desirable to use Equity in the context of the problems discussed in the first two parts. Secondly it served as a brief impulse for a different kind of debate of the subject matter: moving away from old-fashioned views of property, it is shown that the Law of Equity has excelled at developing new forms of property concepts when circumstances have required. The same mechanism is deployed in this instance. Initially introducing Equity as a concept, the genesis and historical development of the Law of Equity is described. Then, equitable property concepts are discussed and illustrated in detail and the different types of new property created shown. Looking at the excellent remedies and mechanisms of Equity, in particular in terms of inherent civil financial sanctions in cases of dishonest appropriation,[2] the text

2 In the shape of defendants having to account for all of their profits.

culminates in a discussion of the potential of Equity using the example of the *Moore* case, as discussed further above.

It is evident that the law is wanting in its current state: the spectre of exploitability leads the law to prohibit profiteering *using our own bodies* but at the same time licenses legal and illegal profiteering of *other individuals' bodies*. The classic notion of exploitation is satisfied and from a libertarian stance, the comparably less problematic idea of exploiting ourselves in turn is prohibited. Where physicians take material which is not theirs during the course of lawful activity (such as the splenectomy in *Moore*), they can subsequently invest the material without consent and have no adverse effects to fear. Even where the excision is unlawful, it will carry no civil law consequences – it is simply a balancing exercise between the risks of a criminal conviction for the assault and the possible benefits of generating immense social prestige and profits from research. New legislative approaches, such as the Human Tissue Act 2004 and the European Union's Human Tissue Directive, though controversially debated and often seen as a first step towards an undesirable commodification or propertization of the human body, do no such thing. The Directive declines responsibility by delegating important aspects of the question to domestic law. The Human Tissue Act is merely a response to public outrage and does no more than enshrine existing, fragmented norms in one instrument. Its only two contributions to the debate are the implementation of the requirements of consent in relation to the issues arising from Alder Hey and the introduction of live organ donation without an element of proximity between donor and donee. The common law, with *Doodeward v. Spence* and *R v. Kelly* still stands where it stood one hundred years ago.

The Law of Equity, in turn, provides existing remedies in cases where property is appropriated and invested in a way which the common law does not see fit to provide actions for. It also does not hesitate to recognize property in assets which were previously not property (such as *choses in action* and debts). It is only natural to use the Law of Equity as a starting point for a possible civil law solution to the problem. Criminal law questions, such as the notion of the law of theft in circumstances such as those in the case of *Moore*, will follow Equity: when Equity has convincingly established human tissue and body products as proprietary, this transition will mean that – inevitably – the 'someone else's property' aspect of the law of theft is satisfied. Giving full criminal and civil property protection to the individual whose tissue is in question is an increase in rights and protection of that individual and is as such highly desirable. The best way to achieve such a protection is by moulding the law to the new complexities of society using the mechanism which the law itself foresaw for such a time.

> For when the thing is indefinite the rule is also indefinite, like the leaden rule used in making the Lesbian moulding; the rule adapts itself to the the shape of the stone and is not rigid. And, so too the decree is adapted to the facts.[3]

---

3 Aristotle, 'Nicomachean Ethics', Bk V, § 14 [1137b].

Bibliography

Books

Andrews, L.B. and Nelkin, D. 2001. *Body Bazaar: The Market for Human Tissue in the Biotechnology Age*. New York: Crown Publishers.

Aquinas, T., Leftow, B. et al. 2006. *Summa Theologiae: Questions on God*. Cambridge and New York: Cambridge University Press.

Arens, W. 1980. *The Man-eating Myth: Anthropology and Anthropophagy*. Oxford: Oxford University Press.

Aristotle, Dirlmeier, F. et al. 1969. *Nikomachische Ethik*. Stuttgart: Reclam.

Austin, J. 2005. *Lectures on Jurisprudence, Or, the Philosophy of Positive Law*. New Jersey: The Lawbook Exchange.

Becker, L.C. and Kipnis, K. 1984. *Property: Cases, Concepts, Critiques*. Englewood Cliffs: Prentice-Hall.

Bentham, J., Dumont, E. et al. 1843. *Principles of the Civil Code. The Works of Jeremy Bentham*. London: J. Bowring.

Bergmann, A. 2004. *Der entseelte Patient: Die Moderne Medizin und der Tod*. Berlin: Aufbau-Verlag.

Bernstorff, C. 2000. *Einführung in das Englische Recht*. München: C.H. Beck.

British Medical Association. 2004. *Medical Ethics Today: The BMA's Handbook of Ethics and Law*. London: BMJ Publishing Group.

Chacon, R. and Dye, D. 2007. *The Taking and Displaying of Human Body Parts as Trophies by Amerindians*. New York: Springer.

Deutsch, E. and Spickhoff, A. 2008. *Medizinrecht: Arztrecht, Arzneimittelrecht, Medizinprodukterecht und Transfusionsrecht*. Heidelberg: Springer.

Dickens, C. [1852-3] 2003. *Bleak House*. New York: Signet Classic.

Dickenson, D. 2007. *Property in the Body: Feminist Perspectives*. Cambridge and New York: Cambridge University Press.

Dickenson, D. 2008. *Body Shopping – The Economy Fuelled by Flesh and Blood*. Oxford: One World.

Douglas, D., Young, G. et al. (eds), 1996. *English Historical Documents*. London: Routledge.

Douglas, H. 1973. *Burke and Hare*. London: Robert Hale.

Frost-Knappman, E., Shrager, D.S. et al. 1998. *The Quotable Lawyer*. New York: Checkmark Books.

Giudice, L., Santa, E. and Pool, R. 2007. *Assessing the Medical Risks of Human Oocyte Donation for Stem Cell Research: Workshop Report*. Washington DC: National Academies Press.

Griew, E. 1978. *The Theft Act 1968 and 1978*. London: Sweet & Maxwell.
Harris, J. 1992. *Wonderwoman and Superman: The Ethics of Human Biotechnology*. Oxford: Oxford University Press.
Herring, J. 2006. *Medical Law and Ethics*. Oxford: Oxford University Press.
Hood Phillips, O. and Hudson, A.H. 1988. *A First Book of English Law*. London: Sweet & Maxwell.
Institute of Medicine (US). Committee on Assessing the Medical Risks of Human Oocyte Donation for Stem Cell Research, L. Giudice et al. 2007. *Assessing the Medical Risks of Human Oocyte Donation for Stem Cell Research: Workshop Report*. Washington, DC: National Academies Press.
Kant, I. 1974. *Grundlegung zur Metaphysik der Sitten*. Frankfurt: Suhrkamp.
Kant, I. and Gregor, M.J. 1996. *Practical Philosophy*. Cambridge and New York: Cambridge University Press.
Keller, M. 2008. *Ausgeschlachtet – Die menschliche Leiche als Rohstoff* [Butchered – The Human Body as Raw Material]. Berlin: Econ.
Kemp, D.A.M. and Kemp, M.S. 2000. *The Quantum of Damages in Personal Injury and Fatal Accident Claims*. London: Sweet & Maxwell.
Kumar, P. and Clark, M. 1998. *Clinical Medicine*. Edinburgh: W.B. Saunders.
Lenk, C., Hoppe, N. and Andorno, R. 2007. *Ethics and Law of Intellectual Property: Current Problems in Politics, Science and Technology*. Aldershot: Ashgate.
Maddicott, J.R. 1996. *Simon de Montfort*. Cambridge University Press, Cambridge.
Martin, E.A. 1997. *A Dictionary of Law*. Oxford: Oxford University Press.
Martin, J.E. and Hanbury, H.G. 2005. *Hanbury & Martin Modern Equity*. London: Sweet & Maxwell Ltd.
Mason, J.K. and Laurie, G.T. 2006. *Law and Medical Ethics*. Oxford: Oxford University Press.
Mayberry, M. and Mayberry, J. 2003. *Consent in Clinical Practice*. Oxford: Radcliffe Publishing.
Nozick, R. 1974. *Anarchy, State, and Utopia*. Oxford: Blackwell.
Nwabueze, R.N. 2007. *Biotechnology and the Challenge of Property: Property Rights in Dead Bodies, Body Parts, and Genetic Information*. Aldershot: Ashgate.
Pattinson, S.D. 2006. *Medical Law & Ethics*. London: Sweet & Maxwell Ltd.
Pollock, F. 1896. *A First Book of Jurisprudence for Students of the Common Law*. London and New York: Macmillan.
Rawls, J. 1971. *A Theory of Justice*. Cambridge, MA: Belknap Press of Harvard University Press.
Ritchie, R., Norris, W., Aldous, G., Allen, A., Kennedy, J., Lewers, N., Hickey, N., Petts, T. and Rowley, J. (eds) 2005. *Kemp and Kemp: Personal Injury Law, Practice and Procedure*. London: Sweet & Maxwell.
Roach, M. 2004. *Stiff: The Curious Lives of Human Cadavers*. New York: W.W. Norton and Co.

Roper, W. [1626] and Singer, S. (ed.) 1822. 'The Life of Sir Thomas More'. London: R. Triphook.
Rousseau, J.J. and Cress, D.A. 1992. *Discourse on the Origin of Inequality*. Indianapolis: Hackett Pub. Co.
Schneede, M. 2002. *Mit Haut und Haaren : Der Körper in der Zeitgenössischen Kunst*. Köln: DuMont.
Sperling, D. 2008. *Posthumous Interests: Legal and Ethical Perspectives*. Cambridge: Cambridge University Press.
Treitel, G. 1995. *An Outline of the Law of Contract*. London: Butterworths.
Van den Haag, E. 1975. *Punishing Criminals: Concerning a Very Old and Painful Question*. New York: Basic Books.
Vines, P. 2007. *The Sacred and the Profane: The Role of Property Concepts in Disputes about Post-Mortem Examination*. Sydney: University of New South Wales Faculty of Law Research Series.
Watt, G. 2006. *Trusts and Equity*. Oxford and New York: Oxford University Press.
Wilkinson, S. 2003. *Bodies for Sale: Ethics and Exploitation in the Human Body Trade*. London: Routledge.
Winter, H. 2005. *Trade-offs: An Introduction to Economic Reasoning and Social Issues*. Chicago: University of Chicago Press.
Worthington, S. 2006. *Equity*. Oxford and New York: Oxford University Press.

Book Chapters

Andorno, R. 2007. Population Genetic Databases: A New Challenge to Human Rights. In: *Ethics and Law of Intellectual Property: Current Problems in Politics, Science and Technology*. Edited by C. Lenk, N. Hoppe and R. Andorno. Aldershot: Ashgate, 27-45.
Brownsword, R. 2007. Biobank Governance: Property, Privacy and Consent. In: *Ethics and Law of Intellectual Property: Current Problems in Politics, Science and Technology*. Edited by C. Lenk, N. Hoppe and R. Andorno. Aldershot: Ashgate, 11-25.
Dickenson, D. 2006. Philosophical Assumptions and Presumptions about Trafficking for Prostitution. In: *Trafficking and Women's Rights*. Edited by C. Anker and J. Doemernik. Basingstoke: Palgrave Macmillan, 45-53.
Edelstein, L. 1987. The History of Anatomy in Antiquity – Ancient Medicine. In: *Ancient Medicine*. Edited by O. Temkin and C.L. Temkin. Baltimore: The John Hopkins University Press, 247-301.
Hoppe, N. 2008. Normative Modelle zur Regelung der Kommodifikation Menschlichen Gewebes in Forschung und Therapie: Fragen der Zustimmung aus der Common Law Perspective. In: *Kultur und Bioethik: Eigentum am Eigenen Körper*. Edited by C. Steineck and O. Döring. Baden-Baden: Nomos, 51-53.

Hoppe, N. 2009. Reflections on Entitlements in the Human Body from an Equity Perspective. In: *Altruism Reconsidered: Exploring New Approaches to Property in Human Tissue*. Edited by M. Steinmann, U. Wiesing and P. Sýkora. Aldershot: Ashgate.

Macklin, R. 1996. What Is Wrong with Commodification? In: *New Ways of Making Babies: The Case of Egg Donation*. Edited by C. Cohen. Indianapolis, Indiana: Indiana University Press.

Sawyer, C. 2001. A World Safe for Mortgages? Registering a Scintilla of Doubt. In: *Modern Studies in Property Law*. Edited by E. Cooke. Oxford: Hart Publishing, 201-214.

Journal Articles

Adams, G. 1917. The Continuity of English Equity. *The Yale Law Journal*, 26(7), 550-563.

Akuffo, K. 2006. Equity in Colonial West Africa: A Paradigm of Juridical Dislocation. *Journal of African Law*, 50(2), 132-144.

Anderson, L., Newell, K. and Kilcoyne, J. 1999. 'Selling blood': Characteristics and Motivations of Student Plasma Donors. *Sociological Spectrum*, 19(2), 137-162.

Bell, M.D.D. 2006. The UK Human Tissue Act and Consent: Surrendering a Fundamental Principle to Transplantation Needs? *Journal of Medical Ethics*, 32(5), 283-286.

Bellivier, R. and Noiville, C. 2004. The Commercialisation of Human Biomaterials: What are the Rights of Donors of Biological Material? *Journal of International Biotechnology Law*, 1(3), 89-97.

Berg, J. 2001. Risky Business: Evaluating Oocyte Donation. *American Journal of Bioethics*, 1(4), 18-19.

Bjorkman, B. and Hansson, S.O. 2006. Bodily Rights and Property Rights. *Journal of Medical Ethics*, 32(4), 209-214.

Boyes, M. and Ward, P. 2003. Brain Donation for Schizophrenia Research: Gift, Consent, and Meaning. *Journal of Medical Ethics*, 29(3), 165-168.

Brazier, M. 2002. Retained Organs: Ethics and Humanity. *Legal Studies*, 22(4), 550-569.

Brazier, M. 2003. Organ Retention and Return: Problems of Consent. *Journal of Medical Ethics*, 29(1), 30-33.

Brazier, M. and Miola, J. 2000. Bye-bye Bolam: A Medical Litigation Revolution. *Medical Law Review*, 8(1), 85-114.

Calabres, G. and Melamed, A.D. 1972. Property Rules, Liability Rules, and Inalienability – One View of Cathedral. *Harvard Law Review*, 85(6), 1089-1182.

Choi, J.P. and Thum, M. 2004. The Economics of Repeated Extortion. *The RAND Journal of Economics*, 35(2), 203-233.

Cohen, C.B. 1999. Selling Bits and Pieces of Humans to Make Babies: The Gift of the Magi Revisited. *Journal of Medicine and Philosophy*, 24(3), 288-306.
Curcio, C.A. (Research Tissue Acquisition Working Group) 2006. Declining Availability of Human Eye Tissues for Research. *Investigative Ophthalmology & Visual Science*, 47(7), 2747-2749.
de Castro, L. 2003. Commodification and Exploitation: Arguments in Favour of Compensated Organ Donation. *Journal of Medical Ethics*, 29(3), 142-146.
Dewar, S. and Boddington, P. 2004. Returning to the Alder Hey Report and Its Reporting: Addressing Confusions and Improving Inquiries. *Journal of Medical Ethics*, 30(5), 463-469.
Dickson, D. 2002. Human Tissue Samples More Difficult to Obtain for Academics. *Nature Medicine*, 8(6), 543-543.
DiPiero, T. 1988. Buying into fiction. *Diacritics*, 18(2), 2-14.
Dworkin, G. and Boddington, P. 1997. Should There Be Property Rights in Genes? *Philosophical Transactions of the Royal Society of London Series B-Biological Sciences*, 352(1357), 1077-1086.
Dworkin, G. and Kennedy, I. 1993. Human Tissue: Rights in the Body and Its Parts. *Medical Law Review*, 1(3), 291-319.
Erin, C.A. and Harris, J. 2003. An Ethical Market in Human Organs. *Journal of Medical Ethics*, 29(3), 137-138.
Fox, D. 2008. Paying for Particulars in People-to-be: Commercialisation, Commodification and Commensurability in Human Reproduction. *Journal of Medical Ethics*, 34(3), 162-166.
Franklin, M. 1951. A New Conception of the Relation between Law and Equity. *Philosophy and Phenomenological Research*, 11(4), 474-488.
Friedman, E.A. and Friedman, A.L. 2006. Payment for Donor Kidneys: Pros and Cons. *Kidney International*, 69, 960-962.
Gairdner, J. 1899. The Fall of Cardinal Wolsey. *Transactions of the Royal Historical Society*, 13, 75-102.
Gassner, U.M. 2007. Legal Aspects of Tissue Banking. *Pathobiology*, 74(4), 270-274.
George, M. 2001. An Overview of Issues in Charity Litigation in Malaysia. *International Journal of Not-for-profit Law*, 4(1).
Gerrand, N. 1999. The Misuse of Kant in the Debate about a Market for Human Body Parts. *Journal of Applied Philosophy*, 16(1), 59-67.
Goff, R. 1995. A Matter of Life and Death. *Medical Law Review*, 3(1), 1-21.
Harris, J. 2002. Law and Regulation of Retained Organs: The Ethical Issues. *Legal Studies*, 22(4), 527-549.
Herring, J. and P. Chau 2007. My Body, Your Body, Our Bodies. *Medical Law Review*, 15(1), 34-61.
Hilden, J. 2008. A Contractarian View of Animal Rights: Insuring against the Possibility of Being a Non-Human Animal. *Animal Law Review*, 14(1).
Hoffenberg, R. 2001. Christiaan Barnard: His First Transplants and Their Impact on Concepts of Death. *British Medical Journal*, 323(7327), 1478-1480.

Holdsworth, W. 1915. The Early History of Equity. *Michigan Law Review*, 13(4), 293-301.

Jamrozik, K. 2000. The Case for a New System for Oversight of Research on Human Subjects. *Journal of Medical Ethics*, 26(5), 334-339.

Jones, M. 1999. Informed Consent and Other Fairy Stories. *Medical Law Review*, 7(2), 103-134.

Jones, M.M. and Bayer, R. 2007. Paternalism and Its Discontents: Motorcycle Helmet Laws, Libertarian Values, and Public Health. *American Journal of Public Health*, 97(2), 208-217.

Kaul, R., Gao, G., Aloya, M., Balamurugan, K., Petrosky, A., Michals, K. and Matalon, R. 1994. Canavan Disease: Mutations among Jewish and Non-Jewish Patients. *American Journal of Human Genetics*, 55(1), 34-41.

Kerridge, I.H., Saul, P., Lowe, M., McPhee, J. and Williams, D. 2002. Death, Dying and Donation: Organ Transplantation and the Diagnosis of Death. *Journal of Medical Ethics*, 28, 89-94.

Laffitte, E. and Revuz, J. 2004. Thalidomide: An Old Drug with New Clinical Applications. *Expert Opinion on Drug Safety*, 3(1), 47-56.

Lewis, T. 2002. Human Earrings, Human Rights and Public Decency. *Entertainment Law*, 1, 50-71.

Liddell, K. and Hall, A. 2005. Beyond Bristol and Alder Hey: The Future Regulation of Human Tissue. *Medical Law Review*, 13(2), 170-223.

Loff, B. 2000. Melbourne – Informed Consent for Tissue Retention Discussed in Australia. *Lancet*, 356(9242), 1663-1663.

McGovern, T.F. 2002. Flawed Proposal for Universal Conscription of Cadaveric Organs Neglects Moral, Long-term, and Societal Implications. *American Journal of Kidney Diseases*, 39(3), 609-610.

McHale, J. 2000. Waste, Ownership and Bodily Products. *Health Care Analysis*, 8(2), 123-135.

Merle, J. 2000. A Kantian Argument for a Duty to Donate One's Own Organs. A Reply to Nicole Gerrand. *Journal of Applied Philosophy*, 17(1), 93-101.

Merz, B. 1990. Biotechnology: Spleen Rights. *The Economist*, 30.

Miah, A. 2004. The Public Autopsy: Somewhere between Art, Education, and Entertainment. *Journal of Medical Ethics*, 30(6), 576-579.

Morrison, D. 2005. A Holistic Approach to Clinical and Research Decision-making: Lessons from the UK Organ-retention Scandals. *Medical Law Review*, 13(1), 45-79.

Moser-Jones, M. and Bayer, R. 2007. Paternalism and its Discontents: Motorcycle Helmet Laws, Libertarian Values, and Public Health. *American Journal of Public Health*, 97(2), 208-217.

Munger, R. 1915. A Glance at Equity. *The Yale Law Journal*, 25(1), 42-57.

Munzer, S. 1993. Kant and Property Rights in Body Parts. *Canadian Journal of Law and Jurisprudence*, 6(2), 319-341.

Nwabueze, R. 2008. Donated Organs, Property Rights and the Remedial Quagmire. *Medical Law Review*. Doi:10.1093/medlaw/fwn004. 15 April 2008 at p. 20.

O'Neill, O. 2003. Some Limits of Informed Consent. *Journal of Medical Ethics*, 29, 4-7.

Plant, R. 1977. Gifts, Exchanges and Political Economy of Health Care. *Journal of Medical Ethics*, 3(4), 166-173.

Price, D. 2003. From Cosmos and Damian to Van Velzen: The Human Tissue Saga Continues. *Medical Law Review*, 11(1), 1-47.

Putnam, B. 1913. Early Records of the Justices of the Peace. *The English Historical Review*, 28(110), 321-330.

Radcliffe Richards, J. 2003. Commentary: An Ethical Market in Human Organs. *Journal of Medical Ethics*, 29(3), 139-140.

Rocha, J. 1994. Thalidomide Given to Women in Brazil. *British Medical Journal*, 308(6936), 1061-1061.

Savulescu, J. 2003. Is the Sale of Body Parts Wrong? (Reprinted from Australian Medicine, vol 14, 2002). *Journal of Medical Ethics*, 29(3), 138-139.

Silingardi, M., Iotti, M. et al. 2004. Thalidomide, Deep Venous Thrombosis and Vasculitis. *Journal of Thrombosis and Haemostasis*, 2(11), 2062-2063.

Smith, B. and Zaibert, L. 2001. The Metaphysics of Real Estate. *Topoi-an International Review of Philosophy*, 20(2), 161-172.

Spital, A. 2003. Conscription of Cadaveric Organs for Transplantation: Neglected Again. *Kennedy Institute of Ethics Journal*, 13(2), 169-174.

Spital, A. 2005. Conscription of Cadaveric Organs for Transplantation: A Stimulating Idea Whose Time Has Not Yet Come. *Cambridge Quarterly of Healthcare Ethics*, 14(1), 107-112.

Spital, A. 2005. Conscription of Cadaveric Organs: We Need to Start Talking about It. *American Journal of Transplantation*, 5(5), 1170-1171.

Spital, A. 2006. Conscription of Cadaveric Organs for Transplantation: Time to Start Talking about It. *Kidney International*, 70(3), 607-607.

Spital, A. and Erin, C.A. 2002. Conscription of Cadaveric Organs for Transplantation: Let's at Least Talk about It. *American Journal of Kidney Diseases*, 39(3), 611-615.

Van Diest, P.J., Lopes Cardoso, N.W.J. et al. 2003. Cadaveric Tissue Donation: A Pathologist's Perspective. *Journal of Medical Ethics*, 29(3), 135-136.

Various 1998. Theft of Body Parts: Property and Dead Bodies. Case Commentary on *R v. Kelly and Lindsay*. *Medical Law Review*, 6, 247-261.

Wallace, H. 2006. The UK National DNA Database. *EMBO Reports*, 7, S26-S30.

Womack, C. and Gray, N.M. 2007. Providing Human Tissue for Research: 1996-2006. *Pathobiology*, 74(4), 212-217.

Reports

Department of Health 2002. *Human Bodies, Human Choices – The Law on Human Organs and Tissue in England and Wales*. London: HMSO.

Department of Health 2005. *The Human Tissue Act 2004 – New Legislation on Human Organs and Tissue*. London: HMSO.

Law Commission Report 1998. *Liability for Psychiatric Injury*. London: Law Commission.

Nuffield Council on Bioethics 1995. *Human Tissue - Ethical and Legal Aspects*. London: Nuffield Council on Bioethics.

Redfern, M. 2001. *The Report of the Royal Liverpool Children's Inquiry*. London: HMSO.

The Health Authority 2004. *Code 2 – Code of Practice – Donation of Organs, Tissue and Cells for Transplantation*. London: Human Tissue Authority.

UK Transplant 2007. *Transplant Activity in the UK*. London: HMSO.

Other Sources

American Association of Tissue Banks website, http://www.aatb.org/content.asp?content_id=453, accessed 3 June 2009.

BBC News, 17 May 2007. Seven Charged over US Bone Theft. Available at http://news.bbc.co.uk/2/hi/americas/6667875.stm, accessed 3 June 2009.

Department of Health 2005. The Human Tissue Act 2004 – New Legislation on Human Organs and Tissue. Available at: http://www.dh.gov.uk/en/Publicationsandstatistics/Publications/PublicationsLegislation/DH_4109578, accessed 3 June 2009.

Frankfurter Allgemeine Zeitung, 8 November 2002. Wirbel um den Verbleib von Ulrike Meinhofs Gehirn. Available at http://www.faz.net/s/Rub02DBAA63F9EB43CEB421272A670A685C/Doc~E817795BD38B545C49C8E6156BDB20E13~AT pl~Ecommon~Scontent.html [Quick URL: http://alturl.com/6ssb], accessed 3 June 2009.

German Heart Institute Berlin (DHZB) 2008. Long Term Results after Heart Transplantation. Available at http://www.dhzb.de/aktuell/veranstaltungen/long_term_results_after_heart_transplantation/, accessed 19 May 2008.

Gillis, J. 2000. The Human Blueprint: Patenting Life? *Washington Post*, 30 December. Available at http://www.canavanfoundation.org/news/12-00_humanblueprint.php, accessed 3 June 2009.

The Guardian, 21 June 2005. Former Alder Hey Pathologist Struck Off. Available at http://www.guardian.co.uk/uk_news/story/0,,1511058,00.html, accessed 3 June 2009.

Hoppe, N. 2007. Bioequity: Applying the Principles of Equity to Resolve Conflicting Interests in Human Tissue. Paper presented at the PropEur Final Conference, University of Birmingham, 22 September 2007.

Human Tissue Authority. Codes of Practice. Available at http://www.hta.gov.uk/guidance/codes_of_practice.cfm, accessed 3 June 2009.

The Leukemia and Lymphoma Society. Available at http://www.leukemia-lymphoma.org/all_page?item_id=8507, accessed 3 June 2009.

Merz, B. 1990. Biotechnology: Spleen Rights. *The Economist*, 11 August 1990.
Presentation given by K. Shearn of Opinion Leader Ltd. at the IQPC conference on Biobanking and Sample Management, Frankfurt, 26 May 2009.
The Sun, 21 June 2008. Tot Body Snatcher Banned. Available at http://www.thesun.co.uk/sol/homepage/news/article108908.ece, accessed 3 June 2009.
Tiss.EU. Available at http://www.tisseu.uni-hannover.de., accessed 6 June 2009.
Tissues and Cells – Legal Documents. Available at http://ec.europa.eu/health/ph_threats/human_substance/legal_tissues_cells_en.htm, accessed 3 June 2009.
The UCL Bentham Project. Available at http://www.ucl.ac.uk/Bentham-Project/Faqs/auto_icon.htm, accessed 3 June 2009.
The UK Biobank Project. Available at http://www.ukbiobank.ac.uk/faqs/results.php, accessed 3 June 2009.
Vines, P. 19 March 2007. The Sacred and the Profane: The Role of Property Concepts in Disputes About Post-Mortem Examination. University of New South Wales Faculty of Law Research Series 13, available at http://www.austlii.edu.au/au/journals/UNSWLRS/2007/13.html, accessed 3 June 2009.
Zalta, E. (ed.). Equality. *Stanford Encyclopedia of Philosophy*. Available at http://plato.stanford.edu/entries/equality, accessed 3 June 2009.

Index

AB v. Leeds Teaching Hospital NHS Trust 85
actus reus 83, 87, 123
Alder Hey hospital scandal 13, 16, 18, 33-43, 63, 92-93, 96, 123-124, 161-163
Alcock v. Chief Constable of South Yorkshire Police 124
altruism 52, 77, 96, 102, 105
anatomy, cadavers for study 83
Andrews, L.B. 3, 27
anonymization 28, 41, 81, 106, 119
anthropophagy 9, 62
appropriation 3, 14, 24, 83, 108, 123, 128, 159, 162
Aquinas, T. 138-139
Aristotle 139
art, body parts used for 86
artful work 86-87, 133
Ashkenazi Jews 110
Attorney General's Reference (No. 6 of 1980) 17
autonomy 8, 36-37, 41, 78-80, 117, 120-122, 157

bailment, law of 57, 113-114
Bateman, R v. 37
Bellivier, R. 30-31
benefit sharing 107
Bentham, J. 48, 53, 83, 151
biobanks 4, 18, 41
bioequity 138, 155-158
bioethics 7, 37
Björkman, B. 49-50
Blackstone, W. 82(n32), 138-139
blanket consent 18-19, 39-40
blood 3(n4), 22, 25-26, 30, 45-46, 62, 71, 88, 108, 127, 132
Blood, R v. Human Fertilisation and Embryology Authority, ex parte 97
body parts 10, 19, 27, 31, 69, 76, 80, 84-85, 94, 127, 132
body-snatchers 83
Bolam v. Friern Hospital Management Committee 37(n19), 37(n20), 118
bones 27, 126, 132
Bowman v. Secular Society Ltd. 112
brain 16, 27, 93
Brazier, M. 61, 65
Bristol Hospital Enquiry 34, 37, 93
Brown, R v. 19, 24, 36, 71, 73, 127
Browning v. Norton Children's Hospital 36
Brownsword, R. 4
bundle concept of property rights 49-55, 62, 82, 114
burial 35, 81-83, 87, 96

cadavers 80
Calabresi, G. 46-47, 70
Canavan disease 110
cancer treatment 89(n63), 108, 111
Catalona *see Washington University v. Catalona*
cell lines 27, 41, 109
Cheere, R v. 82
Chester v. Afshar 121-122
children 14, 16(n10), 34-35, 85(n47), 110, 118, 124, 124(n34), 154
cloning 109
commercialization 6, 22, 30-31, 50, 86, 127, 129-131, 155
commodification 5-6, 62, 62(n2)
common law (legal system) 4, 10, 20, 37, 61, 75-89, 113, 139, 140
common law (as opposed to equity) 138, 140-2
consent 14-19, 36-41, 71, 73, 77-80, 94-95
contract 70, 87, 112, 114, 129, 131, 137
control right 56
conversion 80, 108-110, 154-156

corneas 26, 30, 46
corpses 13, 64, 81-85
Cooke, A. 27
cosmetic surgery 22, 102
criminal law 67-68, 70, 80, 97, 123, 128, 133, 163
Curia Regis 141, 143-148

data protection 106
death 9, 17, 38, 57, 82-83, 93-99, 119, 129
Department of Health 60, 93, 94,
Dickenson, D. 11, 23, 72, 75
dignity 7, 73, 93-94, 94(n12), 119
DNA 23, 26, 41, 81, 99, 110, 119, 119(n11),
Dobson v. North Tyneside Health Authority 85, 87
Doodeward v. Spence 10, 83-84, 86-87, 114, 132, 157, 163
Dworkin, G. 4-5, 34, 78, 83, 138, 156

eggs *see* gametes
Einstein, A. 27
enhancement 76
entitlement 8, 10-13, 26, 46-48, 49, 55-56, 64-65, 67-73
epikeia 138-142
European Tissue Directive 96, 100-106, 125, 162-163
Evans v. Amicus Healthcare Ltd. 87
exploitation 6, 13, 50-54, 72, 133, 137, 163

F v. West Berkshire Health Authority 79
F, Re *see* Re F
fairness 55, 139, 144, 150, 156, 158-9
flak jacket, consent as a 36-41
fraud, Moore case 68(n2), 155, 156

gametes 3, 6, 19, 23, 25-26, 46, 71, 88-89, 97, 113-115, 125, 130
Genetics Institute Inc. 155
German Heart Institute Berlin 9(n24)
Gibson, R v. 84
gift 16, 88, 91, 96, 111-112, 128, 133
Gillick v. West Norfolk and Wisbech Area Health Authority 79, 118
Glass v. UK 118
Greenberg v. Miami Children's Hospital Research Institute 110-111, 128-129, 137
GWW and CMW, Re *see* Re GWW and CMW

Hadley v. Midland Fertility Services Ltd. 87
hairy-cell leukaemia 107
Harris, J. 17, 21, 62(n3), 77, 79-80, 118, 125
Hecht v. Kane 89
Herring, J. 9, 98
Honoré, A.M. 114
Human Fertilisation and Embryology Authority 97(n26)
Human Tissue Act 2004 17(n13), 18(n17), 28, 81, 92-100, 109, 119, 127, 131-133
Human Tissue Authority 93-95, 98

impact 19-20, 23, 25, 122-124
informed consent 18, 37-40, 78, 94-95, 96, 121-2, 155, 157, 161
intellectual property 10, 49, 54, 154, 157
in vitro fertilization 25

justice 55, 68, 111, 122, 138-145

Kant, I. 7-8, 75-77
Kelly, R. v. 83-87, 128

labour, and property rights 5(fn13), 31, 56
land ownership 48, 53, 143
Laurie, G. 51, 121, 123(n22)
Law Commission Report 124(n31)
Leukemia and Lymphoma Society, The 107(n4)
libertarianism 8, 35, 67, 163
Liddell, K. 27-29, 37, 39-42, 109
limited property rights 52-53
Lockean ideas of property 48(n9)
Lynn, R v. 81, 84

natural law 93, 142

McHale, J. 23, 91,
Macklin, R. 6-7

Marx, K. 5
medical research 20, 23, 27-28, 29
Melamed, A. *see* Calabresi
mens rea 24, 83, 87(n52), 88(n61), 123, 162
mind-body dualism 26(n44), 80
Miola, J. 118
Moore v. Regents of the University of California 4, 29(n61), 33, 42, 86, 107-111
moral entitlement 10, 82, 142, 151

nervous shock 39, 113, 114, 123-124
no-property rule 82, 84-85, 110
Noiville, C. 30-31
Nozick, R. 48, 71
Nuffield Council on Bioethics 43, 91

objectification 35
organ sale 13, 129-130
ova *see* gametes
ownership 9-10, 47-48, 50, 54-56, 75, 109, 114, 157, 162

paternalism 33(n1), 34, 38, 63, 78, 120, 132
Pattinson, S. 17(n15)
pecuniarity 14, 22, 24-25, 77, 129-132
personal rights 6, 70-73, 119(n10)
post-mortem 14, 33, 92-94, 99, 118-119
property rights 5, 16, 48-55, 70-73, 112, 114, 137, 153, 161
pseudonymization 41, 106, 119-120
psychiatric injury *see* nervous shock
public good 41

Quick v. Coppleton 82
Quintavalle *see R (on the application of Quintavalle) v. Human Fertilisation and Embryology Authority*

R (on the application of Quintavalle) v. Human Fertilisation and Embryology Authority 87
Redfern Report, The 4, 29, 34
Re F 79, 118
Re GWW and CMW 18
Re W 37
res communis 7, 35(n11)
research subjects 126, 157
restitution 67-69
Roche v. Douglas 89
Rothery, R v. 3, 88
Royal Liverpool Children's Inquiry 4(n6), 28(n56), 35-36

Schloendorff v. NY Hospital 78, 117
self-determination 63, 117
self-exploitation 133, 137
Sidaway v. The Board of Governors of Bethlem Royal Hospital 38, 78, 121
slavery 26, 71-72, 86
sperm *see* gametes
stare decisis 152-153, 156
surrogacy 31(n72), 125

terminology 3, 5-6, 8, 31, 45-58, 137, 161
theft 3, 24, 25, 79, 81, 83, 86-87, 88, 123, 128, 162-163
therapeutic vs. non-therapeutic 15, 18-21, 24, 29, 38-40, 65, 69, 79-80, 102, 118, 121, 127
Tiss.EU project xiii, 101
tissue banks 27, 30, 39, 43, 64
tort 67-69, 70, 91, 109, 114
transferability 62(n2), 133, 151(n3), 153
transplantation 7, 9(n24), 13, 21, 26, 27, 30, 76-77, 93, 97, 125, 129-130
trust 142-143, 154-155, 157-158

UCLA Medical School 107
UK Biobank 4, 41(n33)
UK Transplant 30(n68)
unjust enrichment 111, 155(n19)

Velzen, D. van 35, 92(n4)
voluntariness 21, 102, 132

W, Re *see* Re W
Washington University v. Catalona 16(n7), 111-113, 128, 128(n49), 137, 162

Yearworth 57(n40) and others v. North Bristol NHS Trust 80, 113-115